BALANCING ACT:
MOUNTAINS, FAMILY, CAREER

1978 Family Hike Italian Side of Mont Blanc

Elizabeth "Betsy" White

Cover Photo: at 16,000 ft above Shimshal in Pakistan, 1984, photo by Gene White

All photos except my baby photo, by

Gene White

Dedication

This book is dedicated to my grandchildren:

Elliot, Cosmo, Athena, and Chase

Acknowledgment

First I must recognize the contribution of my late husband, Gene. His diaries, project reports, expedition accounts and thousands of photographs were essential sources for my writing. For three years my dedicated writing group of Doris Ash, Nina Duhl and Jeannette Larsen read and critiqued chapters. Retired professional editors Caroline Herrick, Katherine Duane and Thomas Farber provided additional guidance. Friends Dean Lobovits, Emily Benner, Barbara Peterson and sisters Louise Wheatley, Susan Tyson, and Elena White reviewed many sections. For several months a writing group of the University Section Club helped with final revisions.

I must thank those who helped me create a multi-faceted life: The many professors, mentors, colleagues, and inspiring women I have known, starting with my grandmother. For many years our mountain adventures were made possible by other parents who shared childcare responsibilities at campsites in the Rockies, Wind Rivers, Big Horns, Sierra Nevada and Yosemite. Thanks go to the Benner, Burns, Church, Goss, Harrower, and Menocal families, Jim and Elena White and my brother Bill. I must also thank my fellow alpinists who shared summits and sorrows, and the porters, donkey drovers, horse wranglers and yak drivers without whom we might have not reached our basecamps. Finally, I thank my children and grandchildren who rarely complained about being taken along to mountains or foreign countries and have been patient with my endless writing.

Introduction

My blond ponytail blowing in the wind, I straddled the knife-edge ridge of Capitol Peak, inching towards the summit of my first Colorado 14,000 ft. I stared at the plunging granite on either side. Then I heard a shout from behind: "You can do it! Just don't look down." It was Gene... four years older and an experienced mountaineer, he had boundless, contagious confidence. We hugged on the summit and descended safely. This was the beginning of over half a century of sharing our love of mountains, creating a family, and developing our careers. We encouraged each other to look up, not down. As a mountaineer, wife, and mother, international development professional, runner, and linguist, I experienced success and failure in all categories. I pursued knowledge and adventure from New York to New Guinea, Alaska to Patagonia, and fifty countries in between. I tried to minimize damage to the world and make a positive impact.

Much of my international work and living experience was in Pakistan and Indonesia, two large Muslim-majority nations. My focus was human rights and social and political development. I have been appreciative of the strengths and faults of my own society and those I have studied. Gene was a civil engineer working on water resources. We were a supportive and complementary team at work, as we were in the mountains.

With this book, I hope to encourage younger people to create multi-focused lives. Never let someone tell you, "You can't do that because you are a woman, or too young, or too old, or have children, or have a job." With sufficient energy, focus, appropriate training, and an equally energetic partner, you can try and perhaps succeed at almost anything. Ensure that your ambition does not endanger yourself or others.

Unsolicited advice I have received over the years included:

1959 "You two should not try to climb Mont Blanc alone."

1961 "Two young people should not drive around the Mediterranean in a little car."

1961 "You cannot drive from Cairo to Nairobi." The advice was valid-we had to take the Nile service boats and trains.

1962 "Going to Pakistan in the Peace Corps is not a good idea. You should stay home and start a family."

1964 "You can't take a five week old baby to Pakistan."

1967 "So soon after losing twins, you should not become pregnant again." I did and had a healthy 8-pound boy.

1969 "As the mother of two little boys, it is irresponsible to join an expedition to the Andes." I reached the highest summit in Peru.

1970 "With a newborn daughter and two sons under six, you can't possibly pursue a PhD." I completed the degree in 1975.

1974 "It is not safe for a young blond woman to do fieldwork in the North-West Frontier Province of Pakistan." I completed my research with no problems.

1975 "You can't train for a marathon because you have three small children." I ran 30 marathons.

1977 "It is irresponsible to leave your three children with their father and servants in Sulawesi, eastern Indonesia, while you lead a trek in the Hindu Kush." Gene thought I needed a break from homeschooling.

1974 "A course about women in developing countries won't appeal to students." "Women in the World" attracted enthusiastic students every semester.

1978 "The course title you propose, "Islamic Civilization" won't attract students. The course has become a requirement for a major in Middle East Studies.

1980 "You should not go to the Himalayas again when starting a new job and leaving three children with a friend who has never had children." The children survived, and so did we.

1985 "A woman with children can't fill the responsibilities of a country director." I successfully directed the Indonesian Program of The Asia Foundation for almost three years.

1989 "A woman should not be the director of a program for Afghans." I could meet with Afghan men and women. A male program director would not be able to meet with women.

2000 "You are too old to run the Pike's Peak Marathon". I finished second in my age group.

2011 "At 72, you are too old to join a dating app." I did and found a wonderful companion.

Chapter 1 Inspiring Antecedents

My maternal grandmother, Dr. Josephine Hemenway Kenyon, was important in my life from my birth until her death in 1965. I remember her as short and stout, with a quick smile and a lively interest in everything: music, art, nature, and politics. My mother, my sister Josie, and I lived with her in her New York apartment from 1941 to 1945, and we visited her house on Long Island in the summers until 1952 when she retired and moved to Colorado. She was a respected pediatrician and a childcare expert.

Josephine was born in Auburn, New York in 1880. She had three younger brothers. In 1891 the family moved to Glasgow, Missouri, because her father was invited to become president of Pritchett College. Josephine received a B.A. from Pritchett at age eighteen. She was determined to become a physician, and her family agreed, even if others thought a woman doctor couldn't expect to marry and have children.

She was considered too young to begin medical studies at Johns Hopkins University, so she went to Bryn Mawr College for one year. When asked why she did not enroll in a women's medical college, she wrote, "I need the same preparation as men if I am to hold my own in the profession." In 1904, she graduated second in her class of 42 men and three women. In addition to her pediatric career of 45 years, she was involved in public health issues and worked for the Social Hygiene Division of the U.S. War Department during

World War I. She traveled coast to coast, visiting communities impacted by the presence of military camps. This was during the 1918 flu epidemic, so her letters home to the family describe efforts to contain the flu and other diseases, including smallpox. Her husband, my grandfather, was serving in General Pershing's 106th Field Artillery in France. He wrote home regularly, though he could not mention his location. My mother saved his letters, in which he wrote: "from somewhere in France."

For decades, Josephine Kenyon wrote a column on child and infant care for Good Housekeeping magazine. Her writing appeared in other publications. She served on the editorial board of the Journal of the American Medical Women's Association. She wrote *Healthy Babies are Happy Babies: A Complete Handbook for Mothers"* in 1934. It had five editions, the final two authored jointly with my mother, Ruth. I took this book to Pakistan in 1964 to help me deal with health issues for my newborn son, Eric. When a rash, diarrhea, or fever appeared, I reached for my grandmother's book!

Grandmother Kenyon, whom we called "Mangie," was interested in all her grandchildren. Josie and I were the first and second and benefited from her focused attention. After she retired and moved to Colorado, I appreciated that I could have long conversations with her about any subject, including current affairs, my studies and friends, art and music. Now that I am a grandmother, I try to spend time with each grandchild alone as well as in groups with their siblings or cousins.

My mother, Ruth Talcott Kenyon, was born in New York City on June 6, 1912. Two years later, her sister, Dorothy, was born. Their parents were Dr. Josephine Hemenway Kenyon, a pediatrician, and Dr. James Henry Kenyon, a neurosurgeon. Both worked full-time, so they relied upon family and hired help to raise their daughters. Mother wrote a few pages entitled "Ruth and Dorothy Growing Up." These and our conversations gave me a sense of her childhood. My grandfather's unmarried sister, Addie, frequently visited. Mother remembers her playing games like checkers and parchesi and reading to her and Dorothy daily. Among the books she read aloud were Alice in Wonderland, the Thornton Burgess animal books, James Fenimore Cooper, Sir Walter Scott, and many Dickens. My mother would later read these books to me and my siblings. Ruth and Dorothy attended the Spence School for Girls in New York. There were no traffic lights in New York in those days.

Ruth, Dorothy, and their nanny had to cross busy 57th Street on the way to school. "We often walked behind a bunch of grown-ups when traffic was heavy," she wrote. In the apartment, they had a wind-up record player with cylinder records. The girls spent a lot of time in the kitchen, where they could snack on fresh Irish bread with the maids who drank tea and read the tea leaves. There seems to have been a series of nursemaids and a housemaid. The laundry was sent out, taken by a "black lady and her son" in a wagon. Grandfather James's shirts went to a Chinese laundry.

My grandparents loved the seashore. They first bought a tiny house on a spit of land in Long Island Sound. They found it difficult to access in a small boat in variable weather. In 1927, they built a house on sandy ground near Island Park, Long Island. They spent many happy weekends and holidays there, as did I eventually. They put in an asparagus bed and built a nice dock.

Ruth graduated with honors from Vassar College in 1933 and then entered medical school at Columbia University. She interrupted her education to marry my father in 1935 and resumed medical studies in 1941 after their divorce. Echoing the stories of Mother's childhood, thirty years later, my sister Josie and I lived with our mother and grandmother Kenyon in an apartment at 72nd Street and Madison Avenue. My grandmother and Mother were practicing pediatricians at that time. Like Mother and her sister, Josie and I walked to the Spence School with our nanny, but in the 1940s there were traffic lights, and the streets were much busier. My childhood memories of my mother are of a pretty, active, busy woman. Until I was seven, some of my early care, like that of many children of the era, was provided by nannies. Despite her demanding studies and medical practice, Mother always made time to read to us before we went to sleep. She also created stories. My favorites were those that involved a dog named Frank, who participated in historical adventures.

Frank sailed to Troy in the Trojan Wars; he crossed the Alps with Hannibal; he sailed to England with William the Conqueror; he traveled through Persia to India with Alexander the Great; and he carried secret messages across the lines in European wars. My love of geography and history began with the stories of Frank the dog.

Chapter 2 My Early Years

I was born in New York City on June 12, 1938. My birth certificate read "Elizabeth Talcott Herrick," but I was known as Betsy from the first day. My parents, William Herrick, Jr., and Ruth Kenyon, were from well-respected New England families. My father graduated from Yale, the fifth generation of his family to do so. My mother had graduated from Vassar and completed two years of medical school. Their parents were listed in the New York Social Register. My father was working for a chemical company in Terre Haute, Indiana. However, the address on my birth certificate is 14 East 90th Street, New York, New York, my paternal grandparents' address. I guess my parents did not trust the medical establishment in Indiana, or they just really wanted me to be born in New York, not the "hinterland". Two weeks after I was born, we went to Sharon, Connecticut, where my father's parents had a lovely big house. My father returned to Terre Haute shortly thereafter. Mother, my sister Josie (eighteen months older than me), and I joined him in Terre Haute at the end of the summer. I lived in Terre Haute until I was two, with summer and Christmas visits to Connecticut and New York. I remember nothing of Terre Haute, though I have seen photos and home movies of our lives there.

My best childhood memories are of "Boscobel," my grandparents' house in Sharon. It was a large white wooden house on extensive grounds, with a barn, stable, and gardener's cottage. It was a wonderful place for a small child, with many rooms to explore, even an attic. There was a playroom, a library, a huge living room, and a music room with two grand pianos and an organ. Upstairs were five large bedrooms with attached baths, and in the kitchen wing were four maids' rooms and a maids' sitting room. Each room had a button that, when pressed, would sound near the kitchen. A wooden box on the pantry wall contained four rows of small brass arrows that moved when someone buzzed from another room. This system was an invitation for mischief by small girls. I think the maids learned to ignore the random signals we girls created, but they did pay attention to the dining room, where the button was under the carpet. My grandmother could press it with her foot during dinner to signal that it was time to clear the table for the next course. When Grandmother Herrick was alive, there were at least two maids, a butler, a driver (whose room was in the attic), and Adolph, the gardener, who lived in the gardener's house near the barn with his family. The main house had three stairways: a dark wood, narrow stair from the kitchen to the maids' rooms; a stairway between the library and the playroom leading to the bedrooms at the east end of the house (the walls of this stairway were decorated with five Herrick Yale diplomas); and, at the front door's entrance was a sweeping, wide wooden staircase with a huge window that led up to the three largest bedrooms. Even when I last visited the house, in 1978, after my father's death, I could find my way around the house with my eyes closed.

Josie and I loved exploring the house and grounds. On hot days, we would hide under one of the pianos or stretch out on the cool, red leather couch in the music room. There was a big old barn behind the gardener's house. It contained a collection of vehicles, some functional, some not. Attached to the barn was my grandfather's woodworking shop. I loved sitting on a stool and watching him fit furniture pieces together or carve elaborate designs. I cherish a walnut panel upon which he carved the family coat of arms in deep relief. Between the house and the log guesthouse our grandfather built himself, there was a vegetable garden and a huge raspberry patch where a small girl could get lost. The raspberries were so sweet I did not mind the scratches and mosquito bites that occurred during the picking. Beyond the guesthouse, a stable and a pig pen were at the end of the gravel drive. After dinner, Grandfather would take "slops"– food leftovers–to the pigs. I enjoyed walking beside him even if the slops smelled strange.

Our cousin Emily, who was two years younger than I, joined us for the summers in Sharon. Emily tagged along with us on our explorations of the fields and forests near our house. Two years later, her brother Tommy joined the group, though he could not really keep up with eight-year-old Josie. Tommy amazed us by demonstrating his ability to pee in a Coke bottle. None of us girls could do that! We made up stories about a dangerous bull in the farthest pasture, then would race back to the house to hide for safety. On many hot summer days, someone would drive us to a pond with a small sandy beach, a boathouse, and a float with a small diving board. It was a natural pond, so the aquatic weeds grew in proliferation just beyond the sandy area. Even after learning to swim well, I remained a little frightened of those weeds, wondering if I would get my foot caught in them or if dangerous fish or turtles were hiding in them.

My parents separated in 1940. I never discovered the reasons, but in the summer of 1941, Mother took Josie and me to Nevada to facilitate the divorce. In New York, the only valid grounds for divorce were proven adultery. Nevada had fewer requirements. I remember riding a pony and seeing Lake Tahoe.

After the Japanese bombed Pearl Harbor in 1941, America declared war against Germany and Japan. My father joined the army and was soon shipped to North Africa. His regiment fought the Germans across North Africa and then north through Italy. I would see my father only once during the next four years. I remember him being very handsome in his uniform. He was a tall, slim man with slightly stooped shoulders. He was shy and had a stutter. I think he felt overshadowed by his father, the famous internist and diagnostician. My father had a mixed career, trying different businesses, ending with a successful travel agency in Lakeville, Connecticut, near Sharon.

When we returned to New York after the divorce, my grandfather, Dr. Herrick, encouraged my mother to continue her medical studies. There was a great need for doctors because of the war. Mother, Josie, and I lived with my Herrick grandparents for a year in their spacious apartment at 14 East 90th Street on the twelfth floor. There was a doorman, an elevator operator, maids, and a series of nannies to take care of Josie and me. I remember the entry hall had a marble floor where we enjoyed pushing around our ice-skating dolls. When a maid noticed the scratches of the skate blades, that pastime ended.

My mother graduated with distinction from medical school, an admirable achievement for a single mother. She immediately joined the pediatric practice of her mother, Dr. Josephine Kenyon. We moved into Grandmother Kenyon's apartment, becoming a three-generation female household. Josie and I were enrolled at the Spence School for Girls, which our mother and her sister had attended. Our nanny would walk to school with us, carefully crossing the busy streets of New York. I have fond memories of excursions to Central Park and visits to Sharon in winter and summer. Josie and I were close pals in those days.

I remember looking out the window of the seventh-floor apartment on the Upper East Side with Josie. We could see the pointed tower of the Chrysler Building. Every day, we heard the name Hitler on radio news programs. We knew our father was somewhere "over there." Josie said, "Hitler should be punished by being speared on the Chrysler Building tower." I agreed. We were in the care of Beth, an

Irish governess, while we waited for our mother and grandmother to return from their busy pediatric practice.

We spent happy days at Grandmother Kenyon's house on Long Island. She taught Josie and me to find clams in the mud with our toes. She also taught me to knit when I was five. We knitted squares, which were sewn together to be blankets for soldiers. I wonder if soldiers ever received any of those blankets. We were very aware of the war, whether from the radio news, saving bacon fat, or using margarine instead of butter. I loved squeezing the white margarine, which came in a bag in which there was a little orange coloring bubble. Occasional postcards from my father were personal reminders of the war.

In 1945, my beloved grandfather William Worthington Herrick died at age sixty-five. My mother rushed to his apartment to sign the death certificate. Grandfather Herrick had been very supportive of her continuing her education, and he was loving and generous to his grandchildren. A year later, Grandmother Herrick died. Dr. Herrick's memoriam in a leading medical journal was written by my Grandmother Kenyon. It demonstrates the friendship and professional respect that remained between the two families even after my parents' divorce. Grandfather Herrick was a successful internist and a professor of medicine at Columbia College of Physicians and Surgeons. I remember watching him playing the organ and grand piano and woodworking. In my memories, he is a large, friendly figure, typically standing in front of the fireplace, smiling, the Yale Glee Club charm on his watch chain glowing. These grandparents gave each grandchild US savings bonds on birthdays and Christmas. That money was more than enough for my sister and me to pay for college.

Chapter 3 Colorado And The Rockies

Mother married William Russell on June 2, 1945. They had met when she was on rounds at a hospital, and he was an intern. As Mother's bridal attendants, Josie and I wore flowers in our hair. Bill Russell brought a lively male presence into our female household. He welcomed Josie and me as enthusiastically as he welcomed each subsequent child born into the family. He had just completed medical school and was serving in the Army. Soon, we left New York for army bases in Pennsylvania and California. When the army sent him to the occupation in Japan in 1946, we settled in Denver, Colorado. As an undergraduate, Bill had transferred from Dartmouth to the University of Denver because he suffered from asthma. He and Mother thought Denver would be a good place to live. By this time, the first of my Russell siblings, Louise, had been born. There were to be eight more! Returning to civilian life, he joined the staff of the National Jewish Hospital in Denver, working with a team developing treatments for tuberculosis. He also served Indian reservations in the Southwest as a visiting specialist in lung diseases.

Bill Russell was an enthusiastic falconer. He brought home a series of birds, ranging from tiny sparrow hawks and kestrels to a golden eagle. I enjoyed tagging along when he took the birds out to the prairie for training exercises. He got free chicken heads from a poultry processing plant to feed the birds. During a New Year's Eve party, he flew the eagle across the living room over the heads of the guests. The sport brought to us interesting falconers, including the famous naturalists Olas and Mardie Murie, who were early leaders of the Wilderness Society, and Captain Knight, a popular lecturer from England who traveled the world with his golden eagle. Captain Knight's eagle would soar over the audience during his programs, producing gasps of awe.

After her second marriage, Mother did not practice medicine. She wrote articles on childcare for various magazines. With her mother, Dr. Kenyon, she created revised editions of *"Healthy Babies Are Happy Babies: A Complete Handbook for Modern Mothers."* Eventually, five editions were published, as well as translations in Spanish, French, and German. It was a practical guide for parents.

Instead of the private Spence School in New York, Josie and I attended public schools in Denver. In New York, we lived in apartments accessed by elevators. My sister Josie and I were accompanied by a nanny as we walked to the private Spence School for girls wearing school uniforms. The streets were noisy, crowded with cars, buses, and trucks, and lined with towering apartment buildings. In Denver, Josie and I walked to school with neighborhood children, unaccompanied by adults, on quiet residential streets along shady sidewalks past modest one-story houses. The public schools were coed, of course, and we did not have to wear uniforms. We could choose our own dresses and skirts to wear to school: girls were not allowed to wear pants. I preferred the schools in Denver and the freedom to walk to school with friends, not nannies.

Our small house in Denver was a big change from the apartment in New York. It had front and back yards, with a picket fence. By 1949, when I was eleven, my Denver family moved to a larger brick house. It had three bedrooms and a bath on the main floor, as well as two bedrooms, a bath, laundry, and a recreation room in the basement. There was a laundry chute from the main floor to the basement laundry room. Over the years, several pets and small children descended by the chute, but there were no serious injuries. There was always a basket of laundry below to soften the landings. By the time Josie left for college, there were twelve of us living there: Mother and Bill Russell in one of the upstairs bedrooms; Louise, Abby, Jean, and Peggy in another with bunk beds; Bill, John, Charles, and Steve in the third, also with bunk beds; and Josie and I in one of the basement-level bedrooms. Contrast that with my family in Sharon, Connecticut: My father, Bill, and stepmother Mary, with daughters Caroline and Suzy, in a twenty-three-room house with five large bedrooms, each with its own bath, four maids' rooms, and two other baths.

As young girls, Josie and I wore matching clothes and had the same hairstyle (braids for several years, then short hair with home permanents). As the years went by, our interests differed. She was quieter and more reserved. I grew taller, excelled in school, and became devoted to my chosen sports, skiing, and mountain hiking. Josie's academic record was average, but she never disturbed a class. I received high grades for academics but low marks for conduct. I would finish my assignments in half the time allotted, and then I would fidget, talk, pass notes, and sometimes disturb the other students. In modern times, I might have been considered to have attention deficit disorder. Thank goodness no one prescribed drugs for a hyperactive student in those days! I was always tall and thin and poorly coordinated, and therefore hopeless in gym class. On the rope-climbing test, I could not get both feet off the ground, and playing softball, I rarely caught a ball that came my way.

After World War II ended, my father came once to visit us in Colorado. He took Josie and me to a dude ranch near Rocky Mountain National Park. He brought us home to our house. He said goodbye and told Mother that we had a good time. Those few minutes are my only memory of seeing my father and mother together. After that year, Josie and I traveled by train to visit our father in the summer. The train left Denver in the afternoon, arriving in Chicago in the morning. Our great uncle and aunt would meet us at the Chicago train station, take us to the aquarium and out for lunch or to their home in Evanston, then put us back on the train in the afternoon. The steward on the train watched over us with care. I am sure that he received a tip from whichever adult was putting us on the train. We loved the excitement of the train, buttoning the curtains of our Pullman berths for the night. Our father would meet us in Amenia, New York, near Sharon. We usually stayed for a month or more.

My father had married Mary Hammerel from Minnesota in 1944. They moved into my grandparents' big house in Sharon, Connecticut, and soon had two daughters, who were eight and ten years younger than me. Mary was tall and had red-brown hair. She wore pretty clothes with matching high heels and seemed very glamorous to me. She arranged tennis and golf lessons for us and drove us to ponds and lakes to swim. She was always generous to Josie and me, and she was happy to buy us clothes and shoes when we needed them. Aunt Eunice (my father's sister) and her husband, Uncle Tom Trowbridge, had bought another house in Sharon, so we were reunited with their children, our cousins Emily and Tommy, and their two little brothers. There was also quite a crowd of children in our age group.

Summers on the East Coast included a week or more with Grandmother Kenyon at her little house on Long Island. These were very enjoyable times. We played board games, read, and swam in the muddy salt water of Long Island Sound or in the surf at Jones Beach.

During my fourteenth summer, my father taught me how to drive. I practiced on several vehicles that were in the barn: an army surplus command car, a station wagon, a yellow Jeepster convertible, and Dad's diesel Mercedes sedan. I was allowed to drive the cars between the house and the barn. If he or my stepmother mentioned going somewhere, I would run up to the barn to get the car. When they returned, I would drive the car back up to the barn. It was only about three city blocks distance but long enough for good practice.

When a teenager in Sharon, I assisted at the local summer stock theater, painting sets and props. Josie and I went to dances at nearby country clubs. We wore prom dresses and were escorted by local boys. Fourth of July in Sharon was a Norman Rockwell-style celebration. Admiral Hart, the oldest veteran in town, sat ramrod straight in an open car, wearing his white uniform and medals. Children pulled red wagons decorated in red, white, and blue bunting. One year, my father had a flatbed truck decorated in Hawaiian style to advertise his travel agency. Josie and I wore grass skirts and leis and threw candy to the crowds along the parade route. Denver also celebrated the Fourth of July with a parade, but the Frontier Days celebration and the Stock Show were the biggest events of the year.

Connecticut and Colorado were very different places to experience in my teen years. I attended large, coeducational public schools in Colorado, where the student population included Christians (Protestant and Catholic), Jews, and, some African Americans, Asians, and Hispanics. One of the most popular boys in my high school class was an African American, Ronnie Shanks. He was elected Head Boy in my senior year. Sharon, Connecticut, was basically a white, Protestant town. There were a few Catholic families and hardly any Jews. The only blacks in town were servants. The teens I knew in Sharon attended single-sex private schools, which required uniforms. The New England teenagers, segregated in boarding schools all winter, went "wild" during summer vacations. They wore skimpy clothes, stayed up late, drank, flirted, and drove too fast across the state line to New York, where the drinking age was eighteen. We tall sixteen-year-olds could buy a beer in any small-town New York bar. In Colorado, I was accustomed to going to class with boys, participating in sports and clubs with boys, being able to drive when I needed to, and taking trips to the mountains to ski and hike in mixed groups. The New England of two-hundred-year-old stately homes, tall elm trees, village greens, and exclusive country clubs contrasted with the more egalitarian, down-to-earth, western society of Denver. Within my family, there were contrasts, too.

The family differences became more evident as the years went by. In Connecticut, drinking increasingly became the focus of social life. Every evening in summer, my father and stepmother consumed half a bottle of gin before dinner. In winter, whiskey took the place of gin. I learned to mix my own "gin and tonic" by omitting the gin. On weekends, the drinking began at noon as friends would often gather around the pool or in the living room. Mary and my father smoked. I would search for cigarettes in the coat pockets of the closets. In Denver, I had to hide my smoking from my parents. (In 1976, my stepmother died on a Sunday night. Eighteen months later, my father died on a Sunday night. I believe that the double drinking on Sundays contributed to their deaths.)

When I was in eighth grade, I learned three skills that have been important to me throughout my life: sewing, typing, and skiing. In-home economics, I learned to sew. Ever since, I have made clothes, upholstery and slipcovers, costumes, curtains, men's ties, stuffed toys, and sleeping bags. Two friends competed with me in sewing. We'd purchase fabrics after school and then race to see who could appear first wearing a new dress. Popular in the 1950s was the "Lanz" dress, vaguely Austrian in design. Typically, it had flowers or stripes in the fabric, a full skirt, and lots of tiny buttons down the front. To avoid the tedium of making lots of buttonholes, I developed a system of sewing snaps under the buttons or, when in a rush, using safety pins.

Knowing I was skilled at sewing, Mother would sometimes come home with an armload of fabric and announce, "I thought we would make new curtains." In the eighth grade, I also learned to touch type. That skill has been useful throughout my life. I am using it to write today. My typing teacher, Mr. Eggleston, was a sponsor of the Eskimo Ski Club. He recruited students in the typing classes to join the ski club. I enthusiastically enrolled. Every Saturday morning in the winter, we would get on the ski train from Denver to the Winter Park ski area. The train parked for the day on a siding so we could eat lunches in the train and return when the lifts closed.

In skiing, I found a sport I could do. I was not the best, but I took the lessons seriously and gradually rose through the skill levels. I became an alternate on the high school ski team. By the second winter, I was able to earn the cost of my train ticket by supervising younger skiers and handing out tickets. It was through skiing that I would meet my husband, Gene, and through skiing, that I developed a deep and lasting interest in mountaineering. My high school years were busy and generally happy. Although I was a failure at team sports, I skied every winter Saturday and, in summer, went hiking and climbing in the Rockies with the Junior Colorado Mountain Club. I enjoyed most of my classes and did well. During my senior year, I served as an assistant to the biology teacher. I focused on helping the handsome football players complete their assignments. I was in the honor society "White Jackets," whose members led cheers at athletic events and assisted the school administration. I was on the planning committees for the junior and senior proms but did not have a regular boyfriend for my date. At a planning meeting for the senior prom, a boy committee member and I admitted that neither of us had a date, so we went together and had a good time.

Art was my favorite subject. I took fashion drawing one semester. My teacher encouraged me to submit work to the National Scholastic Art competition; I won two awards. The gold keys were nice, but even better was the reward of a summer job dressing windows at the May Company, a large downtown department store. Window dressing called upon my sewing and ironing skills as much as my artistic talent, as each mannikin had to be perfectly dressed without a wrinkle.

I got my driver's license on my sixteenth birthday, thanks to the instruction provided by my father. Before I could drive a family car in Denver, my stepfather required me to demonstrate the ability to change tires. The challenge took a long time; it grew dark. I worried that someone might think I was stealing tires rather than rotating them. After I passed that test, I took advantage of every opportunity to drive. Some girlfriends and I took Josie's car north to Fort Collins for the Frontier Day celebration at the agricultural university. We hoped to meet handsome cowboys. However, the drive was longer than expected, so we had to return an hour after arriving. Other unapproved excursions included driving to a mountain town to find a certain guitar for my classmate, the singer Judy Collins.

Chapter 4 Gene The Man Of My Life

Christmas vacation in 1954, when I was a junior in high school, I drove my parents' 1946 Chrysler to Winter Park with my good friends Betsy G. and Kathy. Kathy was a senior and an excellent skier. She was meeting her boyfriend, Bob, a student at Colorado State University. As we approached the ski lift, Bob waved to Kathy, and she got on the lift with him. He was followed by two friends, Val Thompson and Gene White. Betsy got on the lift with Val, I stepped in place beside Gene. He was tall, blond, and colorfully dressed: oversized parka, baggy knickers, bright-red knee socks. He had green eyes and a wide smile. I thought I was sophisticated in my black stretch pants and parka. But this was no match for his outfit.

As the T-bar pulled us up the hill, we started talking. He told me he was from South Denver and was a junior at Dartmouth. I was impressed with that and with his skiing: fast and with few turns. Other skiers try to do perfect "S" turns or, with a partner, make a figure-eight track. Gene specialized in figure "11s": skis side by side and straight down the hill, sometimes airborne. In those days, ski boots resembled hiking boots with square toes. They were made of leather and laced to a few inches above the ankle. Gene was using "long thong" bindings, the three-foot-long leather straps holding his boots to the ski with no chance of releasing. Since the straps went around his ankles, he did not bother to tie the laces of his ski boots.

We skied together at Winter Park for the next few days and went to a nearby bar on New Year's Eve. Though we were both underage, we managed to get served beer. We danced until midnight, alternating between twirling your partner "disco" and "slow dancing." We kissed at midnight, and as we walked to the bunkhouse where I was staying. All too soon, it was time to return to Denver, and for Gene to drive across the country to Hanover, New Hampshire. I was smitten but unsure when I would see him again. He seemed to already have at least one girlfriend in Denver. However, he said that we would be getting together to do some climbing in the Colorado mountains in the summer. This was the start of half a century of an often long-distance relationship. We exchanged letters during that spring semester, but we never telephoned. Long-distance calls were too expensive. We spent many weekends together that summer, hiking and climbing in the Colorado mountains with our Colorado Mountain Club friends.

Meeting Gene was a life-defining event for me. I knew when I met him that he was special. I sensed that we had complementary levels of energy and curiosity about the world. He was born in Denver and attended South High School, graduating in 1952. His mother was an elementary school teacher; his father, who had not finished high school, had a varied career, starting in the Marines, then as a letter carrier, barber, and eventually real estate investor and collector of Packard cars. Both were Christian Scientists.

Gene was very athletic and competitive. At age eleven, he was an all-city champion in the high jump, broad jump, and 50-yard dash. In high school, he jumped over six feet. On an early date, he impressed me by jumping over my head; I was five feet nine inches tall, and he did not even brush against my hair as he soared over me, though I may have stooped down a little. He was an Eagle Scout. He had started climbing when he was a Boy Scout. Colorado has fifty-four mountains over 14,000 feet high. At age 16, he climbed Long's Peak, one of the more challenging "Fourteeners," and thus began a lifelong quest to scale summits over that altitude.

He also excelled at academics. His French teacher invited him on a trip to France with five other students when he was sixteen. Until then, he had had no inoculations due to his parents' Christian Science beliefs. He told me the smallpox and other vaccinations were very difficult and the reactions painful. "It almost killed me," he said. That experience ended his confidence in Christian Science. As practiced by his parents, the faith allowed going to dentists but not to use any painkillers. Wearing glasses was tolerated as a sign of weak faith. Of course, alcohol and tobacco were forbidden. Caffeine also banned. His mother drank tea, saving the tea bags for later cups of increasingly weak brew. On the trip to France, Gene began to appreciate wine. Later, when we were dating, he would hide a bottle of wine or whisky in the trunk of his car under the spare tire. Several times, his mother searched the car and destroyed the bottle. The contrast with my family was extreme. My mother, stepfather, and three of my grandparents were doctors. We all drank coffee and alcohol. I smoked cigarettes, too. It took a few years for Gene's mother to accept me with my sinful habits.

At Dartmouth, Gene participated in inter-fraternity track and ski competitions. He had hoped to be on the college ski team but discovered there were two team members who had already been in the Olympics. He joined the Dartmouth Outing Club, renowned for the difficult climbs and explorations. In 1953, Gene and other Outing Club members explored the interior ranges of British Columbia, Canada. They made the first ascents of several peaks in the Purcell Mountains, which are noted in guidebooks. Gene was a calm, cheerful person, always looking on the bright side of things, in contrast to his brother, who had a more negative attitude toward life. Gene wasn't artistic or musical, but he enjoyed all kinds of music and expressed his originality in his clothing. He was famous at Dartmouth for wearing shorts (Bermuda length) every day, rain or shine. In the snowy months, he wore long underwear and knee socks under the shorts. A few months after I first met him, I knitted a pair of red argyle-pattern knee socks for him. To guarantee he did not take them off when with other women, I knitted "Betsy" on the sole of each sock.

In 1956, he graduated from Dartmouth and enrolled in the University of Denver for an additional one-year Bachelor of Science in Engineering degree. His thesis at the University of Denver was a structural analysis of different types of ski-lift towers. That research was very enjoyable for him since it entailed riding the lifts at many ski resorts to compare the structures. Gene studied civil engineering because he wanted an occupation that would allow him to be outdoors most of the time. Long months of office work were tedious for him. He thrived on rough travel through jungles or deserts to remote sites for irrigation channels or dams. He spent one summer working in Alaska on the Distant Early Warning Line of radar stations. Then, he signed up for six months of active duty in the U.S. Army.

Also, in 1956, I graduated from high school and began my studies at Smith College in Massachusetts. Gene and I spent most of the next four years long distances apart. Our letter writing was regular; we did not talk on the telephone long distance more than once a month. When we were both in Colorado in the winter, we skied together. In the summers, Gene and I joined Junior Colorado Mountain Club trips or arranged for our own teams of friends to summit high peaks every weekend. I loved being outdoors and high in the mountains alone with him in a tent or with other friends.

Gene loved to read. Usually, he would be actively reading three books at a time: one fiction, one nonfiction, and one about mountaineering. On long hikes and treks, he would get ahead of the group. We would find him, beside the trail, reading a book. He was mildly dyslexic, so his spelling was innovative. He was left-handed, so his handwriting could pose an additional challenge to the reader. In Muslim societies where he worked, the left hand is considered unclean when used in the latrine. Gene was able to explain, in several languages, that he had been raised to use his right hand for unclean tasks, so it would be acceptable for him to use his left to write and eat.

Chapter 5 My Family

My mother and stepfather had nine children. Bill Russell had dark hair and brown eyes. My mother was a blue-eyed blond like me. The children alternated inheriting their parents' coloring. The first was Louise, blond, born in 1946 at Herlong army base in California. Louise was a jolly, chubby baby. I was eight years old, so I could pick her up and carry her like a big doll, but this one was alive and had real needs, not just pretend ones. The next year, Josie and I caught German measles (rubella) at school. Mother became infected. Rubella, or "three-day" measles is especially dangerous for pregnant women. It can cause severe birth defects. Even in 1947, it would have been possible for a mother to have an abortion for that reason. However, she chose to complete the pregnancy. Therefore, our next sister, Abigail, called "Abby," was born with a degenerative neurological condition. She had poor eyesight, limited physical strength, and slow mental development. She was a blue-eyed, cheerful child despite having to wear thick eyeglasses and braces on her legs and eventually using a wheelchair. When she was a teenager, her condition had deteriorated so much that she moved to an institution where she spent the rest of her life. In 1948, Jean Russell was born. She was a normal, healthy, dark-eyed baby. In 1950, William (Billy) was born. It was a big change to have a little brother in addition to the three Russell little sisters! Bill had his mother's blond coloring. He was twelve years younger than me, but we have remained quite close over the years. Brother John was born exactly a year later, almost an "Irish twin." A year after John came Margaret Ann Russell, known from birth as Peggy. Then, in January 1954, Charles Russell was born, followed by Steve in 1955. When I graduated from high school in 1956, there were four Russell boys and four girls at home. As teenagers, Josie and I were called into service to help with the younger kids. We did not resent the responsibilities. I do not remember a time when helping at home interfered with something I really wanted to do at school or with my friends. I became skilled and very efficient at domestic chores. I could mass-produce peanut butter and jelly sandwiches, braid hair, and put wiggly small hands in mittens.

I had a special method of getting the boys to go to bed. Each would have an orange. I would break into the peel with my thumbnail and leave the boy to peel the rest. The peels accumulated under the bunk beds and gave the room a citrus odor. Knowing I could not spank them, I would threaten to throw cold water on them if they would not quiet down. Only twice did I follow through on the threat. Fifty years later, brothers John and Bill recall my water attack.

Transportation for such a large family was a challenge. I remember a station wagon or two, then a limousine purchased from a funeral home. It had a window between the driver's area and the back, a row of jump seats, extra floor space, and a luxurious three- or four-person seat across the back. The rear doors opened outward from the middle of the car. Once, when I was driving, the right rear door opened, and Jean and Bill clung to the open window. I was horrified and slowed down, but before I came to a full stop, the door had swung closed without any fingers or toes being crushed. When I broke my leg in 1957, I was able to sit on the elongated backseat floor with a full-length splint. I did not need an ambulance to get from the ski area to a hospital in Denver. Finally, the family bought a used school bus.

Josie and I had the basement bedroom with daylight windows. We shared a room until she left for college. We painted the room a bright green and made curtains of fabric with jungle foliage. It was our tropical abode. We could come and go through the back door of the house and go straight downstairs to our room. She left for college in 1954, so for one of the few times in my life, I had a room of my own. After college and marriage, our paths diverged. Josie and I were no longer close. I went off to study in Europe, to do international work and pursue my athletic interests—mountaineering, skiing, and running. Her adventurous nature was expressed in homesteading in Alaska for a few years before settling in the foothills of Colorado.

The youngest Russell, Susan, known to the family as Sioux, was born in 1958 when I was twenty years old and a student in Geneva. Sioux is only six years older than my son Eric. I never had the experience of living a full year with all my younger siblings, only vacations during my college years. One summer, we drove in two vehicles to Grand Teton and Yellowstone National Parks. We stayed at the ranch belonging to the Muries, naturalists who shared Bill Russell's interest in falconry. In Yellowstone, I carried the movie camera. To film the full height of Old Faithful's eruption, I turned the camera on its side. As a result, the film depicts Old Faithful spewing steam sideways.

In 1962, the Russell family moved from the house in Denver to the cabin they had built in Conifer, near Evergreen. The house was very small, with one tiny bathroom. Bill Russell and the boys enlarged it with a living room and a two-bedroom annex. There was an outhouse for additional toilet needs. On forty acres of mountain and meadow land, at 8,000 feet, it was a beautiful but challenging place for a large family to live. Heavy snow often blocked the road. Elk, deer, and bear visited frequently. In fact, once Bill Russell got deputized by the sheriff so he could kill a bear that had been harassing the chickens and trying to break into a porch where the family kept a freezer. He shot the bear through the window of the boys' bedroom one night, and none of the boys woke up!

The Russell boys and girls were active in 4-H, raising rabbits, sheep, and chickens for the annual stock show and prizes. They built a barn, chicken coop, and shed for the falcons. After the stock show, most of the animals were sold. Once, my mother served a chicken stew (after the sale of animals). Brother Charles asked, "Where are the wings?" They realized that it was a rabbit stew made of animals they had raised with such affection.

My children loved visiting the Conifer house, which they called "the Big Boy's house," associating it with my four brothers. With so much forest to explore and the various animals including, horses, sheep, chickens, and falcons, it was very entertaining. My sister Sioux was happy to lead her little nephews and niece around.

Chapter 6   College, Geneva And The Alps

Arriving at Smith College freshman year was a big transition. Going from a large, coed public high school to a women's college, living in a house with thirty-two girls, eight from each class, was a big change from living at home with younger brothers and sisters. Many Smith students had attended boarding schools, so they were accustomed to dorm living. After being near the top of my class in a large student body, I was now competing with girls who had all been at the top of the class. I lived in a small, traditional house, one of the oldest on campus, with students, a house mother, and a resident faculty member. The kitchen staff prepared and served meals. We were required to wear skirts or dresses for evening meals, except on Sunday evenings, when we could wear casual clothing for a meal of leftovers. During the day and for classes, we could wear pants or long shorts—Bermuda shorts.

One early ordeal was the famous Smith "posture picture." Naked, we were each photographed from the side and back. A bold, straight line was drawn on the photos to illustrate posture problems. A physical education teacher discussed these with us individually. Girls who failed the posture pictures had to take remedial physical education classes. There were rumors of (male) students from Amherst or Yale stealing these posture pictures to review the physical traits of the Smith students. I doubted these stories as the photos were kept in a locked file. Yale, Princeton, Wellesley, and a few other colleges did posture pictures in the 1950's and 1960's. Some scholars of social Darwinism and Eugenics studied these photos to categorize body types. Fortunately, the procedure was abandoned by 1970, and the photos were burned. There was also a swimming test. Those who could not swim the required number of laps had to take swimming classes. Those whose posture pictures were problematic had to take special gym classes to correct the faults. I passed the posture picture and swimming tests and was able to take crew as my sport.

The classes I took were interesting and challenging. I especially liked art and history. I had the privilege of taking studio art with the artist Leonard Baskin. One assignment was to draw a complex seashell in ink, repeating the process until we and the professor were satisfied. The impact of that course is with me today as I do figure drawing and landscapes with ink and watercolors. My history major allowed me to explore other subjects, such as philosophy, aesthetics, and economics. I decided to continue to study French so that I could do a junior year in either Paris or Geneva.

College social rules were strict. Men visitors were allowed only in the sitting room at certain hours, never upstairs. I spent weekends at men's colleges: Yale, Dartmouth, and Harvard, and sometimes weekend dates in New York. These outings required permission applications at the college, and there were occasional lies about where I was staying. Sometimes, men came to Northampton for the weekend, but we girls were required to check in to our houses before midnight.

During Christmas vacation of my freshman year, I broke my right leg skiing in Colorado. We were skiing in a group, arcing across the hill in wide, fast turns. Val and I collided. His ski hit my right leg, and the tibia shattered. I was brought down the mountain in a toboggan by a ski patrolman who was a good friend, Andy. It was a bad fracture, requiring surgery, screws, and wires. I had a hip-length cast and used crutches for six months. I missed classes in January, including physics labs, which were on the third floor of the science building. This resulted in a low grade and turned me away from any thoughts of a career in science. Negotiating the Massachusetts winter on crutches was a challenge that I overcame. I did not allow the cast and crutches to restrict my social life. I continued to go to men's colleges for weekend dates, including Dartmouth Winter Carnival. I rented a big wicker wheelchair so my friends or a date could wheel me over icy streets to a local bar. I learned to negotiate all sorts of terrain on those crutches! In June, back in Colorado, the orthopedist operated on my leg again, removing the screws. I was put in a knee-length walking cast so that I could put weight on the fracture area. In a few weeks, the pressure of my weight and the absence of metal made the bone thicken and heal. I wore a brace for a few weeks that summer. I hated the brace because it made me look like a cripple, a polio victim perhaps, while the plaster cast signified a sports injury. Without further physical problems, my sophomore year at college was smooth. I enjoyed my classes and concentrated on French to qualify for junior year in Geneva. I dated several young men from nearby men's colleges. Of course, during Christmas and summer vacation, I returned to Colorado to spend time with Gene, skiing, hiking, dancing, and going to movies.

Junior year in Geneva was a turning point in my life. I developed a love for immersion in a different language. My roommate for the year was a friend from Denver, Marybelle. We sailed on the French Line ship Flandre. The first evening on the ship, we shocked a middle-aged American couple sharing our table by accepting the wine offered by the waiters. We had intensive French lessons in Paris for a month before going to Geneva. Marybelle and I had rooms in the apartment of a very gracious widow in the 16th arrondissement. She did not have a car, but she did have a full-time maid. Except for my wealthy paternal grandparents, most families I knew in America had cars, but none had full-time maids. The furnishings in the apartment were elegant but faded. Breakfast was coffee, hot milk, bread, and jam. Dinners were three or four courses. There were always two carafes on the table at dinner. One red wine, the other water. Madame diluted the red wine with water and encouraged us to do the same.

We took the Metro to our classes near the Sorbonne and to museums and monuments. I remember the strong scent of garlic and tobacco in the Metro, even in the early morning. Some of the cars had wicker seats whose rough surface ruined our nylon stockings. I learned to be wary of male passengers on crowded trains. When a hand would rest on my hip, I learned to twist aside quickly.

When we arrived in Geneva, we lived in the apartment of a French professor of constitutional law, M. Robinet de Clery, and his wife. They showed us how to eat cheese and fruit with a knife and fork and to put a "little butter" on the Gruyere if it was hard and dry. We enrolled as foreign students at the university and signed up for whatever classes we wanted. We rented bicycles and abandoned our white bobby socks that marked us as Americans. Even on the coldest days, we were bare-legged or wore stockings. All classes and exams were in French, so my language skills improved rapidly, and I enjoyed the challenge. I joined the climbing club and made friends with Swiss climbers, including Rene, a medical student who took me to the dances and picnics of the Faculté de Médecine. When you tie on a rope with someone, you automatically switch to the familiar pronoun; "tu" replaces "vous." Formality is reduced, and friendships quickly develop. After all, one is putting one's life in the hands of the climbing partner. Our leader was a famous Swiss guide, Jean Juge. I followed his exploits in mountaineering journals for years.

Marybelle and I met other students who were skiers, some of whom had cars to drive to the nearby famous ski resorts: Megève, Les Houches, Saint-Gervais, and, most spectacularly, Chamonix. Two French brothers who often drove us to Chamonix were puzzled by the flat shoes we wore after skiing. They expected girls to dress up in heels for dinner and dancing. Our American sense of not wanting to be taller than our dates was hard to explain when they asked, "Why are you wearing bedroom slippers?" I learned from them that French men prefer their women to wear stylish clothes and shoes without concern for who is taller.

Gene and I decided since I would be so far away, we should feel free to meet other people and ignore our relationship. (No blue aerograms or phone calls.) Despite this, in December, I got a postcard from him asking for the dates of my spring vacation. He arrived in March to join me skiing at Val d'Isère in the French Alps. Leaving the resort, we tried to hitchhike but it was difficult with skis, so at Albertville in the foothills, we pooled our travelers' checks and bought a Vespa scooter. With two pairs of skis and poles and two big backpacks lashed to the back, we roared off to Geneva, looking like a giant insect on wheels. We stored our ski equipment there. Then, we rode the scooter to Rome for Easter. It rained heavily as we approached Rome. I was wearing a blue wool skirt. When it got wet, it weighed about fifteen pounds. As soon as we found a cheap hotel, we dashed up to our room so we could hang all our wet clothes around the room and jump in bed to get warm. We emerged from the hotel long enough to see the Pope (from a great distance) blessing the crowds. We trudged for hours through the Vatican Museum. By the time we approached the Sistine Chapel, Gene was worn out. He left the museum and sat on a stone wall and read Time magazine while I enjoyed the frescos.

During the year in Geneva, I became a frequent sender of blue aerograms to my friends and family in the US. These had fixed postage and folded inward. One could not insert another page or photo, but the aerograms were inexpensive and not as likely to be stolen or censored as would an envelope with expensive stamps on the front and a tempting flap for steaming open on the back. For many years, my connection with friends and family was maintained with blue aerograms.

When my classes resumed after Easter, Gene continued ski-mountaineering until the snow melted. One day, at the top of the cable car of the Aiguille du Midi, he and his pal Stu (recently mustered out of the U.S. Army) were approached by an American speaking with a Long Island accent. It was Harvey Edwards, a sports journalist living in Chamonix. They skied together, and Harvey generously invited them to stay at his tiny chalet. (Harvey, a bachelor then, became our lifelong friend, as did his wife and their two sons.) Several weekends, I took the train to Chamonix to join Gene, Harvey, and Stu for some alpine ski tours. If

Harvey did not have a date for the weekend, he let Gene and me stay in the master bedroom. As the snow declined in quality, Gene left his ski equipment in Chamonix and rode the Vespa to Arctic Norway.

Finally, my classes were over in June. When I told my Smith classmates I planned to spend the summer traveling around Europe on a Vespa and climbing mountains, they asked, "Why aren't you visiting the great museums and cathedrals of Europe? When will you have a chance to visit them again?" I replied, "The great mountains of Europe are unique, and when might I have a chance to visit them again?" My memories of Scotland and Wales are of rain and fog on the summits of Ben Nevis and Snowdon. I bought some Shetland wool in Scotland and knitted sweaters for both of us. Sixty years later, mine is still wearable. Gene's sweater succumbed to moths. I was so relaxed on the back of the Vespa that I took short naps as we rolled along. One day, a wasp flew up Gene's shorts. He stopped the Vespa immediately and jumped off to shake the wasp out of his shorts. I woke up quickly that time.

"You two should not try to climb Mont Blanc alone."

Before our American friends arrived to meet us, Gene and I decided to climb Mont Blanc, the highest point in Europe. He had skied and hiked to the summit in the late winter, so he was familiar with the route. We got into mountaineering mode by climbing the Aiguille du Moine, a moderate rock climb approached from a glacier. Here, we established a pattern that we followed for decades. On rock, Gene would lead because he was more skilled. After belaying him from below, I would follow, bringing along any pitons or other equipment he had used to protect the route. On snow and glaciers, I would lead, being lighter. It was more likely Gene could pull me out of a crevasse if I fell in. As he was heavier, it was unlikely I could extract him. On the Moine, I hiked ahead to cross the rimaye, the crevasse between the horizontal glacier and the steeper snow and ice slope. As I was tiptoeing across the snow bridge, it collapsed under my weight. I fell up to my armpits and screamed. Gene was below me on the horizontal glacier. He reacted quickly, jamming his axe in the ice, pulling the rope taut, and pulling until I was out. I gasped a sigh of relief when I stood beside him in the sun, pleased to be out of that icy blue hole where slipping lower could mean serious injury or death.

On Mont Blanc, we took the standard route from the mid-station of the Aiguille du Midi cable car, crossed the crevassed Bossons Glacier, and stayed the night in the Grands Mulets refuge, so named because it was originally supplied by mules walking up the glacier. There were only a few other climbers in the refuge. We took off at 3 a.m., saying goodbye to hutkeepers. The other climbers said the "Meteo" (the weather report) was unfavorable. However, we were confident, the stars were bright, and we felt strong together. We tied on the rope and followed tracks on the glacier. We avoided the crevasses and reached the long rounded ridge in the late morning. As we turned left toward the summit, clouds and snow blew in. Soon, there was zero visibility and no chance of reaching the summit. We turned to the right and felt our way down the ridge to the tiny Vallot emergency hut at an altitude of 14,400 ft (4,362 m). We pushed open the door to discover a dirty entryway with frozen garbage in the corners. In the inner room we found frozen blankets. Not elegant, but at least we were safe from the storm. We ate the last of our lunch food, drank water, and settled in for the night.

A pale dawn did not bring clarity. The clouds and whirling snow obscured our views. We had no more food and little water. We needed to descend. We knew there was a refuge on the Goûter Ridge only 1650 ft lower, whereas the Grands Mulets, where we had stayed on the ascent, was 4,300 ft lower, and our tracks up the glacier would be completely hidden by the new snow. The Goûter refuge was on a ridge, which should be easier to follow in the limited visibility. We, put on every piece of clothing we had, strapped on our crampons, tied the rope, and set out. I was confident that we would find our way down. I went in front, probing the snow with my ice axe to avoid a hidden crevasse. After about an hour, the clouds opened briefly. I could see we were descending a narrow snow ridge with steep fluted sides. It was the Aiguille de Bionnassay! I turned around, walked back to Gene, and shouted over the wind that we were on the wrong ridge. We retraced our steps to the junction with the Gouter ridge and slowly descended.

Finally, we reached the hut late in the day. It was a normal refuge, not an emergency shelter. There was no hut keeper, but there were bunks, blankets, a stove, and some basic foods. We were able to melt snow on the stove and prepare a dinner of soup and pasta. After another chilly night, we trudged down the steep, loose rock of the Aiguille du Goûter to the valley. We rested in Chamonix for two days, then went back up to the Grands Mulets. The hut keepers thought we had returned from the dead since it was five days after we had departed at 3 a.m. This time, the weather was clear; we reached the summit of Europe's highest peak at noon and returned happily to our camp in Chamonix.

We were staying in a big campground full of French and Swiss families, beautiful bikini-clad girls playing badminton, paunchy old men playing chess, and young athletic types striding off with their ropes to scale the peaks. I loved being a part of that scene. The European families had multi-room tents in which they could stand upright. Gene and I had a tiny two-person tent about two feet tall and hardly longer than our sleeping bags. With two American friends, Gene set off before dawn one day to climb one of the Aiguilles (rock spires or needles) looming above Chamonix. In the afternoon, a storm came up. They did not return. The next day, I went to the Guides' Office to ask about a rescue. The Chief Guide calmly told me that more than two hundred climbers had been caught overnight by the storm. "Don't worry until the fourth day," he said. Fortunately, Gene and the team did show up, bedraggled and hungry, on the third day.

Too soon, I had to leave them in Chamonix to return to America on the Liberté, a great French ship. It had been a wonderful year. I was so charged with enthusiasm that when I saw a handsome young man with dark hair and piercing blue eyes among the many students boarding the boat train in Paris, I was determined to find him on the ship and did. The first evening, we danced and spoke only in French. On the second evening, we admitted we were American. He was a Yale graduate who had spent a year at a medical school in Germany, and I was a student at Smith. We had a whirlwind shipboard romance. We were desperate to find some private space on the boat. His cabin mates came and went at irregular hours, occasionally bringing girls back to the cabin. I could easily have asked the two college girls in my cabin to vacate for a few hours, but there was also a middle-aged woman from Eastern Europe in the cabin. She rarely left her bunk, and because we had no common language, I could not ask her when she might leave the cabin. We met some evenings in an upper deck alcove. Where we could hug, standing. Every twenty minutes or so, a cloud of smoke from the ship's funnel would waft over. We met in New York at Thanksgiving, but I ended the romance in December. I came to my senses and realized Gene was the man for me. I saw the Yale man a few times in subsequent years. He lived in New Jersey and had a successful medical practice on Park

Ave. If I had married him, I would not have traveled the world, lived in Asia, learned exotic languages, or had adventures for 48 years.

My father met me when the ship docked in New York. To celebrate my twenty-first birthday, he and his best friend took me shopping and out for lunch. I bought a silky black shift dress and high-heeled shoes, which made me almost six feet tall. After my European experience, I felt sophisticated in the dark-paneled dining room of the 21 Club with two older men.

Junior year in Europe was formative: I expanded my intellectual horizons. I studied, lived, and had a social life immersed in the French language. This was preparation for living in Pakistan and Indonesia, immersed in the languages and cultures of those countries. Gene and I faced dangers and challenges together, in the mountains, on the Vespa, and camping with minimal equipment. These experiences confirmed the effectiveness of our partnership. Despite this, I pursued a shipboard romance. It was a temporary lapse of judgement.

Chapter 7   Marriage and The Great Getaway

I graduated from Smith in June 1960, planning to marry before the end of June, though I had done no preparation. We were overwhelmed by the thought of a wedding, wondering who would pay for what. (My father offered to buy a case of champagne.) Another complication was our seven parents. My mother, stepfather, and grandmother were doctors. Gene's father, stepmother, and mother were Christian Scientists. My family drank; his family considered alcohol sinful. I did not know whether my father or my stepfather should "give me away." So, we cancelled the wedding.

We tried to distract ourselves for two weeks by going out with other people, but we were miserable. Gene and I realized that we were meant for each other. On July 8, 1960, we were married by a Justice of the Peace in Denver. My best friend, Betsy, and Gene's brother, Jim, our witnesses. I was studying for my teaching credential at the University of Colorado in Boulder, so we did not have time for a honeymoon. Gene presented me with a new bicycle as a wedding gift. Cycling up Boulder Canyon was our honeymoon. At the end of August, we drove to British Columbia with a few friends. We backpacked to Lake O'Hara, west of Mount Victoria. The weather was damp, the marmots and chipmunks were ferocious, the rock was crumbly, but the scenery was beautiful. We managed to climb some minor peaks and hike up to the hut on the saddle of Mount Victoria, but a snowstorm descended, and so did we. Our week was over too soon. Going and returning, we drove past Grand Teton National Park, an area that would become a lifelong favorite for us.

I returned to my old high school in September for student teaching. It was strange, just four years after graduating, to be back in the same school on the other side of the desk. I had to wear stockings and heels instead of bobby socks and loafers. I worked with a social studies teacher and a French teacher. The social studies classes went well. I was working with a man who had been my teacher five years earlier. The French classes were problematic. The education courses I had taken during the summer emphasized oral/aural learning, avoiding translation and written material until the second semester after the students had memorized several dialogues with good pronunciation. The teacher I was assisting used an outdated method of language teaching. Each Monday, she gave the students French vocabulary lists to memorize and then tested them on Friday. My supervisor from the University of Colorado did not approve of that teaching method but realized that I was obliged to follow the directions of the experienced teacher. I received a passing grade for my student teaching, which I completed in January 1961. It was time to take a real honeymoon trip.

The Great Getaway began at the beginning of February 1961. We emptied our apartment, packed up our things, sold Gene's car, and drove my car to Connecticut, where I sold it. We had two essential books, *Ski Heil: Die 100 Schönsten*

Skiabfarten in den Alpen (Good Skiing: The Hundred Best Ski Runs in the Alps) by Walter Pause and *Trans-African Highways*, published by the Automobile Association of South Africa. Our plan was to ski until snow conditions deteriorated and then drive around the Mediterranean, climbing the highest mountain in each region as we went along, culminating in East Africa with Kilimanjaro and Mount Kenya.

Gene made this ambitious plan without really investigating the practical details of the journey. We embarked on the Maasdam, a Holland American Line ship. It was a long, rough crossing of the North Atlantic in February. We rationed ourselves to a daily ten-cent beer and a shot of Dutch gin to prevent sea sickness. I played bridge to fill the ten rough days at sea. Gene read several books. February 20, we docked at Le Havre and took the train to Paris, anxious for meals that no longer included two members of the cabbage family, boiled. A day later, we took a train to Munich and picked up the bright red Volkswagen convertible that we had ordered in advance. The car had seats that folded flat so we could sleep in it. Gene was six feet two inches tall. When he stretched out, his feet were touching the dashboard while his eyes looked up through the back window.

In Innsbruck, we bought new skis, boots, and poles and put the vertical part of the back seat in storage. The skis were fitted with bindings designed to allow ski touring uphill as well as skiing downhill. We also bought climbing skins. These artificial sealskins had piles facing toward the back of the ski so they would glide upward but not slip back. They were attached with a loop over the tip of the ski and buckle straps around the ski. They worked well for climbing straight uphill, but the straps reduced the effectiveness of the ski edges, making steep traverses risky. (In 1980, glue-on skins were developed, so when climbing, the skier retained the use of the ski edges.)

In Austria, we checked off the first of several of the one hundred best runs. Then, in Cortina, Italy, there are three more famous runs. Returning to Austria via the car-train tunnel, we spent the next week skiing between the towns of St. Anton, Lech, St. Christoph, and Zurs, checking off a few more of the hundred best ski runs. We arranged to meet our American friends Stu Kaufman, a recent Dartmouth graduate, and Alicia Bassett, a Colorado Mountain Club pal. The Arlberg area was my favorite region. We could take a lift in one town and descend to the next. There were no dangerous crevasses or avalanches. We enjoyed meeting our friends and skiing with them. Many of the hundred runs were outside regular ski areas and involved risks of route-finding, avalanches, and crevasses. It is safer to travel such terrain in a group of four than with just two people. Traveling and sleeping in our tiny car gave us plenty of time alone to cement our relationship. I brought along a small portable typewriter for writing a journal and numerous blue aerograms to friends and family as we went along.

We took a couple of days off skis to meet my father and stepmother in Munich, staying in a hotel for the first time in a month. After two days of sightseeing with the parents, we were camping in the car again, back in St. Anton with Stu, Alicia, and Austrian Goetz Koestler. Stu went with us to St. Moritz, where we skied near Morteratsch Glacier and climbed Piz Palü on skis. It is an elegant snow peak above a long, curving glacier. Because we began the ski at the Diavolezza refuge at 10,000 ft, we had to climb only 3,000 ft to the summit. At the end of the day, we had a 6,500 ft descent to the end of the glacier, several miles below. We spent five days in the St. Moritz area exploring long ski tours. Some were gentle, but some were steep and dangerous. Three years later, Olympic champion Buddy Werner was killed in an avalanche on one of those runs.

(There is a German film starring Leni Riefenstahl entitled *The White Hell of Piz Palu*. Every few years, I view it and remember our sunny ascent and long ski run to the valley below.)

From St. Moritz, we went to Grindelwald, Switzerland. We took the train inside the Eiger, crawling out a side tunnel to ski down the Eismeer glacier. That was probably the most difficult and dangerous run we did, but fortunately, there were tracks we could follow, weaving between the seracs and crevasses. After sitting out bad weather for two days, we took the train inside the Eiger to the Jungfraujoch. With Stu and Alicia, we skied down the Aletch Glacier to Concordiaplatz, where four glaciers meet, then turned up the Grosser Aletchfirn, then descended to Goppenstein, more than twenty miles in all. Gene and Stu took a train back to Grindelwald to get the car while Alicia and I slept in the train station until 2 a.m. Then we were off to Chamonix to meet our friend Harvey, whom we met in 1959 at his little chalet. Harvey's sister Joyce and her husband were visiting from Washington, D.C. We had some pleasant dinners and conversations with them. We did another ski tour, "the three passes."

Taking a break from the snow, we went to Geneva for a day to visit with Professor and Madame Robinet de Clery, in whose apartment I had lived when studying at the University of Geneva. They were pleased to meet Gene, though I am not sure they approved of us spending six months on outdoor adventures instead of intellectual or professional pursuits. We arranged a meeting with the professor and his wife by writing a letter in advance and confirming by telephone from Chamonix. I am not sure how we arranged the rendezvous with my father or with our ski friends in Austria and France, probably by letters written to "poste restante" or in the care of American Express. I remember waiting for mail at American Express offices in several cities.

We took some runs at the gentle Flégère area the next morning. After getting snowed-in during an attempt to camp on the Vallee Blanche Glacier, we said goodbye to Harvey and our French friends and drove through the tunnel to Cervinia, Italy.

Finally, on April 24, the weather was getting warm, and we had skied thirty of the best runs in the Alps. We stored our ski equipment in Innsbruck, picked up mail, serviced the car, and took showers at the public baths. We switched to warm-weather clothing but retained a duffle bag of wool and waterproof clothing, gear, boots, crampons, and ice axes for our planned mountain climbs. Two days later, we camped in Trieste and obtained visas for Yugoslavia. We were on our way to Africa! The Adriatic coast of Yugoslavia was beautiful, but the road was unpaved and narrow as it wound through Zadar, Split, and Dubrovnik. We picked up some German hitchhikers, who were good company for two days. Albania was a closed country, so we headed inland toward Titograd via Pec. It was the poorest, dirtiest city we had seen. I saw a bakery and tried to buy a couple of pastries for breakfast. The dough was mixed with mutton fat and had a filling of cold ground mutton and onions. It was not exactly the chocolate croissant I was anticipating!

The roads improved when we crossed into Greece on May 2. We stopped to buy food in Thessaloniki, then continued to Litochoro at the base of Mount Olympus. Inquiring at the office of the Greek Mountaineering Association, we learned that we must hire a guide to use the refuge on the mountain. A man named Kosti, with a donkey, was assigned to us. We shared only a few German words as a means of communication. It was a seven-hour hike to the cold and dark refuge, where we could shelter from the wind and sleep on wooden platforms instead of the snow. In the morning, we prepared for the summit, assuming Kosti would accompany us as our guide. No, he demonstrated that we would "opsteigen" and "aufsteigen" by ourselves, so we set off up through the forest to a wide snow plateau. We thought we were near the summit, but the fog thinned, so we could see a higher point in the distance. In four more hours, we reached the cement pillar marking the Throne of Zeus (at 9,300 ft). There was a precipitous cliff on the other side of the summit. We descended to the refuge and all the way down to Litochoro, where a large crowd gathered to watch us cook dinner on our little camp stove. The next few days were devoted to culture and history, visiting Athens and Delphi, camping overlooking the Acropolis, and at the temple of Poseidon at Cape Sounion.

On May 12, we entered Istanbul and discovered the worst traffic we'd ever experienced. The monuments and bazaars of Istanbul were my introduction to the Muslim world. Hagia Sophia, the Blue Mosque, the forts on the Bosporus, and the palaces were all stunning and so different from the architecture of Western Europe. Crossing the Bosporus by ferry, we drove to Ankara. Police awakened us in the night as we slept in the car. The large water containers we had put outside to make enough room inside for sleeping had been stolen. That was the bad news. The good news was the next day, we met a very nice Turk, Amil, and his friend Jerry, a guy from Montana, for drinks and dinner. Amil helped us find a room in a nice hotel. The next day, we drove to the Taurus Mountains to hike, then on to Adana, where one tubeless tire got punctured. The auto repairmen in the village were shocked when they pulled the tire off the rim. They had never seen a tubeless tire, so they vulcanized it.

We were unable to get a permit to climb Mount Ararat, the highest peak in Turkey, so we sped to the southern border, where we were turned back because we did not have the correct "trip ticket" for the car. Gene took a taxi to Aleppo for the permit while I relaxed for several hours at the border with some Swiss tourists and Arabs.

In Beirut, a charming city, we stayed with a former colleague of Gene in a spacious apartment with a view of the sea. We enjoyed the restaurants and went to a French movie. It seemed we were back in France but with a more varied ethnic population. We drove to the Cedars of Lebanon to hike to the highest point in the country.

Then, we drove to Damascus, the "oldest city in the world," according to our guidebook. It smelled like the oldest city. Strings of camels sauntered down the streets, causing traffic to stop erratically. The camel droppings contributed to the odors. We visited the Roman ruins at Baalbek on our way back to Beirut. From there, we arranged to go by ship to Egypt. We had to avoid driving through Israel, or we would not have been permitted to enter any

Arab countries. Boarding the ship for Egypt was not simple. The passport officials, the export controllers, and the boat crew had demands. Our cabin was dark and grim, but the food was good. We arrived in Alexandria the next day. It took four hours and several official fees, plus bribes, to get our car and baggage through customs. Every man on the dock, from the laborers lowering our car from the ship with fraying old ropes to the uniformed officials, held out a hand for a tip. We found the greed of the Egyptians so annoying we almost stopped our journey there.

"You cannot drive from Cairo to Nairobi."

Fleeing Alexandria and the port, we drove south to the pyramids and camped in the desert, deciding cold beer and Coca-Cola were our only hopes for survival in Egypt. We set off to climb up one pyramid in the morning. A toothless Arab in a long robe insisted we must pay him to guide us to the top. After some bargaining, we paid and proceeded. However, like our guide on Mount Olympus, this man stayed behind and below us. I realized he was concentrating on my legs as I clambered up the two-foot-high stones. I was wearing a dress to be as cool as possible in Egypt's summer heat. Egyptian women all wear ankle-length robes. I was an exotic contrast. Our escape from the heat, dust, and curious Arabs was having tea at the Cairo Hilton hotel. We could sit in the air-conditioned lobby for hours, reading or writing postcards. The only challenge was dealing with the attendant in the ladies' room, a formidable Egyptian woman swathed in black. She doled out tiny squares of toilet paper, and her attitude was threatening if the tip offered was too small.

We went to the Egyptian Museum, several mosques, and the Memphis and Sakkara monuments. Consultation with the tourist office and the automobile association confirmed that it was impossible for a Volkswagen to drive from Cairo to Nairobi. A convoy of four-wheel drive vehicles was required, so we got visas for Sudan and bought train tickets: Cairo to Nairobi on East African Railways, second class since the first class was sold out. The East African territories of Uganda, Kenya, and Tanganyika were English colonies, scheduled to receive indendence later in the year. Therefore, the entire trip was on a single ticket, which included trains, several kinds of boats, a Ford station wagon, and even a small airplane.

We bought some brocade cloth from a talkative old shopkeeper in the great bazaar of Cairo. He invited us for dinner with his family. His three sons offered to keep our car safe while we went south. We trusted the old man to watch what his sons did with our car. It was better than leaving it at the train station, at any rate. We boarded an 8:00 p.m. train for Luxor. Cold beer on the train raised our spirits as we spent the evening in the dining car with a Hungarian and an Egyptian engineer. We arrived in Luxor in the morning. Known as Thebes in ancient times, it was the capital of Egypt for five hundred years starting in 1570 B.C. The towering columns of the temple of Karnak were awe-inspiring with their elaborate carved designs. The half-mile approach lane is lined with six-foot-tall sphinx statues. I was awed by the sophistication of the Egyptians of thousands of years before. The decorated tombs across the river in the Valley of Kings showed elaborately dressed and coifed people and complex hieroglyphic writing. Our northern European ancestors were illiterate hunters and gatherers in that era.

On June first, a train took us from Luxor to Shellal, where we boarded a boat. Our tickets were second-class, so we had to sleep on the deck with the Arabs and Africans. Being white, we could eat upstairs. We dined with Mr. Lambert, an Englishman traveling to Cape Town and an American doctor. The next day, we stopped at Abu Simbel temples, which would later be transported inland to avoid flooding from the Aswan High Dam. There was a pleasant group of tourists from Cairo visiting the temples. They got back on their boats and sailed north while our boat continued upstream toward the Sudan.

Two days later, we left the boat and boarded a train to cross the Nubian Desert. Two miserable days on the train, dusty, hot, and crowded, full of Arabs staring at me, the only visible woman on the train, resulted in dysentery and discouragement. We sat in Mr. Lambert's compartment for much of the journey, but Arabs would squat outside the door, hoping for a glimpse of my legs. Arriving in Khartoum, we checked into the El Shark hotel. We took turns rushing to the toilet. A travel agent told us we had to get special permits for South Sudan and tickets to fly out of East Africa to be permitted to continue our journey south. So, we bought air tickets from Nairobi to Cairo at an unfavorable exchange rate. Those days in dusty Khartoum, struggling with stomach cramps and nausea, were probably the low point of our trip. We did manage to keep relatively cheerful and supportive of one another. I do not know many other people who would have survived that experience with a sense of humor intact.

My father was an enthusiastic member of the Rotary Club. He had written to several Rotary Club chapters on our itinerary. The Khartoum club had answered with an invitation for Gene and me to a Club dinner on an island in the Nile. We dosed ourselves with Lomotil, donned our most respectable outfits, and went to the event. It was the first time the group had hosted a woman. Most of the men wore long white robes, but a few wore business suits. Only one or two dared speak with me! It was a contrast to my father's Rotary meetings in a white clapboard hotel facing the green in Sharon, Connecticut.

After that surreal event, we were informed the Nile was blocked by floating plants, the "sudd." Continuing by boat was impossible, so we were put on a DC-3 plane from Khartoum to Juba, stopping at Malakal and Wau. Mr. Lambert, the large, jovial Englishman from the train, was with us. Juba's only hotel cost four pounds a night, which we felt was expensive, but since lions and armed rebels had been seen on the streets, we did not want to camp in our little tent. There was a small zoo in Juba, but more exotic than the wild animals were the tall, spear-carrying Nubian men clad in ashes while wandering the streets. Even in 1961, there was an ethnic conflict in Sudan between the Arab Muslim north and the African animist/Christian south. To continue south with Mr. Lambert, we hired an old Ford van to take us to Nimule, close to the Uganda border. There, we boarded another boat to continue south on the Albert Nile. We entered East Africa at the shore of Lake Albert. There were no border officials to stamp our passports. The people of Uganda wore simple clothing in contrast to the naked men we had seen in Juba. The banks of the river were a solid wall of vegetation. Each day, we saw the heads and ears of elephants above the trees and sometimes a crocodile in the water. We continued up the Albert Nile and changed to an uncomfortable Lake Albert steamer at 10 p.m. On June 12, my twenty-third birthday, we took a bus to the town of Masindi, where we had a lovely lunch.

From Masindi, a steamer, took us across Lake Kyoga to the town of Namasagali, where we waited for a 6 p.m. train to Nairobi. At 9,000 feet in the East African highlands, it was quite cold, a welcome change from the heat of Egypt and the Sudan. All the second-class seats on the train were full, so we were put in a first-class sleeper, which was very comfortable. The next day, we crossed the equator at 9 a.m. and finally arrived in Nairobi at 5 p.m. We stayed at the

Princess Hotel one night but soon returned to camping in a city park.

On we went to Kilimanjaro, with fresh information from the tourist bureau. We took a bus to Moshi. We saw giraffes, zebras, deer, ostriches, baboons, and Masai tribesmen. We looked across the plains, trying to see Kilimanjaro in vain until another passenger on the bus pointed almost straight up. There was white snow floating above the clouds. After a night in Moshi, a local bus took us to the Marangu Hotel, the starting point for hiking Kilimanjaro.

At the Marangu, we met some English residents of East Africa who would be our companions on the Kilimanjaro hike: Morris and Muriel, Derick, Colin, and Jeff. They were having a fully supported, catered trip, while we hired a minimum of one porter and took our own food. We started on June 18, walking through cultivated fields and villages until noon, then entering the forest. We reached the Bismarck Hut at 4:30 p.m. and waited for the porters. It was a dirty hut, but it was sheltered us from the rain. The next day, we left at 9 a.m. and emerged from the rain forest to heather and grassy slopes. The weather was cool and foggy. We arrived at Peter's Hut at 1:30 p.m. and had tea with some Royal Air Force men who were descending. Only half of their party had reached the crater of the mountain at Gilman's Point.

We departed Peter's Hut in the morning rain. Another descending party passed, including a sixty-eight-year-old man using hiking poles. Across the endless sand and ash saddle, we shuffled, arriving at the Kibo Hut at 15,300 ft at midday. We had headaches and little appetite but tried to sleep. At 1:15 a.m., we began our climb to the summit. Telesphor, a guide, led us up a long scree slope in the cold dark. We reached the edge of the crater, Gilman's Point, at 6:15 and watched a spectacular sunrise. Telesphor turned back to help the others while we walked easily around the crater to the highest point in two hours. This was an example of the "Murphy's Law" of volcanos: the route always goes to the lowest point of the rim. Climbers must circle the crater to reach the true summit. We felt strong when we reached the 19,340 ft summit. When we returned to Gilman's point, we were tired. There, we met Telesphor with Jeff and Colin-None of the others had succeeded in climbing that far.

As we rapidly descended the scree, we both felt nausea and fatigue and headaches. We took an hour's nap at Kibo Hut and then walked down to Peter's Hut. This was a twenty-mile day and very exhausting. We left Peter's Hut at 8:30 a.m. the next day and walked slowly down the mountain, stopping for lunch at the Bismarck Hut and arriving at the Merangu Hotel at tea time. The porters made wreathes of flowers for those of us who had gotten to the summit. I was pleased to have gotten to the true summit when no one in the other group had gotten beyond the low point in the crater.

We had a gay supper with our companions from the mountain, with liberal servings of beer and wine. The next day, we took a bus to Moshi and another to Nairobi, which broke down near Arusha. Finally, on Sunday, June 25, we arrived in Nairobi and had dinner with the group from Kilimanjaro. Jeff and his wife kindly invited us to stay at their home, where we met their two small children. The next two days, we took care of urban issues, including surgery to remove an infected wart from my thumb. We helped Jeff and Jan pack their tiny plane for a flight. Then, the rest of the group picked us up, and we drove north in two cars toward Nanyuki, stopping for a festive picnic along the way.

Our friends helped us locate the farm of Mr. Raymond Hook, a legendary "white hunter" and one of the early European settlers of the area. He looked the part. He was over six feet tall, with a massive chest, and was clad in a khaki shirt and wide-legged shorts. His skin was tan, and his knees were as wrinkled as an elephant's. He was gruff but cordial and confirmed that he could arrange for our approach to Mount Kenya. We stayed at his farm and had interesting discussions about the recent Mau-Mau insurrection. He provided three "boys" -African men, two mules and a horse to go up the mountain with us. We followed a dirt road for seven miles to the ranger station, passing Kikuyu villages. Then, we walked into a dense forest where the men cut our way through the overgrowth with their pangas (machetes). The trail was a muddy elephant track. Elephant footprints were like serious potholes that we had to step around, and the steaming piles of elephant dung proved that the animals were close. We knew an elephant could come through the bamboo like a locomotive at any time, while we could only move slowly through the dense vegetation. The trails were overgrown because the Mau-Mau rebellion had made the area off-limits to hikers for several seasons. At 3:30, we put up our tent at 10,000 ft and made a fire of bamboo. The next day, we hiked above the last bamboo and entered a zone of giant heather, groundsel, and grass tussocks protruding above a sea of mud. We tried to balance on the grass tussocks but often slipped off into the deep black mud.

After lunch, we went over Two Tarn pass (14,500 ft) then descended to a Hut in the valley below. There, we met four Royal Air Force men descending. We were all wet from rain and fog, but as the sun set, we had views of the peaks. In the morning, we hiked up to Top Hut in two and a half hours, then on to the 16,355 ft summit of Lenana, the lower peak of Mount Kenya. This gentle snow summit was our goal because the rock faces of Kenya's highest points, Batian and Nelion, were plastered with ice making it impossible for us to climb with the equipment we had. As we descended, we met one of our men at the Top hut, then dropped down to the valley, over the ridge, and down to camp in the grass at 13,000 ft. On July 2, we walked seven hours through forest, bamboo, and cultivation to Mr. Hook's farm. As we ate a long and delicious dinner, he lectured about Africans, politics, big game, and the wars in Africa. The showers and comfortable beds of his guest room were most welcome after our soggy little tent.

Back in Nairobi, I got the stitches out of my thumb and had lunch at the home of Jeff and Jan, where we stayed overnight. We watched their children while they went out dancing at the Equator Club. On our last day in East Africa, having climbed our mountains, we went to a Nairobi game park and saw lots of animals, including Nile crocodiles. I was pleased to see them in the zoo instead of swimming beside our boat on the Nile.

On July 5, Jan drove us to the airport for our flight back to Cairo. We were sorry to leave East Africa, which has beautiful scenery and friendly people. (We were saddened three years later to learn of Jeff's death in a crash of his small plane.) The passport control officers were angry when they discovered we had no entry stamps in our passports. We had entered East Africa at Lake Albert, where there were no officials to stamp them. A lengthy discussion and map consultation convinced them to let us board the plane. After stopping in Addis Ababa and Asmara, we arrived in Cairo and went to a small hotel. The next day, we got our car from the Arab family. They had put two hundred miles on the car and a few minor dents, but otherwise, it was OK. We got visas for Libya and drove to Alexandria. From there, we continued west. While waiting for passport control at the Libyan border, we went for a swim in the ocean. I was wearing my Swiss blue-and-white-check bikini, oblivious to Arab sensitivities about modesty. The Libyan army officer processing our passports was very interested in our swimming.

On July 8, our first wedding anniversary, we drove to Benghazi and Sirte through the desert. On the way, we passed several spectacular but unidentified Greek and Roman architectural remains. We cooked tuna and rice sitting and camped on the sand. Not a very festive anniversary celebration. We were sleeping in our Volkswagen with our heads looking up at the stars through the rear window. After midnight, the head of a large camel appeared above us. We were startled; so were the camel and his rider. Gene did the universal pantomime for sleeping, hands clasped beside his tilted head, and the man rode away to our sighs of relief. The next day, we continued to Tripoli and Sfax. No one in Tunisia would exchange Egyptian money, to our disappointment. In Tunis, it took two days of persistent effort to get reservations on a boat to Sicily, but we finally succeeded. We swam at a "family" beach at Carthage, where women swathed in black burkas shared the surf with French women in bikinis like mine. It was a relief to be with a few people in similar bathing attire. We were always ready for conversation in French or English, so as we rested on a bench near the beach, a Tunisian professor engaged us in conversation and then invited us to dine with him at a nice restaurant.

We returned to Europe on an overnight ship to Palermo. The next morning, we drove across Sicily to the ferry to Italy. In Florence, I bought two pairs of the most beautiful shoes I had ever owned. One was green leather with little straps across the top of the foot; the other was tan woven leather. Both had two-inch heels. Quite a change from my traveling shoes– flip-flops and climbing boots. Happy to be back in Europe, we continued to Zermatt to climb several summits of Monte Rosa, the second-highest peak in the Alps. From the Zumsteinspitze summit, we traversed the Gniffeti Col to the Margherita Hut, spectacularly situated above a cliff descending 3,000 feet into Italy. The hut-keepers shared their grappa with us, and we slept soundly despite their tobacco smoke. The next morning, we continued over two more snow summits, belaying carefully on the steep and crevassed sections. By 4 p.m., we were on the train down to Zermatt to celebrate with wine and hamburgers in the campground. We picked up our ski things in Innsbruck and detoured to the Arlberg Pass, where we met our friend Alicia and Goetz Koestler, her new husband. We returned to Geneva to celebrate Gene's birthday in the campground and pick up our films and slides.

We met my father in Paris, had a fancy dinner, and then went to a "Folies" show. I was not interested in the topless dancers, but I guess my father thought it was a special experience. The next day, we drove to Normandy to meet my half-sister, Caroline Herrick, who was traveling with another family. We spent a day visiting Mont St. Michel with them and then headed for Calais and the Dover ferry. We had a ship to catch back to the U.S.A.

We ended the trip so that I could begin teaching French and social studies at a junior high school in Denver. Gene went back to Tipton and Kalmbach, the engineering firm where he had worked since 1958. T & K, as it was known, specialized in water-related engineering issues and had many international projects. One of the partners, Mr. Tipton, had participated in the creation of major water treaties, including the Rio Grande Treaty and the Indus Waters Treaty.

Our travels in Europe and around the Mediterranean made us restless for more international experience instead of making us ready to "settle down," as our parents hoped. Gene's father, Frank, dealt in real estate. He found a small brick house for us to buy for $9,000. Built-in 1910, it was in central Denver, near my high school. It needed work but would have been very comfortable for a small family. We plunged into home improvement, steaming off wallpaper and painting.

Chapter 8   First Pakistan: Peace Corps Volunteer

Several events early in my life had lifelong impacts on my personal, educational, and professional life. My marriage in 1960 to Gene changed my life to a shared one. Our 1961 trip, driving around the Mediterranean, gave me a superficial introduction to the Muslim world and the culture of Arab societies. The Peace Corps experience in Pakistan was an immersion in the cultures of South Asia, particularly the Muslim society of Pakistan. It was the foundation for our careers. I went to graduate school, studying the history of the Indian subcontinent for an M.A., followed by a Ph.D. in International Studies, concentrating on social and political development in Muslim societies. Gene worked on irrigation and water resources projects that would eventually take him to twelve developing countries in Asia and Africa. Among those, only Nepal and India were not Muslim-majority countries. (Ironically, his only job in Europe was in Albania, a Muslim majority country!)

At a party in the spring of 1962, our friend Peter announced he had joined the Peace Corps and was going to Nepal. "Some of America's most accomplished mountain climbers were serving as staff for the Peace Corps in Nepal and India," he said. Gene and I were intrigued. Peter gave us a number to call for applications. We called, submitted our applications, and, in a few weeks, received letters saying we were accepted. The Peace Corps wanted us to go to Pakistan, not Nepal. We hastily consulted an atlas to confirm that the

Himalayan Mountain chain extended across Pakistan. In fact, five of the world's highest mountains are in the Karakoram range of Pakistan.

"Going to Pakistan in the Peace Corps is not a good idea. You should stay home and start a family."

My parents and Gene's mother were proud of our decision, though a bit worried about us going so far away for two years. Gene's father was dismayed. He thought we were going to settle down in the little brick house and have children. By the end of June, we sold the house, stored our belongings in Gene's mother's basement, and went for our training in St. Paul, Minnesota. Our group of volunteers included three other couples like us: an engineer husband and a liberal arts wife; several single engineers, ranging in age from twenty-five to seventy; four teachers; two nurses; and two farmers. Some were assigned to East Pakistan, now Bangladesh. We were fortunate to be assigned to Peshawar in the North West Frontier Province of West Pakistan, a few hours away from the high mountains.

The Peace Corps wisely decided to have volunteers selected for Pakistan to study the language of their specific area of assignment rather than Urdu, the national language. We studied Pushto, an Indo-European language that is spoken by some 40 million *Pathans, Pukhtoons, or Pushtoons,* in the North-West Frontier Province (NWFP) of

Pakistan and eastern Afghanistan. Other volunteers studied the language of their assigned location: Punjabi, Sindhi, or Bengali. Our instructors were native speakers. We studied language every morning. They used the modern approach of having us memorize dialogues without translating them into English for the first three weeks. This resulted in excellent pronunciation and the ability to speak basic sentences without hesitation. In the afternoons, we had classes on the history, culture, and religion of Pakistan, health issues, and physical training. We were required to pass basic swimming, lifesaving, and first aid tests. We had a series of inoculations and medical exams. Peace Corps rules required that couples not have dependent children during their years as volunteers. Because we were training in Catholic St. Paul, Minnesota, we did not receive any contraceptive advice or supplies!

After two months of training, we were on our way. The flight was endless; it was a propeller plane, not a jet. We landed in Karachi and then flew north to Lahore. The person most fluent in each language was asked to make a little speech when coming off the plane. I was selected to give the greeting in Pushto. Of course, none of the officials in Lahore, in the heart of Punjab (an area where Punjabi is the local language), could understand Pushto or the Bengali spoken by one of the volunteers going to East Pakistan. In 1962, Pakistan had been independent for only 16 years. There was residual respect for English-speaking foreigners. Sahib and Memsahib continued to be polite in terms of address. Our group of volunteers, male and female, old and young, were generally treated with respect, along with some puzzlement of why we had come and occasional accusations of working for the CIA.

After a briefing in Lahore, the NWFP group left by train for Peshawar, near the Afghan border. There were eight of us, including Gene and me; Millard, assigned to Ismailia College for men; Nancy, at the home economics department of the University of Peshawar; Martha and Barbara, at Frontier College for Women; and engineer Ralph Cole and farmer Norman House, working in Mardan an hour north of Peshawar. We attended a two-day orientation at the Academy for Rural Development, where two volunteers from the first Peace Corps group had been working for a few months. The academy was modeled on the very successful Comilla (East Pakistan) Academy for Rural Development, but its programs appeared more theoretical than practical. Finally, we went to our assignments. It was the first of many years of living and working in Muslim-majority countries and of years of boiling and filtering all drinking and cooking water, taking anti-malarial medication weekly, and living without a telephone or television.

Peshawar's population was over 250,000. Like many cities in the former British Empire, it was divided into two distinct areas: the cantonment and the old city. The streets of the cantonment, built by the British, were wide and straight, lined with tall trees. Some of the trees were mulberry. In the early summer, the fallen mulberries coated the roads with dark purple slime. Once, my bike skidded on the mulberries, and I fell. I was bruised, and my clothes were dyed purple. Behind iron gates and spacious lawns was the State Guest House, where Queen Elizabeth, Jackie Kennedy, and visiting heads of state had stayed. There were several schools, a market area, an English library, the Peshawar Club, the Anglican Church, the Christian cemetery, and the governor's residence. The military facilities included parade grounds, barracks for the soldiers, and bungalows for the officers. There was also some housing for civil servants and a food market. The cantonment gave one the impression of orderliness and planned development.

In contrast to the cantonment, Peshawar City was surrounded by a massive wall, with a huge fort on the western edge to ward off attackers from the wilds of the Tribal Areas and the Khyber Pass. Until the 1950s, the gates of the Peshawar wall were closed at night. Enclosed by the wall, the city grew upward instead of outward, with a maze of tiny streets, many impassable for automobiles. Buildings five or six stories high haphazardly lined the narrow lanes. Streets were often blocked by huge timbers supporting the upper floors of mud-brick buildings.

The center of the old city was the *Chowk Yadgar* or Memorial Square. It was fascinating to watch the constant parade of people and animals there. At any time of day, colorfully robed holy men, water buffaloes, two-wheeled horse carts (*tongas*), three-wheeled scooter taxis, laborers hauling wooden carts of freight, barefoot villagers in baggy pants carrying their shoes to rest their feet, Punjabi businessmen in suits, drink vendors with carts holding citrus squeezers, dusty glasses and sugar cane, legless beggars on little carts, and small boys scurrying to deliver trays of tea to offices and stores could be seen. (Business deals and discussions always required a cup of "Peshawari chai," green tea with sugar and cardamom.) Afghan merchants carrying rolled red carpets would stride past peddlers selling spicey fried vegetables and meats. Herds of goats, sheep, and cattle occasionally blocked the way, followed by children collecting dung for fuel. Strings of camels added to the traffic confusion. Always, there were groups of Pathans, tall, swaggering, hawk-nosed men bristling with pistols and rifles, wearing turbans, long shirts, and baggy pants. Amid the variety of life on the city streets, one segment of the population was conspicuous by its absence, the women. Now and then, a faceless figure in black silk or white cotton cloth would pass on foot or in a tonga. The only visible women were foreigners like me. Rarely would a woman from Karachi or Lahore pass through the street in the back seat of a car, shielded from view by tinted windows. The cantonment was a different world where the wives of military officers and soldiers could be seen in the shopping areas.

The Municipal Committee (City government), to which both Gene and I were assigned, provided our housing. It was an apartment in the Cantonment, about half a mile from the city walls at # 2 NC Road. There were four apartments on the two lower floors occupied by military families. Our quarters consisted of two rooms on the roof, with a bathroom between. Our kitchen was across the roof and down a half flight of stairs. The arrangements were better than we expected. There was electricity, ceiling fans in both rooms, running cold water, and a regular bathroom. To take a bath, however, one had to heat water in the kitchen, carry it up the stairs and across the roof, through the living room, and into the bathroom. The kitchen was black from the soot of the kerosene stove. One time, as I descended to the kitchen, the floor was as black as the walls and ceiling; it was undulating. It was wall to wall cockroaches! They scurried away as soon as my foot touched the floor. Another time, I was carrying a small beef roast from the kitchen. A kite (a species of hawk) swooped down and snatched it from the plate.

There was a kerosene stove and a "food safe," a screened cupboard to protect food from insects and rodents, but no refrigerator. I bought an oven to place over the stove for baking. The kerosene smoke tended to turn baked goods gray. The gray meringue on my lemon pie was not very appealing. We used large, unglazed pottery jars (*matka*), to cool butter, cheese, or meat in watertight containers by immersing them in cool water. We would also cool our weekly bottle of beer. As the water evaporated through the unglazed pot walls, it cooled below the ambient temperature.

Before we arrived in Pakistan in 1962, Gene and I had lived in Europe and traveled through the Middle East and North Africa, tasting and eating different foods. Pakistan exposed us to a new cuisine. We loved the crusty, puffy *tandoori* (oven) naan bread. Hot and fresh, it was delicious. Cool, on the second day, it resembled leather. There were many delicious vegetable dishes determined by the season. Spinach, peas, potatoes, and carrots are in curries in the winter, and okra, eggplant, squash, and tomatoes are in the summer. Each curry involved a different combination of spices, roasted and ground during the preparation. Sometimes, rice was served instead of naan. We liked the *pilau* (pilaf) rice cooked in a broth with vegetables. Lamb was the preferred meat in Pakistan, followed by chicken, beef, and water buffalo. Cubes of lamb (tikka kebabs) on skewers cooked over charcoal were ubiquitous in the markets and at dinners. Shami kebabs were made of spiced ground lamb formed on the skewer like a sausage. *Nargisi* (narcissus) kofta was ground lamb wrapped around hard-boiled eggs, surrounded by a curry sauce. When the kofta was sliced, the yellow-and-white egg was visible in the center of the meat, mimicking the colors of the flower.

Fish was rarely available in Peshawar, a thousand miles from the sea. Once a week, a train arrived with fish packed on ice. It rarely smelled fresh. (In the 1980s, we met a family

76

in Swat who were raising trout. That fish was excellent.) Ground beef mixed with hot chilis, onions, and an egg appeared in the open markets as *chappli* kebabs. A *chappal* is a flat sandal. *Chappli* kebabs were as big as the sole of a shoe. They were deep-fried in a large black pan, like a giant paella pan. This was the Pakistani equivalent of "fast food," strictly snack food. It would not be served in a private home.

When my young adult sons visited us in Pakistan years later, they called these "gristlebobs."The beef was tough. Cattle and buffalo worked pulling wagons and plows or turning the wheels of threshing machines; they were not fattened for eating. I learned to distinguish buffalo from beef after a few shopping trips. Buffalo fat is white, while beef fat is more yellow. In the meat markets, half an animal would be hanging at the butcher's stall. I would shoo the flies away and point out which part I wanted to buy. The butcher squatted behind a block like the stump of a large tree. He would hold a sharp knife with his toes and pull the meat against it. I learned to ask for "undercut," the sirloin. This was the only part of the cow that was tender enough to chew. The meat experience in Pakistan and later in Indonesia pushed us toward a more vegetarian diet, eliminating red meat. Later, Gene explained in France, *"Je ne mange pas de viande, mais je mange la chacuterie"* (I don't eat meat [which is sold by a butcher], but I do eat cured meats which are sold at the charcuterie or delicatessen). Many Pakistani dishes are cooked in clarified butter (ghee) or animal fat.

They are tasty when fresh and hot, but the grease congeals as it cools.

One of my favorite dishes was spinach curry with white cheese -*sag panir*. It was excellent on rice or naan bread. We enjoyed the deep-fried snacks, pakoras or samosas, too. The fruits in Pakistan were excellent– mangos and melons in the summer, all kinds of citrus in the winter, mulberries in the spring, and bananas all year. In the hill villages, excellent apricots, grapes, peaches, and apples were grown. Mountain villagers dried apricots to enjoy in the winter. The lack of good transport or preservation meant that the prices would fall when fruits and vegetables were in season, and the income for farmers low. One of the projects in villages where I worked with college girls was teaching women to bottle ketchup and jam. That helped prevent waste of excess tomatoes or fruit and increased the farm income.

Gene was assigned to work with the city municipal engineer, Mr. Rauf. The city government had requested the Peace Corps send an engineer. They agreed to find an appropriate assignment for me: Social Welfare Officer. This position was listed in the official Colonial documents for municipalities but had never been filled. The duties included supervision of libraries, gardens and parks, the orphanage, the poor home, and the "general welfare" of the population of a city of 250,000.

Gene was immediately put to work designing water systems and structures, supervising construction, and inspecting public works. The City Engineer, Mr. Rauf, settled back to drink tea and smoke cigarettes while Gene did his work for two years. Gene and I shared an office and a peon, Ahmed Baksh. Every office had a peon to sweep, carry messages, and, his most important duty, bring tea. We continued studying Pushto by hiring a tutor from a nearby village, Babu Fazle Elahi. (Babu means clerk. It implies that the person is literate and knows English.) He came to the office half an hour before the official opening time. Ahmed Baksh would bring three tiny cups of green cardamom tea, and we would practice our language skills. Gene would search for engineering terms such as "compacting the soil," "leaking pipe," "lack of concrete," or "slump test." I needed to expand my vocabulary related to health, education, women, and families. During the second year, twice a week, we met with a Pushto poet to learn how to read simple poems and primary-level books. We also studied Urdu, the national language. This proved useful in future years, as our careers brought us back to Pakistan and to India, where Urdu and Hindi are mutually comprehensible at the basic level.

All volunteers were issued bicycles for transportation. After six months, the Peace Corps provided Gene a scooter so he could more easily visit other volunteers in the area. He was considered the leader of the NWFP group. In the second year, the Peace Corps issued him a blue jeep. Each vehicle was supposed to be used for official or emergency business only. I must admit we had some nice excursions to the mountains in that jeep, with two or three other volunteers, of course.

In contrast to 1961, when I had worn a bikini on the beach in Libya, and a short skirt climbing the pyramid in Egypt, oblivious to local customs, I understood the need to wear modest clothing and acquired several shalwar-kameez outfits. These are baggy pants worn under a knee-length tunic. A dupatta, or scarf, draped across the shoulders or head is a required part of the outfit. I respected the need for modesty, but I refused to cover my face in all the years I lived in Muslim areas.

Although I was prepared for a segregated society, passing daily through the streets of Peshawar without ever seeing a woman was disorienting. Only in the gold and jewelry bazaar could I spy a woman lifting her face veil to inspect a bracelet or ring. There were no women in the other markets. Servants, children, or men did the shopping. In the narrow residential streets, peddlers pushed carts of food along. A basket would be lowered from a second or third-floor window, and a feminine voice would ask the price and bargain. When the agreement was reached, the money was lowered, and the vegetables were lifted up. I would often see a bearded, turbaned, bandoleer-wearing Pathan tribesman picking through flowered silk fabrics in the cloth bazaar, selecting material for an outfit for his wife or daughter.

Babu, our Pushto teacher, was a very traditional Pathan. He had two wives; he explained that the second one was the widow of his brother, so it was his responsibility to marry her to keep the children and the property in the family. Babu was very protective of us, always warning us of potential dangers. When we proposed taking a bus trip to Parachinar, a walled border town in the tribal territories near the Afghan border, he insisted on accompanying us. The commanding officer of the local regiment checked our papers. He invited us to stay overnight in the military guest house. Babu's enthusiastic introduction of us as selfless volunteers contributing to development in Pakistan may have facilitated this hospitality. On the other hand, the officers may have been happy to see a young woman and speak some English with us.

The Peshawar municipal staff indicated that the major responsibility of my position as Social Welfare Officer was to ensure there was no graft at any of the institutions under my supervision rather than to try to make improvements. Checking on the gardens each month was fun. The head gardener and I would make the rounds on bicycles. The first time, he told me we had to check the "buffalo allowance." I was puzzled. At the first park, I saw that a water buffalo was pulling the heavy lawn mower. The buffalo allowance was for feed! If the buffalo looked very thin or ill, one suspected the garden staff pocketed the allowance. There was a special area reserved for women at the largest municipal park but not at the smaller ones. I initiated a program of reserved times in the mornings for women and children at other parks. A woman without a male escort would be unacceptable in a park in the 1960s. (even now, it seems)

At the municipal library, the books were locked in glass-fronted shelves. If a book was missing, the value would be deducted from the librarian's salary, so of course, he did not let people take books out. There was a shelf list of books but no catalog. I hoped to introduce a membership program and a catalog system for checking out books after the library moved to the new town hall, which was under construction.

At the orphanage *Darul Atfal,* the concern was auditing, not improving the lives of the sixty resident boys. The orphanage received US Food for Peace wheat, cooking oil, powdered milk, and other items distributed by Catholic Relief Services (CRS) for the United States Agency for International Development, (USAID). I visited once a month, met with the director, inspected the record-keeping and the use of the donated food, and counted the donated blankets to be sure none were missing. The director tried to prevent me from speaking directly with the orphans; as my Pushto fluency improved, I understood them easily. The boys were not happy with the director or with the food. They threatened to run away if there was not a change of staff. I reported the problems to my supervisor at the Municipal Committee, but after two years, not much changed. I suggested the college girls could tutor the younger boys as part of their social work program, but the director feared the presence of young women would be a moral risk. During my two years, there were no boys adopted from Darul Atfal. Several were released at age seventeen.

I was surprised there were orphan boys because male children are highly valued in the local culture. Even if both parents had died or gone to jail, a boy would be cherished by uncles, aunts, and grandparents. Probably, the parents of these boys were too poor to keep them, lacked extended family, or the parents could have committed some terrible sin, such as adultery or murder, to make the child unacceptable.

Frustrated by the limitations of my official job, I investigated other institutions where I could be useful. I joined Martha and Barbara at Frontier College for Women, supervising the social service work of graduating college students. The provincial government had introduced a social service requirement for both men and women college students. The women professors at Frontier College were not interested in giving up their weekly holiday to supervise the students, so we Volunteers spent Fridays taking groups of students to institutions where we made arrangements for them to volunteer. The sites included a women's hospital, the women's jail (children accompany their mothers to jail, so our students organized games and lessons for the children as well as reading and writing letters for the illiterate prisoners), health centers, and a nearby village. We chartered the college bus to take the students to the village, but we three Peace Corps Volunteers usually rode our bicycles, to the amusement and amazement of all.

Other work I found outside the city government was teaching English and typing at the largest girls' high school in the city. The principal, Mrs. Tila Mohammad, was enthusiastic and enterprising. She had obtained a grant from the Ford Foundation for her high school to become a pilot model high school, introducing practical subjects like typing and home economics. I taught there for one year until the Peace Corps assigned a volunteer to serve full-time at the school. At the University of Peshawar, Gene and I met some of the professors. Several wives I met wanted to form a university women's organization. A dozen of us met to discuss the idea. They voted to create the Women's Volunteer Service. The members wanted to assist the rural communities around the university and the non-academic staff. There were two distinct groups of university wives: some were quite educated, had traveled abroad, and could have been professors themselves, while others were country-cousin brides with little education or sophistication. Almost all marriages were arranged by the families, but some clearly considered the need for some equivalency of education for the bride and groom. Others held to the tradition of marriage to the daughter of a cousin to keep property in the family. Women's Volunteer Service members were mostly well-educated. Members of Women's Volunteer Service spoke Urdu, Punjabi, or English. After a few months, some of them decided they needed to study Pushto so they could communicate with the local women they were trying to help. My example of learning Pushto inspired them. They managed to work together on several projects, the first of which was holding a fundraising bazaar to purchase medicines for the clinic serving the nonacademic university employees and their families. I was elected Secretary of the Women's Volunteer Service at the first meeting but was pleased that after a year, the women were ready to take over the leadership. These women and several professors were very helpful to me when I returned in 1974 to do my dissertation research. The principals of Frontier College and the girls' high school were also helpful. In contrast, no one associated with my job at the Municipal Committee became a helpful colleague or friend.

Gene also faced challenges at his job. Several times, he was asked to modify inspection reports in favor of contractors who were friends of local officials. He was ignored when he pointed out leaks in the roof of the new town hall and other, shoddy construction. He soon realized that corruption was common in government-financed construction.

Outside our regular jobs we were invited to be technical advisors to the mountaineering club of the University of Peshawar by a friend, Professor Farzand Durrani, an archeologist and avid hiker. We met with interested students and faculty, discussed mountaineering techniques, and demonstrated mountaineering equipment and clothing. In the summer of 1963, our friend from Peace Corps Nepal, Peter, joined us and three professors, ten students, a cook, and fifteen local porters to make an attempt on Saraghrar, a 24,111 ft peak on the Pakistan-Afghanistan border in Chitral.

After three days of jeep driving and four of hiking, we established a base camp. Gene, Peter, Professors Farzand and Qazi, and I, with three students, found a route through the steep, rocky lower terrain to a flat glacier area, an ideal spot for a high camp. We had five days of food and fuel and thought we had a good chance of getting to one of the several summits of the peak. The next morning, a porter ran breathlessly up to our camp, informing us that the professor who had remained in base camp had died after falling from a cliff while taking photographs. The whole trip was over. All the porters were needed to move the group and the body. We packed up and descended, wearing our heavy mountaineering boots all the way to the hot valley. My toes and heels were covered with blisters as a result. The students had arranged a burial spot in the scenic opening of the valley, but word was relayed from the nearest village with a telephone that the family wanted his body back in his ancestral village. The coffin was carried by horse for two days until a jeep forced its way up the rugged track. It was 110 degrees, so the body was decomposing. The two men driving the jeep covered their faces in cloth to ward off the scent. Because of my blisters, I hiked thirty miles in plastic flip-flops. We were sad that our friend had died and the expedition had failed.

We visited India and Nepal for the first time since we still had a few days of vacation remaining and enough money saved from our living allowance of $70 per month each to pay for flights to New Delhi and Kathmandu. In New Delhi, we met Gene's mother, Stella. She was on a retired schoolteacher tour. I showed my blistered feet to the Peace Corps doctor in Delhi, and he was taken aback. He told me I should not be walking around in the dust of India in that condition but offered no alternative. So, I carried on, changing Band-Aids frequently. After sightseeing in Delhi and Agra, we flew to Kathmandu. Stella's tour group also went to Kathmandu. They were staying in one of the old Rana palaces that had been converted into a hotel; we were sleeping on the floor at the Peace Corps office. We spent a day with Stella, visiting the bazaars and temples in and around Kathmandu. It was monsoon season, so the rain prevented us from flying to Pokhara, where Peter was teaching at a local college.

We were accustomed to the frustrations of our jobs and the satisfaction we gained from making Pakistani friends. I knew some middle-class Pakistani women with whom I did informal cooking and English lessons, but they could not meet Gene. One friend was never prepared for the cooking projects. I would arrive at her house planning we would bake a cake, only to discover there was nothing in her refrigerator but a bowl of loquat fruits. She was waiting for me to tell her the ingredients before sending her servant to purchase eggs, butter, and milk. She had not learned to use the refrigerator to keep an assortment of basic foods. Another friend wanted me to show her how to make salads, as one sees in British housekeeping magazines. Unfortunately, most of the ingredients are not available in Pakistan. Lettuce was not sold in the markets. Tomatoes and cucumbers were available only in season. I was able to show her how to score a cucumber with a fork so that the slices have a scalloped edge and how to make oil and vinegar dressing and potato salad, but not much more.

Among the downstairs neighbors in our building was one couple who were cosmopolitan and very cordial. The husband was a colonel in the Pakistan Air Force, and his wife was an obstetrician. Most Pakistani women would not consult a male physician for any health problems, and certainly not for gynecological issues, so medicine is one profession open to women. They had a teenage daughter who planned to attend a university. We had pleasant visits with them.

We had a visit from the Director of the Peace Corps, Sargent Shriver, accompanied by Richard Goodwin. Seven of the nearby volunteers gathered at our apartment waiting anxiously for about two hours. The Shriver team had come by road from Kabul and miscalculated the time for the journey. We took them to a famous kebab restaurant in Peshawar City for a lively conversation and good food. After dinner, the visitors continued driving east to Rawalpindi.

We were invited regularly to family celebrations by people of all classes in the city, in villages, and in the wild, ungoverned tribal areas. These included weddings, funerals, and circumcision rites. Men and women were segregated at these parties, but I, a foreign woman, was not subject to the limitations of local women. I could shoot guns, watch dancing girls, and drink whisky at the men's gathering, and then join the women and children at their party, drumming and dancing to traditional songs.

Our first visit to Afghanistan was at Christmas 1963. We got a ride in a diplomatic shuttle to Kabul. I was enchanted by Afghanistan. Young women in Kabul wore short skirts and jeans under flowing scarves or capes; the town seemed ancient and modern at the same time. There was one row of modern cement buildings along each major street, but the rest of the city was a mud-walled village interspersed with the blue tile domes of mosques. Louis and Nancy Dupree, who became the foremost American experts on Afghanistan, entertained us at a musical poetry reading in their garden and took us to visit Istalif, a village famous for blue pottery, and to a modern resort at a lake above the city. The villages we passed looked simple, but the fruit orchards and fields looked productive. Afghanistan's major exports in that era were raisins and Karakul lamb skins. Thirty years later, Nancy Dupree and I both lived in Peshawar, where we worked with Afghan refugees. The Peace Corps volunteers in Afghanistan were a lively group, too. We envied their refrigerators, while they envied our ability to access the medical services at an American Air Force base near Peshawar. Restaurants in Kabul were open to women and men and served beer, to men, at least.

Around this time, I decided I was tired of struggling with a diaphragm for contraception. Gene agreed that it was time to start thinking about having children. Since we were 25 and 29 years old. In a few weeks, I was pregnant, though I did not confirm it for a couple of months. Eric may have been conceived on one of those cold nights in the Kabul Peace Corps office. This was another life-changing event!

Tipton and Kalmbach, the firm for which Gene had worked in Denver, had extensive work in Pakistan. Mr. Tipton made a detour to Peshawar to talk with us when he was visiting company projects. He invited us for dinner at the classic British-style Peshawar Club. He offered Gene a job in Pakistan, in view of his experience in the country and impressive language skills. He would be the Team Leader of a project in the Punjab, starting in September 1964. It would be a challenging assignment for a thirty-year-old engineer, supervising dozens of local workers and two American engineers and coordinating with Yugoslav construction contractors. The laborers were Pakistani, and the funders were the US Agency for International Development and the governments of Pakistan and Yugoslavia through a barter arrangement. Our standard of living would change dramatically. Our monthly electricity allowance would equal our Peace Corps monthly living allowance. We would have housing with air-conditioning, hot water, and a well-equipped kitchen. We could buy a car for personal use in addition to the many project vehicles and drivers who would be under Gene's supervision. Our air travel would be in business or first class.

The Peace Corps experience from 1962 to 1964 in Peshawar had a profound impact on us. Gene and I matured. We learned to face challenges together, dealing with people who accused us of working for the C.I.A., dangerous traffic on our bicycles, the death of a professor on our climbing expedition, carrying pots of hot water from the kitchen to the bath, dust, disease, and polluted water. These challenges reinforced our partnership. We learned to bike and drive on the left side of the road, too. We learned two languages, Pushto and Urdu, and passed the Foreign Service exam level three for speaking and understanding both. Though we had low reading skills, we learned the Arabic alphabet sufficiently to sound out words and names on signs. Gene shared his engineering knowledge with laborers and contractors at his job. He was less successful in imparting ideas to the Municipal Engineer, Mr. Rauf. For example, one of the city projects was to improve the water supply with a new elevated water tower. Its size would be determined by the number of buildings with water connections. Many afternoons, we walked through narrow lanes, Gene looking at the pipes and me taking notes on a blueprint of the water system. We counted more undocumented connections than legal ones. Rauf certainly did not want to spend his time stepping over open drains and detouring around bullock carts to count water connections. Gene learned about corruption, which seems universal in Pakistan (and many other countries) when building and contracts are involved. The most ambitious project of the city was the construction of a new city hall. When he refused to certify the shoddy construction of the roof, Rauf and the mayor wrote, "Mr. White is not an employee, so his judgment has no bearing on the certification." Of course, the contractor was a friend of Rauf.

In our interaction with the Peshawar University Mountaineering Club, we imparted some basic climbing techniques, concentrating on snow and ice travel since the overambitious objective they had chosen for their first expedition was largely a snow climb. We also shared ideas for trip organization and camp management. Two professors became long-term friends.

The impact of my presence was scattered among the high school girls to whom I taught typing, the orphans whose rations I monitored, the libraries where I tried to introduce the concept of open shelves, the college students whose social work I arranged and supervised, and the university wives' group whose charitable program I helped launch. I was pleased that I worked my way "out of a job" with that organization, leaving it with local leadership to carry on.

The Peace Corps issued a footlocker of books to each volunteer. We were supposed to donate these to a local institution when our terms were completed. I gave some of our books to the municipal library in the new town hall. Though the permanent collection of books was kept on locked shelves, I insisted that the books we donated be placed on open shelves where patrons could check them out. I donated our remaining books to the fledgling women's college in Charsadda, a town north of Peshawar.

We gained an understanding of Islam. My experience with Christianity was limited to being baptized, attending church occasionally, and participating in a youth church choir. Gene's experience was with Christian Science. In contrast to Christianity, as I knew it, Islam is a system of belief that categorizes all human activities as required, admirable, neutral, or forbidden: Halal to Haram. The five pillars of Islam are required: recognizing Allah as God and Mohammad as the Prophet, praying five times a day, fasting during Ramadan, giving alms, and making a pilgrimage to Mecca. The Haram, or forbidden, activities include adultery, eating pork, and blasphemy. All other human activity is in the middle range of neutrality, argued over by Muslim scholars over the centuries. I heard of religious scholars arguing whether shampoo was halal since it was not mentioned in the Koran, Hadith or other sacred writings. Apparently they did not discuss if the Kalishikof gun was halal or not.

Most Pakistanis we knew had arranged marriages, meaning spouses were chosen by their parents, with extensive research and consideration of different candidates.

Since marriage to cousins is preferred to keep the property in the family, some brides and grooms had known each as small children but had been separated in adolescence. Marriages were intended to provide social stability and fertility, to cement the relationship between two families, and to provide prestige or economic security. Romantic love was not the basis for a marriage but was expected to develop over time. I met many women who were happy in their marriages. Perhaps the careful judgment of the older generation works, as well as the attraction of hormone-charged young people to choose lifelong partners.

Islam permits polygamy. But women are limited to one husband. In some cases, a man is expected to marry the widow of his deceased brother to maintain family solidarity. However, in other cases, a man will marry a second wife because the first wife has not given birth to a son or he is bored with her. I suggested to some women friends that it would be fair for women to have multiple husbands. They were shocked at the idea. I pointed out that in Tibet, it is acceptable for a woman to marry two brothers since some men are long-distance traders and absent for months at a time. Another inequality in marriage in Islam is that a man may marry "women of the book," that is, a Christian or Jewish woman, but a Muslim woman may only marry a Muslim man. I was told of a different kind of marriage, only available to Shia Islam followers, *Mut'ah*. This is a temporary marriage, an agreement between a man and a woman to be married for a fixed time, anything from a few hours to a lifetime. It is egalitarian in theory because the woman enters into the agreement herself, whereas, in a traditional (especially Sunni) marriage, her father or other male relatives must sign the agreement on her behalf.

We hoped our presence had contributed to some appreciation of Americans, just as we'd learned to appreciate the society in which we were immersed. From that time onward, Gene worked internationally in twelve countries. Among them, only Nepal and India were not Muslim-majority countries. The experience of living in a gender-segregated society determined my future studies and career. For my Ph.D., I conducted research on the implications of segregation on economic and social development. At San Francisco State University, I taught courses on women in the developing world, Islamic civilization, and the history of the Indian Subcontinent. When I joined The Asia Foundation, my first title was Advisor for Women in Development and Islam.

The job for Gene, and my pregnancy changed our plans for the summer of 1964. At the completion of our Peace Corps service in July 1964, two other American couples, old friends from Colorado, planned to join us at the "1964 American Hindu Kush Expedition." The goal was a new route on Tirich Mir, the highest peak on the Afghan border. Being six months pregnant, I was not going on the expedition. Gene stayed in the mountains of Pakistan for three weeks while I used my ticket home to visit Europe. I booked my ticket through Brussels, where one of my best friends from college lived, then Copenhagen, Stockholm, Oslo, and Bergen. I traveled through Scandinavia by train and bus to see the countryside and visit small towns. It was a good trip, though some of the other clients on our tour bus were curious about a pregnant woman traveling alone. Adding to their curiosity, for two days, one of the other Peace Corps volunteers from our team joined the tour. I introduced him to other tourists as my "friend," not my husband. That caused more puzzled looks.

After a week in Connecticut, I flew to Denver. Gene met me there, flying directly from Pakistan after the end of the expedition. His job in Pakistan was scheduled to begin on September 20. The baby was due September 10, so we thought we had scheduled everything perfectly. Nature does not always comply. I had false labor pains a couple of times, but by September 19, when Gene had to depart, the baby was not yet born.

Chapter 9   Second Pakistan: Mother and Memsahib

"You can't take a five-week-old baby to Pakistan."

Finally, on September 23, 1964, in Denver, Colorado, I gave birth to a 7-pound, 13-ounce boy. We named him Eric Kenyon White. I was given a mask with gas to use during the final strong contractions. I took a deep breath to push out the head, then felt the little shoulders and slippery body slide out. I had a sense of relief and excitement. Eric's face looked squished after the long labor. His hair was red and invisible against his pink skin.

We stayed with Gene's mother, Stella, for a month, and we had regular visits from my mother and siblings. Stella welcomed her first grandchild to her home. My recovery was accelerated by all the help I got from her and my family during those first weeks. I was prepared to care for a baby because, from the time I was eight, I had helped care for my younger half-brothers and sisters. I did not doubt my capability even in remote Pakistan. In addition to clothes and diapers, I had to get Eric a passport and inoculations, including smallpox, so we could return to Pakistan and join Gene. My sister Josie had given birth to a girl, whom she named Elizabeth, a few months earlier. We introduced these great-grandchildren to our grandmother, Dr. Kenyon. She was pleased.

By the end of October, we were ready to depart, first class on Pan American Airways, to Karachi! I was seated in the front row, where there was a baby bed that folded out from the bulkhead. The flight was long, and I was tired and dehydrated from nursing. When we finally landed in Karachi, I fell asleep again and almost missed disembarking. The plane had landed on a distant runway. A small bus came to get the passengers. I woke up and realized I had missed the bus and frantically waved at the flight attendant. No other passengers in first class were disembarking at Karachi, so I had been allowed to snooze on. If I had not woken, I would have been on my way to New Delhi without a visa for India. The stewardess radioed for a car.

Meanwhile, Gene was nervously searching for me and Eric in the parade of passengers from the flight. It was well after midnight when we were reunited, and Gene met his son. We spent the rest of the night at the airport hotel, then flew north to Lahore in the morning.

I was returning to Pakistan as a true "memsahib," with servants, cars, leisure, and a child. I was no longer a humble volunteer. In addition to my grandmother's *"Healthy Babies,"* I carried Dr. Spock's *"Baby and Child Care"* book to guide my decisions in health crises. A company driver met us at the airport and took us to the WAPDA (Water and Power Development Administration) flats. We had a three-bedroom apartment on the second floor. Gene had recruited Mohammad Ali, a Peshawar Pathan who had worked as a cook for other Peace Corps volunteers, to be our household helper. Mohammad Ali went to the local markets, boiled and filtered our drinking water, prepared food, and did some cooking. He was delighted with little Eric. As soon as possible, he was carrying him around on his shoulders. Tall, turbaned, his grey beard dyed red with henna, Mohammad Ali was a striking figure, especially with tiny, red-haired Eric. We hired an ayah, Sheila, a Christian woman, to help with Eric and do the washing. Muslims do not take jobs dealing with human waste, including diapers. Although previously I disdained the wives who played bridge and drank sherry while their husbands were out at construction sites, I found myself getting close to that pattern. I played tennis with foreign and Pakistani women at the nearby Punjab Club, Sheila pushing Eric along in a stroller as we walked there. I sewed a short white tennis dress for myself but always covered it with a longer skirt for the walk to and from the club. I joined a group of women who enjoyed painting and drawing, but I did not sink into the bridge-and-sherry set.

Even with the increase in income, servants, refrigerators, cars, and the more sophisticated markets of Lahore, food and cooking could be challenging. All our drinking and cooking water had to be boiled and filtered. I learned to substitute ingredients. In Lahore, as throughout Pakistan, vegetables and fruits were seasonal. There was no frozen or prepared food. Throughout the year, we missed the "A" s: Artichokes, Asparagus and Avocados. There is no pork in Pakistan unless you know someone who hunts wild boar. However, we could drive to Amritsar, India, in less than two hours to buy pork. When Eric was ready for baby food, I created it at home, mashing our food with a fork. I learned to disguise the bitter malaria pills in a spoonful of jam so he would swallow them every Sunday. Although my social status changed to that of a dependent wife and mother, I continued to travel and seek adventures with Gene. I had a good baby backpack and a firm belief that babies are portable. We hiked in the nearby countryside and with a couple of Pakistani friends, rock-climbed on an escarpment on the Indus River. We took turns entertaining Eric near the cliff.

Gene had two days off for Christmas, so we planned a day trip by air to Gilgit, the administrative headquarters of the Karakoram Mountain area. The flight went over the shoulder of Nanga Parbat, the tenth-highest mountain in the world. It was far more spectacular than any mountain scenery we had observed in the Alps or North America. Gilgit is a small commercial center with a large military establishment. It guards the northern and western borders of Pakistan. There were no year-round roads through those borders until the Karakoram Highway to western China was constructed in the 1970s. Towering glaciated peaks surround the valley. It was so spectacular in Gilgit that we extended our stay and spent one night at the government tourist guest house. It had fireplaces in every room, but only cold water. In Gilgit in December, it is below freezing at night. The army held a celebratory polo match on a grassy field bordered by stone walls. It was an exciting match. I was the only woman in the audience, holding three-month-old Eric on my lap. Flights were canceled the next day due to weather. By the third day, we were running out of diapers. To ensure getting on the next plane, we camped near the runway in a forest ranger's hut so that when we heard a plane approaching, we could snatch Eric and our packs and race across to the terminal to be first in line for boarding. The plane was a small Fokker and could not fly very high. "When the pilot eased over the 14,000 ft pass near Nanga Parbat. I could count the pine trees."

In early April, we drove to Jammu, India, and flew to Srinagar in Indian Kashmir. We rented a three-bedroom houseboat on the Dal Lake. It was equipped with a "cook boat" and a full set of servants. Men selling vegetables, flowers, souvenirs, and Kashmir shawls rowed their narrow boats to our houseboat all day. Kashmir was beautiful in the spring, with many flowers blooming in the Moghul gardens. The snow-covered peaks surrounding the area made it seem far from the world's problems.

My father and stepmother, Mary, came to visit us later in April. They wanted to meet Eric in person and see our way of life. They stayed with us and enjoyed Mohammad Ali's cooking. One day in Lahore, I was driving them on the Mall, a four-lane wide roadway, when we changed destinations, so I made a U-turn across four lanes of car, bullock cart, truck, and horse traffic. My father was impressed, especially because I was driving on the left side of the road. We took a quick trip to Peshawar and up the Khyber Pass. My father, being a travel agent and fascinated with exotic locations, really enjoyed that.

In the spring of 1965, we moved to Multan, a large city on the Indus plains, halfway between Lahore and Karachi. It was close to Gene's project site, in the area between the Jhelum and the Sindh rivers, tributaries of the Indus River. Multan was known for *"Gabiristan, Garam, Gund and Gharib,"* (tombs, heat, dust, and beggars.) All true, we observed. The project rented a nice house for us, a bungalow in the *Gulgasht* (flower garden) Colony, an upper-middle-class area. It had servants' quarters, a kitchen, dining, and living rooms, and two large bedrooms, each with a dressing room and bathroom. The central rooms had high ceilings with fans and small ventilation windows near the ceiling. The low-ceilinged dressing rooms, bathrooms, and verandahs sheltered the inner rooms from heat, which was over 115 degrees many days. There was a large yard enclosed with a brick wall, with space for lawns and flowers and a large vegetable garden. We had air conditioners in the bedrooms and the living room; however, the power supply was irregular. I loved having enough space for Eric to play indoors and out, as well as for sewing and art projects. The only drawback was the kitchen, which was small. There wasn't room for Mohammad Ali and I to cook at the same time. Our household staff expanded. We hired a gardener, a night watchman, a day watchman, and a new ayah, Mumtaz.

A *dhobi*, or washerman, came once a week to collect large laundry, including sheets, towels, and Gene's pants and shirts. He brought the clean things back the following week. I had a wringer washing machine for Eric's diapers, his clothes, and mine. We also hired a sweeper, a Christian, who came several times a week to wipe all the terrazzo floors with rags that became darker with each visit. When the toilet drain got blocked, the sweeper brought another man to help unclog it. They were amazed that there was paper in it! It was a square brick drain, so of course, the toilet paper got stuck. Pakistanis use water to cleanse after defecating. These sweepers had never imagined people using paper.

Having a small child gave me an advantage in meeting women. All the houses were surrounded by high walls, but news of the arrival of a foreign woman with a baby spread quickly. In a few days three of our neighbors sent servants to invite me to visit. I walked to their homes with Eric in a stroller. I was glad that I had spent some time learning Urdu since women in Multan spoke Urdu or Punjabi and would not have understood Pushto. Three children about Eric's age were living close by.

Through an official associated with Gene's work, we were introduced to one of the most influential families in the area, the Gardezis. They owned large farms and several villages. The blue-tiled tomb of their ancestor, Shah Yousuf Gardezi, was in a square in the center of the city. In 1088 A.D. Shah Yousuf came to Multan from Gardez in present-day Afghanistan. He was regarded as a saint because he converted many people to Islam. My family history in America was three hundred years long; this family had a nine-hundred-year connection to their home! In the twentieth century, Gardezis served in the government in several capacities, including as officers in the armed forces and members of the provincial and national assemblies. A daughter of the family, twenty-year-old Rebab, became my friend. She was smart, beautiful, and eager to learn; she was a college student. Accompanied by a servant or her brother, she occasionally came to my house to cook, sew, and paint. Somedays we played badminton in the garden. During our three years in Multan, the Gardezi family generously hosted us for dinners and took us on picnics at their farms. The picnics were segregated, of course. Strolling in a huge orchard with a group of women watching children playing under the trees while a cook prepared curry and rice over an open fire was pleasant. (No cold sandwiches on these picnics.) In summer mango season, we ate the ripe mangos leaning over tubs of water with the sticky juice running down our chins. In the winter, the servants juiced oranges while we picked the fruit. Meanwhile, over at the men's party, Gene would be drinking whisky, discussing politics, or being challenged to ride a racing camel.

The expatriate community in Multan was very small. There were a couple of missionary families and a mission hospital with two elderly American women doctors. There were four Peace Corps volunteers in nearby rural areas. There was an older British couple who seemed right out of the _Raj Quartet_, fading gently into retirement in an alcoholic haze. Entertainment was limited. The single cinema in Multan showed English language movies only on Sundays. Outside of town, there was a large swimming pool at a power plant constructed by Germans. We got permission to use the pool, where we rarely saw anyone else. The Yugoslavs working on Gene's project lived an hour away, near the work site. The chief of the party had brought his wife, but the others were of bachelor status.

Our good friend, the mountaineer Trevor Braham, lived in Khanewal, thirty miles away, managing a large cotton farm. We enjoyed visiting Trevor and went on several mountain adventures with him. These included climbing peaks in Baluchistan and an excursion to the Karakoram in 1967 when Gene and Norman Norris made the second ascent of 17,135 ft Malika Parbat.

Rebab introduced me to the principal of Multan Women's College. She asked me to teach English conversation. I enjoyed teaching a small group of students each week. After I got to know several faculty members and the principal, they asked if I could teach swimming. I was surprised that a women's college had a pool. The pool was small, about the size of a badminton court. It was surrounded by a high wall to satisfy the need for modesty. I agreed to teach swimming to eight people at a time. I asked that the pool be filled to shoulder depth only. I figured I could rescue anyone in that amount of water. For the first scheduled lesson, I arrived with Eric (age one and a half) and his ayah, Mumtaz. Eric wanted to jump right in. I held him and let him kick and splash, hoping to reduce the students' fear of water. Mumtaz took Eric to play on the grass while I encouraged the students to enter the pool. They stood around the edge, wrapped in large towels or sheets. They modestly dropped the coverings at the water's edge, showing a variety of tailor-made swimsuits. One girl surprised me by wearing an American-style Jantzen stretch one-piece suit. Her mother was from Iran, where such fashionable items were available. There was no place in Multan to purchase ready-made women's clothing, let alone a bathing suit! Households regularly engaged a tailor, who would sit on their veranda and sew whatever garments were needed. The girls had asked their tailors to sew swimming attire consisting of a top like a blouse worn with a sari and knee-length pants. It took several lessons for some girls to put their faces in the water, even if they were standing. I was pleased that after three months, most of them could float, flutter- kick, and paddle across the pool. These lessons might well have saved one or two from accidental drowning.

On September 6, 1965, Pakistan and India went to war. The war had begun as a ground war near the cease-fire line in Kashmir, but soon evolved into an air war. This interrupted our adjustment to life in Multan. Blackouts were imposed. Billboards were smeared with mud in case they would reflect light. The authorities feared that the lights on the ground would show Indian pilots the locations of cities. The army took over the telephones at the hospital and the bishop's office. (There is a small Christian community in Multan. It was the seat of the Catholic Bishop of the Punjab.) We heard rumors of the evacuation of American dependents. The newspapers ceased to be available. We had a radio on which we heard confusing news reports from international sources. For local news, Gene relied upon the office peon who brought his tea in the morning.

We learned on September 15 that U.S. military planes had evacuated American women and children from Lahore and Karachi, but we had not been informed. We did not have a telephone at the house, and Gene's office phone was being monopolized by government and military officials. I had read about the riots in Watts, Los Angeles, and felt perhaps it was safer to stay in Pakistan during the war rather than flee to America. (My mother in Colorado had been buying baby food in case we arrived suddenly.) Bad news in distant places is more frightening than a local crisis. A few days later, American dependents were evacuated from Dacca in East Pakistan.

Police and civil defense patrolled our neighborhood to enforce the blackout rules. They called out if there was a glimmer of light anywhere. One evening, Gene was using a flashlight to go to the bathroom. Someone peered over our wall and saw the light. Then, the patrol hammered on our gate and shouted at us, calling us trouble-making foreigners. The Gardezis invited us to stay at their farm, but we preferred to stay in Multan, where Gene continued to have occasional access to a telephone at his office.

We were worried but did not feel an immediate threat. The war was fought between the two air forces. India lost more planes on the ground than in the air. Indian planes attempted to bomb the Multan airport but instead killed several cows near the runway. This was ironic; cows are sacred to Hindus in India, so those pilots committed sins by killing cows. In Peshawar, Indian bombs hit the Mall Road rather than the airport runway. Parachute troops were dropped on both sides of the border; the soldiers were captured immediately if they survived the jump. Senseless violence spread in other cities: The U.S. Information Service library in Karachi was burned, the U.S. Embassy windows were smashed, and there were demonstrations at the United Nations and United Kingdom offices. A ceasefire went into effect on Eric's birthday, September 23, 1965. Relations between Pakistan and America soured after this war as did relations with India.

A ten-year moratorium on the sale of U.S. military equipment was imposed on both Pakistan and India. India had not relied on the U.S. arms, but Pakistan had. The Pakistan authorities thought they had been betrayed by the U.S. since it was a member of CENTO (Central Treaty Organization, created in 1955, dissolved in 1979. Member states were Iran, Iraq, Pakistan, Turkey, U.S.A., and United Kingdom). No more Peace Corps volunteers were accepted in Pakistan or in India after this war. Indian leadership was angered that America treated both combatants equally. India's leaders felt it should be supported as the world's largest democracy and leader of the nonaligned movement. (I was not familiar with the Asia Foundation in 1965, but I discovered years later, when I became an employee, that the foundation had been asked to leave India. However, it continued its presence in Pakistan.) Those weeks of war, with the occasional sound of aircraft flying low, were a difficult and worrying time, but I was confident that I could protect my infant in a war zone, just as I was sure to find my way up and down the mountains I had climbed.

We drove to Lahore for Thanksgiving to join the other employees of Tipton and Kalmbach. One other wife had refused to be evacuated. She was an older woman of English background. We two organized a Thanksgiving dinner for twenty-five men. Fortunately, we could go to the company commissary to get frozen turkeys and plenty of drinks. Eric kept everyone entertained, running around speaking with the servants in Urdu.

Most of the wives and children who had been evacuated returned by Christmas, so the company Christmas party was a more normal gathering. There was a camel for children to ride and costumed Santa Claus to hand out gifts. Eric was frightened of Santa Claus and of the crowd of American children. His playmates in Multan were all local children.

Chapter 10   Home Leave And Twins

Our first home leave came in 1966 when Eric was almost two. I believe that children are portable when small and capable when ambulatory. Eric was just between those two stages, almost too heavy to carry but not sufficiently reliable to toddle about independently. We wanted to take maximum advantage of Gene's contract, which gave us two first-class round-trip tickets from Pakistan to Colorado. Eric did not get a separate seat or a luggage allowance. However, the seats in first class were so large that either of us could comfortably sit with him. I looked forward to the trip, to adventures in familiar and new areas. It would be a chance to introduce Eric to our friends and families who had only seen photos of him.

On July 16, we flew to Karachi and boarded the Pan Am One flight at midnight. Down the aisle came a stewardess serving champagne, cheeses, and sliced ham. For the past two years, we hadn't seen any champagne. Most cheese and the only ham we had was canned, so we enjoyed this midnight repast. Unfortunately, I was suffering from a persistent Giardia infection and was taking strong medication that made me dizzy. When I got to Geneva, I stopped taking the medicine because I did not want to ruin my vacation with its side effects. I also stopped taking birth control pills.

Gene's brother, Jim, and his wife, Elena, met us in Geneva. We drove to Chamonix for dinner with our friends Harvey and Suzy Edwards. Harvey and Suzy now had a one-year-old son, Frederic, so they were able to recommend childcare and pediatricians, both of which we needed. We left Eric with a sitter for a day and a half so we could climb the Aiguille d'Argentière with Harvey, Jim, and Elena. To access the climb, we took the cog rail train to Montenvers, descended and crossed a glacier, then followed a steep trail up rocks and ladders to the refuge. As in most Alpine refuges, there was a restaurant, bar, and bunks for more than fifty people, even though the building was on the top of a cliff. I was happy to be back in the Alps again. Staying in a crowded refuge with climbers from several countries planning their ascents, sleeping on shelves like sardines, I enjoyed hearing the discussions about the departure time (2 a.m. or 3 a.m.) for each climb. It was a welcome change from being a memsahib in Pakistan. The climb went well and we returned to the valley in good spirits. The following day, we drove through the tunnel to Italy for a four-hour lunch at Chez Filippo. We six people consumed five bottles of wine. When we got back to Chamonix, we found Eric was sick with fever and vomiting, so I stayed with him and visited the French pediatrician while Gene, Jim, and Elena went off for another climb. I did not panic about his illness because we were in civilized France, where it seemed no infant sickness could be too serious. After all, Eric had spent his first two years in the presence of typhoid, typhus, cholera, malaria, dysentery, and smallpox. A fever or rash in Europe seemed trivial in comparison. French antibiotics for his age were administered as suppositories, which were easy to administer. After a few days of antibiotics, Eric was fit and happy.

On July 25, we drove to Switzerland and took the train to Zermatt, where no cars are allowed. We stayed in the campground with an excellent view of the Matterhorn and Monte Rosa. We celebrated Gene's birthday with pork chops cooked on the camp stove. I saw two blond Swiss girls in starched uniforms wheeling an eight-child stroller down the street. I spoke with them and discovered they were from a children's hotel, *Kinderheim* Theresa. We hurried up the hill to enroll Eric for a two-day stay so that we could climb the Breithorn while Jim and Elena climbed the Matterhorn. Eric stayed at the hotel again so we could climb Castor, a pretty snow peak near Monte Rosa. He seemed to fit right in with the European children. One of the staff members said that she had forgotten his name but had called him "darling."

Back in Chamonix we said farewell to Harvey and Suzy, then on to Paris for two days of sightseeing and shopping before stopping in Brussels to visit with my college friend Cecile and her husband, David. They had a two-year-old daughter. Cecile and I had a long conversation about the birth process after dinner. When we got to the part about expelling the placenta, Gene and David retreated to another room!

On August 9, we arrived in Connecticut, visiting my father, stepmother, sisters, cousins, aunts, and various East Coast friends. A blur of parties, picnics, swimming, and cocktails left me feeling so ill that I consulted Dr. Everts, who had been my pediatrician when I was a small child. She thought I had the flu. Eventually, it would be clear that I was pregnant and still suffering from giardia.

Eight days later, we went to Colorado. We stayed first in Denver with Gene's mother, then went up to Conifer in the foothills, where my family lived. The house, built by my stepfather and my four brothers, was on the road where I had learned to rock climb with the Colorado Mountain Club a decade earlier. We left Eric in the care of his grandparents and multiple aunts and uncles while Gene and I went to Aspen and Boulder for four days of climbing and hiking with friends. Too soon, it was time to leave. Overnight in San Francisco, we had a glimpse of the "swinging sixties." Friends who were in graduate school took us on a quick tour of North Beach and Telegraph Avenue. We missed the "summer of love" and those iconic trends because we were living in Pakistan.

Our return was through Japan, where I felt illiterate because all signs and addresses were written in Japanese. This was very disorienting after living in Pakistan, where I could read the Arabic script used for Pushto and Urdu. In Europe, I could speak and understand French and read signs, menus, and train schedules in Italian or German.

Fortunately, Japanese students wanted to practice English and were very helpful. We asked our hotel clerk to write in Japanese the name of the train station and our destination. We could show this to our taxi driver and the agent at the station. We took the train to Kawaguchiko and were directed to a very nice hotel. From there, in the early morning, a taxi took us to Mount Fuji. Each hiker buys a stick at the base and has it stamped at each "station" on the ascent. Eric and I reached only station five because he insisted on walking, not riding in the backpack. A two-year-old does not walk very fast. Gene went on to the summit and took photos.

Our trip ended with a day in Hong Kong and three in Bangkok, where we stayed at the famous Oriental Hotel. Other guests were startled when Eric jumped into the swimming pool and paddled back to the side. He did not know how deep it was, but he knew I was there in the water to catch him. A day of sightseeing on the canals was a good way to end our journey. We arrived in Karachi at midnight, two months after we had departed.

I continued to feel weak and nauseated, so I went to see the missionary doctor in Multan. She told me I was pregnant. The predicted birth date was May 15, 1967. Good news, but the bad news was that I continued to have Giardia parasites in my intestines. I had to take another round of nasty, strong medication.

The trip was wonderful, but it was nice to be back in our own home in Multan. My big project for the fall was making wine with the help of a book on home winemaking and the advice of the Yugoslav contractors on Gene's project. I bought grapes in the fruit bazaar from trucks arriving from Afghanistan. It is essential to have the grapes before their frosty-looking exterior is washed off. This has the yeast that makes the juice ferment. Mohammad Ali crushed the grapes with a potato masher. We put them in big crocks for a few weeks until they bubbled. Then, we siphoned off the juice into glass demijohns and then into bottles. The Yugoslavs encouraged me to add sugar water to the fermented skins for a "second pressing." In six months, I had sixty bottles of quite potable wine. A few exploded in the storage room, however.

I renewed my other activities: teaching English once a week at the women's college, taking Eric on play dates with neighboring children, and entertaining visiting engineers, local Peace Corps volunteers, and our English friends. Occasionally we played tennis in the evening. Sometimes, we drove out to the Yugoslav contractors' living site. The chief engineer, Mr. Skileen, had built a small swimming pool. When we arrived, Eric would call out, "Water is clean, Mr. Skileen?" to everyone's amusement. He loved to jump and play in that pool.

I bought a local sewing machine that operated by turning the wheel manually. The expression "sitting tailor fashion" is derived from the tailors of Asia who sit cross-legged on the floor with their hand-powered machines. Eric was fascinated with the sewing machine, so I taught him to turn the wheel for me. He would sit on the table, turning the wheel, while I adjusted the fabric under the fast-moving needle. Occasionally, he turned too fast, and the needle ran off the edge of the fabric, but it never punctured any of my fingers. Together, we made several patchwork quilts, as well as dresses for me and clothes for him. Pulling together my Peace Corps and later experiences with girls and women in Pakistan, I worked on creating a manuscript, "The Invisible Pakistanis." I also continued to draw and paint.

We had a Thanksgiving party for about fifteen people, and at Christmas, we took a long drive to Peshawar, where we stayed in the classic British-style Dean's Hotel. With glowing fireplaces in the bedroom and the dining room, it seemed a very festive holiday treat. I got food poisoning from the shrimp cocktail. On the way home, I had a diarrhea attack as we drove through the desert. Desperate, I told Gene to stop. We were far from any town or village, so I jumped out of the car and squatted behind a sand dune. After a few minutes, I heard a noise; a man on a camel was approaching. There was no way I could stop what I was doing, so I ignored him. I hope he ignored me, but he probably got a good look at my bare backside.

Paul Smith, an engineer working for Gene, and his wife moved to the Multan area. The four of us and two-year-old Eric planned a trip to Afghanistan in January. We flew to Quetta and took a bus to Kandahar, the second-largest city in Afghanistan. Eric had to pee while we were on the bus, so I held him in front of the door. The driver was amused, but it was not unusual in a country where toilets are few and far between. More than once on a bus, I had seen a trickle emerge from below the hem of a woman's all-encompassing burka. One of my colleagues said, "burkas are portable comfort stations." We toured the mosques and bazaars of Kandahar in horse-drawn wagon for two days.

Every month, I consulted with the doctor at the mission hospital. Her pregnancy management included monitoring and limiting weight gain. She said I was too big and had gained too much for the current stage of the pregnancy. I started doing the Canadian Air Force exercises introduced in our Peace Corps training and tried to eat less. I felt nauseated sometimes, particularly when Mohammad Ali was frying garlic and onions for his curries. After I complained a few times, he resigned and returned to Peshawar. He was not happy in Multan, in the lower Punjab, where the climate and the food were much hotter than in his native North-West Frontier Province.

There may have been racist comments directed toward him in the bazaar, too. At any rate, he missed his family and his fellow Pathans. His departure meant I had more work in the house. I enlisted the help of the gardener and Gene's driver to purchase food in the bazaar. Eric's ayah, Mumtaz helped with the food preparation and boiling and filtering of our drinking water.

I felt there was something different about this pregnancy. There were lots of fluttering movements in my bulging stomach. At one appointment, the doctor said it felt there was a "small head presenting." But I was still too large. Eric's birth had been normal, so I assumed that with the mission hospital and doctor, I should be fine for a second birth.

I was overconfident. On March 13, I did my Canadian exercises and then took a hot bath. Soon after, I started bleeding. Gene came home from work and took me to the hospital, where I was given an injection and told to lie down, so we went home. At home, the cramps turned into real contractions, so we went back to the hospital. The mission hospital facilities were very simple. No fancy monitors or pain relief. Just before midnight, I gave birth to a boy. I pushed his head out, and then the slippery shoulders and body followed. He was tiny, three pounds 10 ounces. The afterbirth came in a few minutes as the doctor and attendants wrapped the baby. Then the doctor felt my abdomen and said, "There is another one!" This baby was breech; instead of his head in the birth canal, it was his backside. However, he was so small that the doctor was able to ease him out quite quickly. He weighed only three pounds, three ounces. I heard these tiny boys make noises in a crib. They both had red hair like Eric. When Gene came into the room, he saw them also and held my hand. We were frightened and worried; I was exhausted, and Gene had to go home to stay with Eric. Since Mohammad Ali had quit, the only person overnight at our house was the illiterate night watchman, dozing by the gate. Mumtaz would come in the morning.

I was put in a dank, dark room, so I shivered in misery. Before morning, a nurse came to tell me the smallest baby had died four hours after his birth. Then Gene brought Eric to visit and cheer me a little. I asked him to bring the box containing baby clothes from the house. It included some embroidered white cotton dresses that Gene had worn as an infant. Gene went home to get the clothes and to find a carpenter who could make a tiny coffin. A nurse told him how to find the Christian cemetery, where he arranged a burial.

During the day, I held the other baby, but he would not nurse; he was too weak. In the early hours of March 15, the doctor brought me to the birth room. There was the baby on the raised bed, struggling to breathe. A tube from an oxygen tank was in his nose; we took turns trying to breathe into his mouth and nose. He could take only two breaths independently. After an hour, he stopped trying to breathe at all. He had lived for forty-four hours. I put one of the baby dresses on his tiny body. We called Gene's office from the hospital so he could repeat the process of having a little coffin made and enlarging the plot in the cemetery.

I went home the next day in emotional and physical pain. Despite an injection to stop it, my breasts were swollen with milk. I was angry with myself for thinking everything would go well for a simple birth in Pakistan. This was not a simple birth. It was premature—at about seven months—and twins. My body was weak from the repeated bouts of Giardia and the toxic drugs used to address it. I had made wrong decisions based on my boundless confidence. My body and my judgement had failed me. I was devastated. Gene was sad and comforted me in my grief, but the loss had less impact on him. He had not felt those stirrings of life for months. With every pregnancy, I enjoyed communicating with my future child by gently pushing at my bulging body and feeling the responding nudge from within. With the twins, there were more fluttering responses. During my other three pregnancies, the responding kicks were more robust, especially as they neared full term. Why do I remember these details half a century later? Pregnancy is a condition at the core of being female. When it ends with death, it is an unforgettable loss.

We contacted family and friends by mail and received many sympathetic letters, including one from the obstetrician who had delivered Eric. He said he looked forward to taking care of me in the future. Gene's mother, a dedicated Christian Scientist, wrote, "The babies had never really lived." Others in my family wrote about the preciousness of their short lives Our local ex-pat friends came by with sympathy and concern, as did Rebab Gardezi. However, it was lonely to be so far from my family during the saddest days of my life. Two-and-half-year-old Eric was my source of joy as I gradually regained my strength. I was determined to have another child as soon as possible. The doctor told me my uterus was tipped back, so it might be difficult to become pregnant, though I had no evidence of that from previous experience.

The Pakistan Water and Power Administration constructed a "housing colony" for the engineering staff of Gene's project. It was located across the Chenab River near the village of Muzaffargarh. It was ready for occupancy in May 1967, two and a half years after the beginning of the project! Government departments prefer to construct housing for foreign-funded projects because there is far more scope for graft than there is for rental housing. The housing colony consisted of a dozen bungalows for the engineers, foreign and Pakistani, and a row of smaller housing units for some of the drivers, mechanics, and foremen. The large motor pool was adjacent. The move to Muzaffargarh shortened the drive for engineers to the project sites. However, there were limited resources for families. There was no big food market, no hospital, no college. It was rather isolated, though near a major highway. That highway proved a curse. One of the Pakistani families we knew lost their five-year-old boy in an accident. Their servant was riding a bike with the boy sitting in front of him when a speeding truck ran into them, killing both instantly. The parents were inconsolable. Having buried our twins recently, I shared their grief. Children are so precious when they die as infants or youngsters; it is devastating for mothers and fathers.

In July, Gene took some time off so we could go to the mountains with our friend Trevor Braham and an Englishman, Norman Norris, a tall young missionary. We drove to the Kagan Valley in Pakistan Kashmir, with camping gear and food for ten days. We hired some donkeys and porters to help us backpack into a high meadow near the goal, a 17,356 ft peak called Malika Parbat, which had been climbed only once before. Eric rode a horse. When the trail became tricky for the animals, a young man who was the religious leader (mullah) of the local community took Eric on his shoulders. After two days of hiking, we reached a lush green pasture where cows and sheep were grazing. Some women, children, and a few old men were staying in rock shelters while tending the animals and making yogurt and cheese. The able-bodied men were down in the villages working on their farms. We set up our tents and cooked dinner on camp stoves. A circle of shy children watched us from a distance. In the morning, Gene, Trevor, Norman, and the Pakistani climber packed up enough food for four days, hired two villagers to help, and headed up toward the peak.

Once the men were gone, the women and children were no longer shy with me. They were very curious about Eric and his red hair. Though their knowledge of Urdu was limited (they speak a local dialect, Kohistani), we were able to communicate. They did not want to be photographed but did not object to my drawing or painting them. Eric played with the children and enjoyed seeing the baby goats and calves. We ate some of their fresh yogurt and shared our sugar and tea with them. The young mullah slept a respectful distance in front of my tent to protect me, perhaps from wild animals or maybe just from curious children. At any rate, I felt very peaceful and comfortable in that high-altitude meadow. Three days later, the men returned. Gene and Norman had made the second ascent of Malika Parbat, so we all celebrated with a little brandy in our tea. I would not have gone on this trip if I had twin babies.

I wondered then, and still wonder, how my life would have been different if I had known I was carrying twins in 1966. I would most likely have moved back to America for the pregnancy. If the twin boys had survived, would I ever have had a daughter? Three boys might have seemed a large enough family, but after a few years, I might have wanted to have another child, hoping for a daughter. Gene had always wanted a daughter, and so had I. My daughter has been a source of great joy. Once, when she was upset, brother Greg tried to comfort her, saying, "Just think, if the twins had lived, you would have been a boy, and we would be twin brothers." I am not sure if this was comforting or not!

**"So soon after losing twins, you should not become
pregnant again."**

By late September 1967, I was delighted to be pregnant
again. The baby was expected in April 1968. Not wanting to
risk the outcome, I insisted that we return to America. Gene
agreed and gave notice that he would be leaving in
November, about a year short of his four-year contract.

During the three years, Gene's project had reached many
of its goals in terms of reducing soil salinity by building tube
wells and drainage canals. I had helped at a college and made
friends in the community. Overall, we hoped to have created
some small measure of understanding between our culture
and that of Pakistan. We had suffered the loss of our twins
and learned to depend upon each other in our grief, isolated
from our families.

Gene developed an interest in rugs and textiles during
our years in Pakistan. He incorporated textiles into his
wardrobe as scarves, vests, and neckties. I sewed the
neckties, of course. Several times, he purchased an entire
six-yard silk sari so that I could make him one bow tie. I
would have the remaining fabric to create other clothes. His
textile fascination extended to carpets. He enjoyed hours of
bargaining with merchants in their shops. In Multan, the rug
dealer would arrive on a camel with huge bags on each side.
He would fling open bags and spread the rugs on the veranda
for our appreciation and eventual purchase. When Gene
returned to America from distant assignments, his luggage

always included rugs. We would then host carpet parties for friends, with wine and cheese instead of the tea and cookies of Tupperware parties. Our parties were far more lucrative. At his memorial service, a friend mentioned, "If you couldn't afford to buy a rug from Gene, he would give you one." At one point, the rugs were five deep in a room of our house. I tried covering chairs with rugs, but they proved too itchy for comfortable seating.

Gene enjoyed shopping so much that he would buy anything typical of the area where he was working: Ikat textiles in remote islands of Indonesia; yak saddle-covers in Nepal; spears, shields, woven bags, and penis gourds in New Guinea. In the bazaars and markets of Asia, we found the competition was between merchant and buyer, not between the merchants. Gene leaped into the fray, offering 20 percent of the first asking price. Several cups of tea later, a final price might be 70 percent of the initial price. Both the merchant and Gene would end the transaction with smiles and a handshake. Fortunately, I have never been a shopper. I am a saver. Gene sometimes called me "a parsimonious New England woman." If we had both shopped as he did, we would have had very little savings for retirement.

Chapter 11   Coming Home: Alps and Rockies

Following our pattern, we flew to Geneva and then drove to Chamonix, where our friends had found a chalet for us to rent for several weeks. We could sit on the balcony having our coffee and gaze at the chain of pointed peaks and Mont Blanc, which is so familiar and lovely. I pursued what my friends called the *cure de fromage* and gained about twenty pounds. I was not planning to restrict my weight gain in this pregnancy! We had a Thanksgiving dinner with Harvey and Suzy and their little boy, Freddie. Gene did some low-altitude rock climbing, and we all took long walks. When there was an early snowstorm, we borrowed skis and poles for Eric to ski around the garden by our chalet. One day, on the highway to Geneva, a little red sedan sped past Gene and Harvey. Gene asked what kind of car it was. "Alfa Romeo," said Harvey. That day, Gene called the Alfa factory in Milan and ordered a car! The next week, we flew to Milan and got into our car, a red, two-door sedan with a small back seat sufficient for two children, at least. It cost $3,005. We shipped the car from Amsterdam and then flew to New York. We visited my father and stepmother briefly, then flew to Colorado for Christmas with Gene's parents (divorced, but both living in Denver) and my mother, stepfather, and younger siblings.

After Christmas, Gene flew back to New York to get the car and drive it west. About five months pregnant, I was feeling fine but a little anxious that Gene needed a job and we needed a home. Before the end of January 1968, Gene had a job with a local engineering firm, and we made an offer on a seventy-year-old brick house. It had three bedrooms (one of them very small) and one full bath upstairs, and on the main floor, a living room, dining room, kitchen, and a powder room (toilet and sink). Price: $19,000. Like many houses in Denver, it had a recreation room and laundry room in the basement. We had saved enough money for a down payment during Gene's three and a half years of salaried overseas employment, not subject to income tax. By February 9, we occupied the house, just in time for our sea freight to be delivered. As we were moving boxes, two blond boys walked in the front gate to see Eric. I walked home with them down the block and introduced myself to their parents, Eliot and Natalie, and discovered we had several mutual friends. They were skiers who loved the mountains as we did. Eliot had climbed with some of our friends. With our children the same ages and our mutual interests, they became lifelong friends.

We enrolled Eric in preschool. He and Gene did some skiing while I got larger and larger. In late April, I became anxious since the due date for my baby had passed. Finally, on May 4, the contractions started at 6 a.m. Gene's mother, Stella, came over to stay with Eric so Gene could come to the hospital. At 9:30 that morning. I gave birth to a beautiful eight-pound boy who entered the world smiling. I had no drugs or injuries. My doctor wanted this to be a good experience for me a year after the loss of twins, so after the placenta was expelled, he asked me if I felt like walking. I stood up, and he handed me the baby. I carried him out to the hallway to Gene. (In those days, fathers were not permitted in the delivery room.) We were delighted with this happy baby, whom we named Gregory Herrick White.

Eric seemed pleased to have a little brother. The grandparents were all happy, too. My father and stepmother came to visit in June. Gene's mother and father saw the little boys regularly, as did my mother, stepfather, and younger siblings.

By 1968, Gene had climbed fifty-three of Colorado's fifty-four peaks over 14,000 ft. One remained, Mount Holy Cross, named for the snow formation on the north face. He wanted to do a celebratory climb on the Fourth of July. Unfortunately, Holy Cross requires a rough backpacking approach. I could not convince anyone to come as a hiking babysitter. My mother was happy to keep Greg and Eric for four days, but she insisted I get Greg accustomed to bottle feeding in advance. We did the climb, straight up the "cross" using ice axes and crampons on the steep snow. Our group celebrated the summit with champagne. Gene was the sixtieth person to have climbed all the 14,000 ft peaks at that time.

When we returned, the boys were fine, but I regret I did not know that one could restart breast feeding after an absence of four days. My mother was a pediatrician, but during her medical school era, breast feeding was not as strongly encouraged as it was in the 1960s and later. I learned two years later from a friend who joined us on a four-day mountaineering trip, that it is possible to restart nursing because she had expressed milk during the time away. Eric had nursed for eight months, and my daughter, born two years after Greg, had continued for a year. I enjoyed breast feeding, though I confess to double-tasking; I always read a book or did very careful knitting while holding the baby.

At the end of July 1968, we set off for Canada with the two boys and all our camping and climbing gear in the little red sedan. We were joined by two other couples, one of whom had two boys aged two and four, in Jasper, British Colombia. We hired horses to pack ourselves the twelve miles to Berg Lake, at the base of Mount Robson. Eric and the other four-year-old boy rode horses; the other mother rode with her two-year-old. I am not confident with horses, so I hiked the with Greg on my chest in a baby carrier and a pack of diapers on my back. I had no problem losing the weight I had gained during the pregnancy with this level of exercise. It was the first of many mountain trips we took with other families. We discovered that sharing the base camp tasks and child supervision among parents enabled everyone to have some time to climb or hike and enjoy the outing.

Only one parent needed to stay in camp with the small children.

We failed to climb Mount Robson. Its infamously steep Kain Face, named for Conrad Kain, the Austrian who climbed it first, was in bad condition. Another party descending it had been swept a long distance in an avalanche, resulting in one seriously injured climber. We helped them bring down some of their abandoned equipment. Several of us climbed Resplendent, a lovely snow peak, and explored the high country to the north of our camp. Alas, one day, heavy, wet snow fell, dampening our camp and spirits! A day later, the wrangler arrived with the horses for our departure. The two dads completed the smoky task of burning a large pile of used disposable diapers just in time to set off on the trail with the horses and hikers.

Back in Denver, after this adventure, I registered for classes at the University of Colorado Denver Center to renew my teaching credential. I really enjoyed the intellectual challenge of the readings, the research, the writing, and the class discussions.

I volunteered to tutor reading at a junior high school and to tutor French for girls at a private high school. Another enterprise, using my sewing skills from 8th grade, was sewing bright, wide neckties and "butterfly" bow ties. I sold these to friends and a couple of shops, earning over $350 a year. I also helped Dale Johnson, founder of Frostline Kits, by sewing prototype down jackets and sleeping bags for children. Our children did the product testing.

We continued to ski or hike on the weekends. Among our climbing friends were two who suggested we go on an expedition to the Andes. Gene and I discussed it. We were tempted. We had climbed Mont Blanc, then Kilimanjaro, 4,000 feet higher, so why not try a peak 3,000 feet taller than Kilimanjaro? The Iowa Mountaineers, a club that organized trips to mountains all over the world (since they have none in Iowa), was taking a group to Peru to the Cordillera Blanca. With our friends, we signed up to go in July 1969.

Chapter 12   The Andes And A Volcano Or Two

"As the mother of two little boys, it is irresponsible to join an expedition to the Andes."

I was happy having two thriving little boys after having lost two, yet I was willing to leave them for three weeks to pursue a useless and dangerous goal: climbing a high mountain. A father would not be subject to as much criticism as a mother.

Gene's mother agreed to take care of the boys with help from my mother. We started training for the climb by running around the track and up the stairs in the Denver University football stadium. Our system was to let Eric play in the sandy high-jump pit and to put Greg in the center of the field. Greg would creep and toddle around. One of us would complete a lap on the stairs before he got to the edge of the field and then put him back in the middle of the field. We also hiked up several of the nearby 14,000 ft peaks to become ready for the altitudes in the Andes.

We four friends, Gene, me, John Larson, and Mark Bostwick, signed up with the Iowa Mountaineers for their 1969 Peru Cordillera Blanca expedition. John and Mark had been among my high school friends in the Junior Colorado Mountain Club. John was a quiet engineer. Mark was a radical historian, planning a thesis on Kerensky. We, the "Colorado Four," soon expanded to five when we met Barbara, an athletic, dark-haired recent graduate of the

University of Colorado, at the Denver airport. As we waited in the transit area of the Miami airport, we encountered a muscular young blond man, Ray Jardine, from Denver, so we became the "Colorado Six." Ray was an electrical engineer and a keen rock climber. He spent his spare time developing climbing equipment. He explained, "I make single cable climbing nuts with a guy named Bill Forrest." Most of us had been using pitons, which must be hammered in and out of cracks tediously. Only recently had the use of "chocks," or nuts, been introduced in America. The first nuts were nuts from the hardware store. A nut with a threaded cable can provide protection for a roped climber when slotted into a crack. A single cable nut has an advantage over a nut with a loop of cable, due to greater ease of placement and removal. Single cable nuts are lighter by an ounce or two. That matters when a climber is carrying 20 or more for a big wall climb. We were fascinated and came to be good friends with Ray. Eventually, Gene and I would invest money and time in Bill's company, Forrest Mountaineering.

When we arrived in Lima, Peru, I anxiously watched our luggage roll off the baggage carousel. My duffle bag was not there! I could probably borrow or buy warm clothing, but climbing boots with fitted crampons would be very hard to find. With despair, I went to our hotel. In the morning, a bus would take the group to the town of Huaraz at the foot of the Andes. Without my gear, what could I do? Gene, Mark, and I went to the airport to wait for the next plane from Miami.

We gave huge sighs of relief when my duffle appeared. The bus had already departed, so we took a taxi to Huaraz, where we reunited with the whole expedition of twenty-five people.

Harold Walton, an experienced scholar and climber, had gone ahead to shop and make arrangements. Later, we discovered he had purchased bubble gum instead of hard candy, corned mutton instead of corned beef, and, worst of all, cheap leaded gas instead of "white" gas for the camp stoves. These mistakes would plague us for the entire trip.

With donkeys to carry the heavy loads, we went into the *Quilquahuanca quebrada* (a valley or canyon leading into the mountains) for acclimatization. The base camp was in an open meadow with a stream on one side. Upstream, we discovered a pasture where cows had been grazing. Therefore, all our water had to be treated or boiled to be safe for drinking. The group had two large canvas tents for storing and cooking food. The meals seemed skimpy to us. Ray developed a talent for sneaking under the edge of the food storage tent to retrieve supplemental cans of fruit and candy bars for us. We, the "Colorado Six," wanted to climb 20,000 ft Mount Chinchey, which loomed above the camp. Since Gene was one of three recognized climbing leaders on the official roster, we thought we could proceed as we wished. However, the leader of the Iowa Mountaineers cautioned us to wait until we had done some lower hikes. Rain delayed our departure, but we had a nice three days exploring the glacier below Chinchey up to 18,000 ft. We were happy to be away from the big group and able to cook our own food. The porters who helped us bring down our equipment became very friendly. The most experienced of them, Antonio Vargas, had climbed with recent French expeditions. I had some good conversations with him about his experiences with other expeditions, mixing his limited French with my fluent French and simple Spanish. I think he respected my determination and climbing skills. He said, "Senora Blanca y Antonio, vamos al cumbre del Huascaran," that great mountain, the highest in Peru, was our next goal. We hiked down the valley, meeting a truck to take us to Hotel Monterrey's famous hot spring pools. After camping and cold sponge baths, it was a luxury to soak in the sulfurous hot water. We ate and drank well in the hotel, but the beds were as saggy as hammocks.

We did some hasty shopping for food to supplement our high-altitude rations and jumped into the truck heading for the highest village, Musho. Burros carried our duffels to the first camp at the edge of the glacier at 14,000 ft. Gene took a rest day there, but I continued with some other climbers and porters to drop loads at the site of our next camp, 2,500 feet higher. We met two young men from Argentina and Peru descending from seven days of climbing. They were very tired and hungry, so we shared our dinner with them.

Gene and I had a two-person tent, while the others shared larger, four-person tents. We established a personal high-altitude record for making love above 16,000 ft. We certainly breathed harder than at sea level. Mark, in a neighboring tent, remarked that he had heard some Cheyne-Stokes breathing during the night. (That is irregular breathing associated with the effects of altitude.) The food for the high camps was not organized well. We found ourselves without sugar or salt. Fortunately, I had purchased extra freeze-dried high-altitude food for our group, supplemented by homemade beef jerky and fudge. On the positive side, at this camp, there were pools of water on the ice, so we were spared the tedious task of melting snow.

Usually, we climbed three people on a rope for safety among the crevasses. More than once on Huascaran, I had a desperate need to defecate when tied in the center of the rope. I had to ask Gene, on one end of the rope, and John, on the other, to stop and brace their ice axes in the snow while I squatted over the edge of a crevasse. It would have been very awkward and dangerous to fall in a crevasse with my pants down.

When we reached the 18,000 ft pass between the two summits, we dug a shallow trench in which to erect our tents to escape the constant wind. Our first summit attempt failed as we came to extremely steep slopes with unstable snow. John, Mark, and I scouted farther across the pass for a better route toward the top while Gene and Ray went back to the windy camp. The next morning, we started at 7, following the tracks that John, Mark, and I made the previous afternoon. It was a good route. The altitude made for slow going. I took two breaths for each step but went steadily, without headache or other signs of altitude sickness, arriving at the summit at 2:30 p.m. Antonio Vargas, with one other climber, met us. He was so excited he hugged everyone. When he was working for the French expedition, Lionel Terray assigned him porter tasks at altitude but did not include him in the summit parties. I was very pleased that we had been to the summit together, "Antonio y Señora Blanca." It was sunny, and it seemed the whole of Peru was spread out below us. I was elated at being so high, 22,205 ft with a group of friends. We congratulated each other in English and Spanish.

The next group heading for the summit had arrived at our camp hours earlier, but they did not melt snow or make tea for us, so I began those tasks when I arrived, tired but happy. After a very uncomfortable night, with three people in a two-man tent, me in the middle, squished but warm, we packed our personal gear and descended, happy with our success. I was the second American woman to climb the Huascaran. The first American woman to climb it was Irene Beardsley, a friend of mine, who was the first American to reach the summit of Annapurna in Nepal in 1978. In 1908, Annie Peck with two Swiss guides, reached the slightly lower north peak. It has subsequently been named for her. Annie is one of my inspirations and heroes. She taught at Smith and flew a "Votes for Women" flag from every summit.

Descending from above 18,000 ft to 10,000 ft in one day was exhausting, made more so because, at two lower camps, we had to pick up our tents. At base camp, we met two American climbers planning a daring, difficult route on the north peak. They had little money and needed some equipment. They agreed to carry our packs in exchange for climbing helmets, some camping gear, and a rope. At 4:30 we arrived at the village of Musho, where there was cold beer! We said goodbye to Antonio there, so Gene gave him his Lionel Terray brand down jacket, gloves, and goggles. He had worn my spare wool knee socks to the summit; he swore to be our friend for life. The young American climbers jogged down the road to find a truck, which roared back to get us just as we were arranging for eggs and potatoes in the village. We piled in the truck and sped to the town of Yungay. As we celebrated our victory over steak, potatoes, and beer, a waiter shouted to look at the TV. There was an image of Neil Armstrong stepping on the moon. A year later, the entire town of Yungay would be buried up to the height of the church steeple in a mud and ice avalanche from the slopes of Huascaran caused by an earthquake. Antonio Vargas survived, but hundreds of people died.

On July 26, we five from Colorado took a taxi from Huaraz to the Lima airport. Arriving at 7 p.m., we booked the last four tickets on an 11:30 p.m. flight to Miami. We had no extra days for tourist activity. Cuzco and Machu Picchu would have to wait for another trip. We rushed to the Savoy

Hotel to shower and change because we wanted to have a birthday and summit celebration at Treces Monedas, said to be the best restaurant in Lima. At the door, the waiters whispered about *el saco,* then came forward with some jackets for John and Mark to meet the dress code. It was a wonderful dinner. We did not miss our flight either.

I was anxious to pick up our little boys. They seemed fine after our three-week absence, but my mother-in-law was exhausted. Staff from the local newspaper came to interview me about the climb. "Denver Woman Scales Peruvian Peak" was the heading of the article. The reporter questioned me about risk-taking and adventure, seated at the dining room table in our home. He did not ask if the male climbers discouraged or disparaged me or if I had doubts about leaving my small sons for three weeks. My ascent of Huascaran became known in the climbing community. Arlene Blum contacted me about joining the first all-women expedition to Mount McKinley (Denali) in Alaska. It was an honor and a challenge. I couldn't go because I was pregnant, expecting our third child.

We had miscalculated the birth date again. The due date was mid-June, so I agreed that Gene could plan to climb Mount Rainier on the fourth of July weekend with his friends. I drove him to the airport in the afternoon, and in the evening went into labor. His mother, Stella, came to stay with the boys while I took a taxi to the hospital. In the parking lot, I met my obstetrician, arriving in a taxi with a cast on his ankle. We hobbled inside together. Just after midnight, Laura was born. I called the Mount Rainier ranger station to relay the happy news to Gene. He was delighted. Between 1964 and 1970, I had four pregnancies five live births, finishing with three healthy children. During those years, I had also climbed in the Rockies and the Alps, trekked in Pakistan, and climbed the highest mountain in Peru.

Before the end of the summer, we packed up everyone and drove to Wyoming to stay at the newly established AAC Climbers Ranch. We shared a rustic cabin with Gene's brother, his wife, and their baby boy. We took turns climbing. I had to be fast to avoid missing more than one feeding since I was nursing, but I managed to summit Ice Point, Storm Point, and Teewinot Mountain before we returned to California.

Mexico was our next south-of-the-border adventure. When he was in college, Gene had climbed two of the highest peaks in Mexico, Orizaba and Popocatepetl; stomach sickness had prevented him from climbing the sister peak of Popo, Iztaccihuatl. He studied the Mexican maps and located other peaks over 14,000 ft: Nevada de Toluca, 15,355 ft; and, La Malinche,14,460 ft. So, in the spring of 1971, we left all three children with my mother and sisters and flew to Mexico City. In a car, we drove to the crater of Toluca and camped. It was more than halfway up the mountain, so we were on the summit before noon. Then we drove to the city of Puebla. It was more difficult to find the road to La Malinche, and the ascent was a more strenuous hike, but we made it. Iztaccihuatl is higher and more complicated. We drove as high as possible, then hiked to a small refuge surrounded by boulders and patches of snow. It was empty and drafty, but we managed to sleep until dawn. We hiked up a rocky ridge and stepped onto a snowfield covered with *nieves penitentes.* These are spikes of ice or hard snow up to two feet tall. It is extremely tedious to step over and between them. It was foggy when we arrived at the high end of the snow field. Then, the fog cleared, and we could see that the true summit was about a mile away. This reminded me of Mount Olympus. A summit hidden by clouds, revealed only when the sky cleared, though we climbers assume we have already reached them. After our climbing success, we spent a day in Mexico City at museums and admiring the wonderful murals in public buildings, then a day at Teotihuacan admiring the architecture. We had accomplished a lot in a ten-day trip. Our children seemed to have not missed us much, either.

Ecuador was our next southern mountain destination. In December 1971, encouraged by our efficiency and success in Mexico, we planned a trip to Ecuador. Climbing pals Mark, John, and Ken agreed to come. At the last moment, Ken's girlfriend, Diane, a pretty, red-haired flight attendant, got a free flight to join us. She was a good addition to the group. Like me, she spoke some Spanish and enjoyed the markets, the handicrafts, and the culture. She became a lifelong friend, eventually settling in California.

Our goal was to climb the high volcanos, Chimborazo and Cotopaxi. We left Laura with one family in Denver while Eric and Greg would stay with my mother, stepfather, sisters, and brothers at their little house in Conifer in the Colorado foothills. We flew to Quito, the capital of Ecuador, on December 29. We hiked up some steep hills near the city to acclimatize before renting a truck to take us to the base of Chimborazo. At the highway's highest point, we left the truck, picked up our backpacks, and hiked to the small mountain refuge. The refuge was crowded with four other Americans, including a Colorado couple, Gerry and Barbara. Diane was feeling the effects of altitude, so she descended to spend New Year's Eve with an Ecuadoran family in a tiny shepherd's hut near the highway.

There was a strong, cold wind blowing when we left the refuge before dawn. It slowed our hiking as much as the altitude. We reached Chimborazo's huge summit plateau, 1,500 ft below the summit. We discovered, to our dismay, that the plateau, which is a mile wide, was covered in deep fresh snow. Progress on that surface, without skis or snowshoes, would be extremely slow. Discouraged by the snow conditions and the gale-force wind, we all turned back. Since even Gerry, the toughest guy, turned back, we felt it was the right decision. We picked up our overnight gear and trudged down to find Diane waiting patiently near the highway. We retreated to the comforts of Quito for two days before heading to Cotopaxi, the second-highest peak in Ecuador. We all hiked up to the newly constructed mountain refuge at 15,700 ft. It was clean and comfortable compared with the hut on Chimborazo. From there, the ascent to the 19,348 ft summit was a steep glacier hike. Numerous open and hidden crevasses made it necessary to keep the team roped together. Gene, John, and I on one rope, Mark and Ken on the other. Diane stayed at the refuge. We reached the crater edge before noon. As on most volcanos I have climbed, we were at the low point of the crater rim. The highest point required an hour-long hike around to the opposite side. It was a lovely day, and it was exhilarating to be high on a peak with Gene and good friends. The steaming, deep crater was on one hand, and the snowy slopes down to the green farms on the other. The beauty of this summit made us forget the disappointment of Chimborazo. We descended quickly. Two days remained before our return flight, so we took a bus down to the coast. Each turn in the precipitous road brought us closer to tropical vegetation and different populations. We started among traditionally dressed highland Quechua people cultivating potatos and corn and ended at sea level, where descendants of African and European immigrants worked on pineapple and coconut plantations. We stayed in a tiny town on the beach, "Sua by the Sea." We ordered chicken at the only cafe/hotel and soon heard the squawk of a bird being butchered. It soon appeared as our dinner. The black sand beach was deserted; the sea was warm with gentle waves. This was a pleasant contrast to the high glaciated mountains. On January 11, we flew back to Denver. It was a whirlwind trip. Thirteen days away, two major mountain attempts, one high summit, and one beach day. No time for the Galapagos.

Chapter 13 Academic Ambition

"With a newborn daughter and two sons under six, you can't pursue a Ph.D."

In the fall of 1968, I'd enrolled in the University of Colorado to take a few courses for renewal of my teaching credential. Professor James Wolf, a specialist in British Colonial history, became my advisor. He recommended that I expand my horizons with a few courses on Spanish colonial history and qualify for a master's degree. I followed his advice and received my degree in 1972.

Professor Wolf encouraged me to continue for a Ph.D. He recommended the Graduate School of International Studies (GSIS) at the University of Denver and introduced me to his friend, a specialist in Indian society, Professor Bayley, who would become my advisor. Though it was late in the academic year, I applied and was accepted. The University of Denver is a private institution with high tuition fees. We would have been unable to pay that from Gene's modest engineer's salary. However, I was granted a tuition waiver! Several sociologists and economists on the faculty included India and the Muslim world in their scholarly research. I wanted to investigate the role of women in the history of the Indian subcontinent and discover more about the Islamic restrictions on women there and in other countries. My concept was that the restrictions on women are an obstacle to the economic, social, and political development of nations. My three advisors, led by David

Bayley, approved. I enrolled in courses in economics, comparative politics, sociology, and statistics. I was very fortunate to find a graduate program in Denver, where I was living, to be given financial assistance, and to have enthusiastic academic support. With three small children, I could not have gone to a university in another location. After two years of courses, I was awarded a Shell International Studies grant for dissertation research.

With my family responsibilities, I did not have time to hang out with other graduate students, though I did become friends with some. Every hour at the university meant paying for an hour of childcare for Laura and Greg. Only Eric was in public school at the time. Of course, we continued to go skiing on winter weekends and to various mountain areas in summer for weekends or a week or two away. I also did some work at Forrest Mountaineering, sewing hammocks and designing soft goods like mittens and gaiters.

Though Gloria Steinem had graduated from Smith the year I enrolled, I was not attuned to the women's movement, perhaps because of being in Pakistan from 1962 to the end of 1967. Nevertheless, my graduate work and thesis on women's roles in Muslim societies was timely and even cutting edge. The discipline of Women's Studies was just forming in the early 1970s. The Decade for Women was from 1975 to 1985.

Graduate study introduced me to organizations where I met people who shared my interests and encouraged me to continue. Elise Boulding was one of the most inspiring. A mother of five, a scholar, and wife of the famous economist Kenneth Boulding, Elise was a leader of the Women's International League for Peace and Freedom. Her teaching and writing emphasized the role of women in history. She believed women in leadership positions could create a more peaceful world. She founded the Peace Studies program at the University of Colorado. Elise gathered a few scholars in her living room once a month to discuss issues of relevance to women's contributions to peace and world history. She always wore Birkenstock-type sandals. A decade later, I met her at an international development conference in San Francisco, and she was still wearing those clunky sandals. She told me, "You must look after your feet. Nobody else will." That was good advice, based on experience.

While searching for other studies of Pakistani society, I found a book by Henry Korson, a professor at the University of Massachusetts. I wrote to him, and he invited me to contribute to the next edition of his book on the sociology of Pakistan. I was honored to send him chapters of the manuscript I had written at the end of our Peace Corps time, "The Invisible Pakistanis," and promised when I came to the East Coast, I would meet him in Amherst, where he was living and teaching. In the summer of 1975, after I finished my Ph.D., I took the children to Connecticut to visit my father and stepmother. I drove up to Amherst to spend a day working with Henry on incorporating my data and concepts into his new book. He and his wife came to Sharon another day to confer. So, just a few months after completing my dissertation, some of my words appeared in print!

"With three children, graduate study, and sports, you don't have time for an affair."   In 1972, I was in graduate school at the University of Denver, raising three children, going to the mountains for climbing or skiing on the weekends, and sewing neckties and climbing accessories. I found the time and energy to get involved with a mathematician /mountaineer who visited Denver three or four times a year. We met through a mutual friend who was a mathematics professor at the University of Denver. I may have been trying to prove to myself that I could "have it all': A family, academic and athletic success, and a lover. Perhaps it was the "12-year itch". He was a dark-haired bachelor, a few years younger than I and about the same height. We had long talks and did some difficult rock climbs during the few hours we could sneak away. The emotional and physical connections with a new person were more exciting than my domestic life. He became very serious about the affair and wanted me to divorce Gene and marry him. Gene was furious but took a gamble by taking care of the kids while I made a three-day visit to my lover at the New York State university where he taught. Gene guessed that when I saw the situation I might be entering, I would come to my senses.

Gene was correct; the visit convinced me that the whole affair was a mistake. We went to a marriage counselor to repair our relationship. After the third visit, we decided to spend the money (and babysitter time) on going out to dinner together. Since then, no other action threatened our union. I learned from this experience that romantic adventures should be avoided, but if one occurs, it should not be taken seriously. The participants should be in the same marital category. This relationship was unbalanced. I was married, a parent, and committed to my marriage. He was a bachelor eager for a partner. I had a brief involvement years later with another man who was as firmly committed to staying with his wife as I was to staying with Gene. That affair was fun for a while and left no regrets. Gene and I proved that brief lapses in fidelity could not threaten our partnership as spouses, parents, and climbers.

Chapter 14   Move to California: Sierra Nevada, Yosemite

Both Gene and I felt we were ready for a change and new challenges in 1973. We also wanted to find a new set of friends who were not aware of our recent marital crisis. He started looking for jobs with an international focus. He was offered a job by International Engineering (IECO) in San Francisco. A long-term assignment in Morocco was a strong possibility. We jumped at the opportunity to take our children to a place where they would learn French and Arabic. An exotic location but close to Europe, Morocco seemed ideal.

In August 1973, we drove west, stopping at the Grand Canyon and Pasadena before arriving in San Francisco. We stayed with friends and drove around the Bay Area looking for a house to buy. A high school friend of mine living in Oakland said we were really "Berkeley people" and should concentrate our house search in the East Bay. Before we made a final selection, it was time for me to drive back to Denver with the children. Gene started his job in San Francisco, staying in a hotel provided by the company. He promised to continue house-shopping, concentrating on locations within half a mile of Indian Rock, the iconic practice site for climbers.

When I got back to Denver, I put the house on the market and finished my requirements at the university. I had to take comprehensive exams and present my thesis concept for approval. The University of Denver required two foreign languages for Ph.D. candidates, so I had to take an exam in French. Pushto was my other language. At the completion of my Peace Corps service, I passed the Foreign Service Language test for Pushto. No one at the university could judge my Pushto fluency! I gained approval of the outline for my dissertation. I was very grateful when the university awarded me a Shell International Studies research grant. That would enable me to return to Pakistan to do field research.

Gene flew out to spend a couple of weekends with us in September and in October. He was not pining away as a bachelor in San Francisco, however. A couple of women friends spent time with him. By the first of November, the house was sold, and I hired a moving van. I packed up the station wagon with the children and essentials. I thought it best to have another driver, so I found a student at the university who wanted to go to California. He could not have known how a journey crammed into a car with three small children would be, but he survived. At highway rest stops, he would walk on his hands to entertain us. When we had an overnight stay at a motel, he slept in the car. I dropped him off near Sacramento where he wished to be and continued to the address Gene had given me. Gene was waiting for us at the house he had purchased. It was raining that afternoon. As I gazed out the window, looking for the overdue moving van, I saw it go by without stopping! It must have continued north to the 600 block in El Cerrito instead of Berkeley. I frantically called the moving company, but in the days before cell phones, it was hard for anyone to track down an errant truck. It finally arrived after dark. The men hastily unloaded the furniture and boxes in the rain but did not unpack. They left before we had a chance to inspect anything for damage or missing items. The living room and dining room were carpeted with pale green shag carpet. We spread our sleeping bags on the carpet among the boxes and slept for the first night in the house we would occupy for decades (and I still occupy.)

Gene's employer had not won the contract for the Morocco project. His first foreign assignment was two months in war-torn Bangladesh, which was not a family posting. So, ten days after the children and I arrived in California, he flew off to Bangladesh with a two-day stop in Chamonix on the way. I was discouraged. It seemed to rain every day in Berkeley. I knew only two other families. Thousand Oaks Elementary School, for Greg's kindergarten, was only a few blocks away, so I hoped he and Eric could walk to school together. However, Eric was sent on a bus to another school for fourth grade. (Kamala Harris was among the children brought by bus to the Thousand Oaks school while Eric went to a school in West Berkeley). I found a preschool across the street from the Thousand Oaks school for Laura.

Each child started and finished school at a different time, so I rarely had more than a couple of hours to do research, write, or run. Fortunately, I met a neighbor, Louise, who had two boys the same age as Laura and Greg, living just up the hill. Her family had moved to Berkeley after five years in Germany. She felt just as displaced and disoriented as I. We shared our dismay at the weather and the cost of preschool but soon discovered we were both interested in running. We read about the Bay to Breakers race and vowed to train for it, even in the rain. A couple of times a week, Louise and I would run for an hour while our children were in their various schools. Otherwise, my training was a mile or two before the children woke in the morning.

We quickly discovered there were running races every weekend, with distances ranging from three miles to full marathons and more. We plunged into the California running scene with enthusiasm. One day, as I was running, two large German shepherd dogs emerged from a house, barking and baring their teeth. They bit me in the rear, and I screamed. I ran home and called the police. When the police arrived, they wanted to take me to the site of the attack to identify the dogs. The baby sitter had just left and Greg and Laura were at home, so I had to take them in the police car. Greg was as terrified as I was when we saw the dogs. From that day on, he and I have been wary of dogs. If I hear a dog barking when I am walking, running, or biking, I change my route to avoid getting near the dog.

My professors at the University of Denver had referred me to scholars at the University of California. I became an Associate of the Center for South and Southeast Asia Studies and joined the Association for Asian Studies and the Society for International Development (SID). At a SID meeting, I met Beatrice Bain, "Bea," founder of the Women's Resource Center at Berkeley and assistant to the university provost. Like Elise Boulding, she was married to a famous economist. She was an adjunct professor at San Francisco State University. Bea was introducing a new course, "Women in the World," to mark the beginning of the Decade for Women. She invited me to apply to SF State as an adjunct professor to teach the course with her, bringing my international perspective to her feminist theory. It was a great opportunity for me. I team-taught with Bea twice and later taught the course myself. Bea taught me to be a better teacher. She was skilled at bringing students from different backgrounds and different levels of academic preparation into the discussions. Women's studies and the feminist cause lost a champion when she died in 1986.

I felt more optimistic about the move to California when I connected with the mountaineering community. I joined the Sierra Club and participated in a cross-country ski weekend. I also contacted some members of the American Alpine Club (AAC). Two members took me to a club meeting in Palo Alto, where I was awed to meet several of the legendary West Coast climbers who were developing new techniques and equipment for rock climbing. AAC members occasionally rented a cabin in the Tahoe area for skiing. One weekend was designated as a family weekend, so I packed up the kids and their ski gear to join the group. That weekend, I met two families with young children about the same age as ours. For the next several years, we spent many weekends together, winter weekends skiing and summer weekends hiking, camping, and climbing together. Through mountaineering contacts, I discovered the Mountain Travel office on Solano Avenue, near our home. For the next two years, I worked a few hours a week at Mountain Travel, answering calls and letters inquiring about adventure trips in Pakistan and India. It was a welcome respite from academic research and home responsibilities.

Since we were in California, I decided we should see Yosemite. Even though it was January, I planned to camp in a tent with warm sleeping bags. The drive took much longer than expected, so we arrived after dark. The children were exhausted and hungry. As I stepped out of the car, my foot sank through a layer of ice into a freezing slush. No tenting for us! I turned the car around towards the cabins beside Yosemite Lodge Hotel, rented one, and turned on the heat. The scenery in Yosemite was beautiful, but winter was not the best choice for our introduction.

In February, I enrolled Eric in a ski club that took children to the Boreal resort on Donner Summit every Saturday. I wanted to give him an experience like mine with the Club 20 years before. We introduced each of our children to skiing at age three. Gene or I would trudge to the top of a practice slope and ski down with the child between our legs. After a couple of descents like that, Eric, Greg, and Laura would bravely cruise down the slope and stop by sitting in the snow with a big laugh. When we got to California, we realized that buying lift tickets for a family of five was extravagant. We concentrated on ski touring and cross-country skiing on our many winter trips to the Sierra. The kids enjoyed traipsing up hills and competing on the downhill. They constructed little jumps to add to the fun and challenge. Every year, in March, the local AAC group organized a trip to Grover Hot Springs near Markleeville. Twenty or more members, friends, and families would meet on Carson Pass to ski up and down some beautiful mountain terrain, then reassemble in the hot springs pool and campground. We took turns preparing a big dinner for the group. It was great fun for all ages, but Sunday morning brought the added challenge of frozen bathing suits to the confusion of packing up tents in the snow!

The first week of February, Gene returned from Bangladesh. Because I was required to utilize my research grant before June, I was making plans to fly to Pakistan on March 2. Before I could depart, I had to plan for the family during my absence. I searched newspapers and bulletin boards at the university for live-in help. I found an English couple who were looking to exchange housing for childcare or other duties. Gene and I interviewed them in a house that reeked of patchouli. Richard and Kathy seemed far more clean-cut than their hippie housemates. Richard was working on computers at UC Berkeley. They agreed to live with Gene and care for the children during my eight-week absence. A desire for foreign experience brought us to California, but it was not what we had anticipated. Instead of the whole family going to romantic, exotic Morocco, Gene had months in desperately poor Bangladesh, and I had my adventure, returning to Pakistan as a research scholar, not a volunteer or a memsahib.

Chapter 15   Third Pakistan: Research Scholar

"It is not safe for a young blond woman to do fieldwork in the North West Frontier Province of Pakistan."

My 1974 trip to Pakistan began with one night in New York City with my brother Bill. I had lunch with my father and stepmother, Mary. I called Gene to say goodbye and was tempted to call my former boyfriend, but I did not. I realized there was no reason to reopen that drama. I was not worried about my safety in Pakistan, but it was a radical step to leave my husband and children to fly halfway around the world to a country I knew well but also a country with a reputation for being dangerous for women traveling alone.

The flight arrived at Karachi after midnight, as usual. I made my way through the pushy gang of red-turbaned porters to the Midway Airport Hotel. I woke early and called my friend from the Academy for Rural Development in Peshawar, Dr. Aquila Kiani. She was frantic on the phone, saying her son Khalid had come to meet two flights from America during the night but had not seen me. Of course, I would not have recognized her twenty-year-old son, whom I had not seen for ten years. Now widowed and a sociology professor at the University of Karachi, Dr. Kiani had a nice bungalow in the faculty housing area. She welcomed me warmly even though she was departing for a conference in Geneva in a few days. She gave me suggestions for my research and fieldwork while I recovered from jet lag. The university campus was a peaceful and safe place for my morning running, though, of course, I wore long pants and a long-sleeved shirt. Downtown Karachi, where we went for dinner and shopping one evening, was chaotic and not welcoming for a woman visitor alone.

Before leaving America, I had written to every contact possible: In addition to Dr Kiani, our language teacher, Babu; the Gardezi family in Multan; our mountaineering friends in Rawalpindi, Hussein and Khalida Mahmud; and Arshad Zaidi in Lahore. Also, several professors at the University of Peshawar, Frontier College for Women, Mrs. Tila, the Girls' School Principal, and Dr. Munir, our neighbor. I hoped to stop in Multan for a day to see the Gardezi family and visit the graves of our twins. However, my travel agent had booked a direct flight to Rawalpindi. That was a disappointment, but the rest of my program went smoothly. I stayed with my mountaineer friends in Rawalpindi. They took me a few miles up the road to the new capital of Pakistan, Islamabad. The highway traversed a meadow where, eleven years earlier, Gene and I had camped. This modern city was built in a grid of blocks designated for residences, commerce, the national government, and foreign embassies. Many of the blocks were empty, so there was little traffic. What would become the largest mosque in Pakistan was under construction. It was startling to see an entire city built by design in a few years, rather like Chandigarh in India or Brasilia. It contrasted with the neighboring ancient city of Rawalpindi with its narrow winding streets, bustling bazaars, and chaotic traffic of cars, trucks, donkeys, motorbikes, and tongas.

My thesis was that restrictions on women impede social and political development. Comparisons of the extent of modernization of Islamic family laws among Muslim-majority nations revealed a correlation between the legal changes and education, population growth rate, and participation of women in the labor force. My plan was to test this relationship in individual women's lives, considering variations in economic class, age, and rural or urban settings. I designed a thirty-item questionnaire to measure the degree of seclusion (purdah) practiced by individual women, their mothers, and their expectations for their daughters. It also included questions that dealt with attitudes toward the education of girls and boys, as well as the actual education of the subject, her mother, and her daughters. The final section had questions about health and family planning. To determine the economic status of my subjects, I used my observation and a checklist. In each household, I noted the type of house construction (was it mud/adobe, wood, or cement), whether the woman had a sewing machine, whether she cooked with a wood or dung fire or had a gas or electric stove, whether transportation by members of the household was by foot, bicycle, motorcycle, or automobile. (Survey questionaire in Appendix I.)

Then and now, the rate of women's literacy in Pakistan is low. The pressure of conservative Muslims to maintain segregated schools greatly limits girls' education. There are fewer girls' schools at all levels, especially in rural areas. A shortage of women teachers and the fact that an unmarried woman teacher could not live alone in a rural area further limits girls' education. The military and a few private organizations operate coeducational schools. They hire as many women teachers as possible to make the schools acceptable to families who are concerned about their daughters' safety and respectability.

Professor Karim Elahi and his wife welcomed me to their home on the University of Peshawar campus for three nights. My hosts were too polite to tell me that it was against University policy, I learned later. My friend from Peace Corps days, Miss Jaleel, Principal of Frontier College for Women, resolved my housing problem. She recommended staying with her friends the Anwar family in University Town. Her driver took me to meet the family. The family consisted of the parents, an eighteen-year-old daughter, a fifteen-year-old son, and seven-year-old twin boys. The older boy vacated his bedroom and slept with his younger brothers, so I could rent his room. Mr. Anwar was a businessman who had managed plantations in East Pakistan but lost everything in the war of independence for Bangladesh. He was looking for new employment. His wife was a teacher. Her salary was meager for a family of six.

They welcomed me with warmth and generosity. I was happy to pay rent and share the cost of food. The daughter and I went on brisk walks or jogs when we could. It was bittersweet for me to be living with twins about the same age as mine would have been, but I enjoyed their youthful energy and antics. Everyone in the family spoke English as well as Urdu and Bengali. The house was across the street from the university. There was a bus service to the old city of Peshawar five miles away; it was a good location for me.

I was happy to be back among the sights and smells of Peshawar. Fresh chapatis from the tandoor ovens in the bazaar, the smell of kebabs roasting over charcoal fires, the sweet milky tea, and the pungent fragrance of curries were welcome. The bougainvillea and flame trees were blooming. Roses in the parks were beginning to fade in the spring heat but were still fragrant. However, I was alone and could not stroll into the old city to buy those kebabs as I had been able to do with Gene. A woman alone had to be circumspect.

Old friends and new ones helped me with my research. For instance, Dr. Munir, our neighbor in the 1960s, introduced me to the Family Planning Department official, who invited me to tour family planning clinics with her. Mrs. Tila had been promoted to District Inspectress of School. She invited me to accompany her on school visits. Naseem Elahi's sister recruited three of her college-educated friends to administer my questionnaire in their middle-class neighborhoods. In Peshawar city, I was able to visit different neighborhoods to interview women, just as I had done as a Social Welfare Officer as a Peace Corps Volunteer.

Babu Fazle Elahi (our Pushto teacher in the 1960s) introduced me to Roo-Afzal, a petite widow midwife from his village. She agreed to be my assistant for a reasonable salary. She would accompany me on survey travels in rural areas. She had two sons and a daughter. To support her family after her husband's death, she established a sewing center in her home. Girls came to learn tailoring and household sewing on the five treadle machines she had set up in the living room or out in the courtyard on sunny days. When we went to villages, she introduced us to each home we visited. She gave a simple explanation for my visit. We showed photos of our children to reassure the women that it was appropriate for us to discuss family planning. She also helped me by speaking with women who spoke different dialects. Roo-Afzal and I did our interviewing in villages accessible by bus, by horse cart, or on foot from Peshawar. In many of these villages, she had a distant relative or knew someone. Being in the company of a respectable woman who wore a full burka flowing white village-style covering lent me respectability. I wore Pakistani clothes, with the required *dupatta* (scarf) over my head, but I did not cover my face.

Each interview took thirty minutes to an hour. I would chat with the woman about families and life in general, then start with specific questions about her life and attitudes. My survey work was sometimes tedious but very interesting.

One woman answered my question about her children by saying that she had four daughters and so assumed that her "boy tube" was blocked. Men and women were unaware that the sex of the child is determined by sperm, not ova. The lack of a male child is justification for a husband to divorce or to marry a second wife. In another wealthy village household, I met two college-educated women who were wives of one man, a doctor. They said each had a "love marriage" with their handsome physician husband. In Pakistan, where dating is virtually impossible, that meant that they had met the man before the marriage. Each of these attractive young wives had two children. They proudly showed me their separate bedrooms, each with a carefully embroidered cover on a large bed. I suppose the husband took turns.

Very few women refused to answer my questions. In some villages, many women would crowd into a courtyard and insist upon being included in the questioning. I was trying to get opinions of individual women, not group answers! My days were busy with traveling and interviewing, while evenings at home with the Anwar family were relaxing. I was invited to other homes for dinners and to several weddings. At weddings, I usually stayed in the women's section, enjoying their singing, dancing, and ribald joking.

I traveled to more distant towns by bus and stayed with people I knew. In Mardan, I stayed with Professor Mrs. Irfan, whom I knew from Frontier College for Women. She had become the principal of the new Mardan College for Women. Some of our donated Peace Corps books were in the library, on open shelves accessible to the students, and I was pleased to see them. One of the towns I visited doing my research was Charsadda. The people of the area are strict observers of the Pathan or Pushtoon code, which includes the protection of family honor, revenge, and hospitality, which are the three most important elements. One of the most powerful families in the Charsadda area is the Durrani, a Pushtoon clan with Afghan origins. The Durrani men say they are more concerned for the honor of their sisters and mothers than that of their wives because "one can always get another wife, but a sister or a mother is of the family's blood." Stories told in the area confirm this commitment to the Pushtoon code.

I was told stories to illustrate the importance of honor. One concerned a family of three brothers and a sister whose parents died. The brothers had married and brought their wives to the family home. They decided their sister should remain single, help their wives, and not ask for her share of the family wealth. One day, she was bringing firewood from the roof of the house, and a young man saw her from the street below. She saw him also, but no words were exchanged. Later, he approached her brothers, asking to marry her. The brothers refused, saying his family was inferior to theirs. The young man made the mistake of saying, "Why not ask your sister herself if she wants to marry me?" The brothers assumed the couple had been in communication. This could bring great shame to the family. The sister protested that she had never spoken to any man. They took her to a deserted field with knives in hand. She pleaded, reminding them how she helped them and their wives, how they had shared childhood joys, but to no avail. Her possible blot on the family's honor was too great. They killed her, cut her body into pieces, and buried it in the field. The police arrested the three brothers. They escaped with a fine, but Allah had his revenge. One brother died of illness, and another was shot a few years later. The remaining brother lived with the widows of his brothers and the guilt of his sister's murder.

A story illustrating revenge, or *dushmani* (keeping enmity), involves another family drama. Twenty-five years ago, a young, childless married woman named Samina was seen by a khan (rich man) of Charsadda. He was already married and had five children, but he insisted that Samina's husband divorce. The khan took Samina away to Kashmir, where they married and had two children. When they returned to Charsadda, Samina lived in a house beside the home of the khan's first wife, who was dark and fat, while Samina was fair and slender. About four years later, the khan went to Peshawar to shop. Returning, he stopped at a gas station and was approached by a beggar. The beggar pulled out a gun and killed him. He had been paid six thousand rupees by Samina's first husband and brother. Samina was left a widow with a newborn daughter and two young sons. She lived in terror from then on. She and her children slept in the watchtower of the house compound. She arranged for her children to be educated in Lahore and Rawalpindi, each accompanied by a faithful servant/guard. Her son Khalid's guard was shot once, but Khalid managed to finish his M.A. Surrounded by enemies, including the khan's first wife, Samina trusted few people. She promised to marry her daughter to the son of a family that helped settle her land disputes. She sought another strong alliance by betrothing Khalid to the daughter of a prominent family. The sixteen-year-old bride lacked education, and Khalid was unhappy with the match but accepted at his mother's insistence. Khalid would have liked to do scientific farming on the family land, but Samina feared for his life when he went out. He was considering seeking work overseas. One act of folly, polygamy, and the custom of revenge made all members of this family unhappy.

In contrast to these sad stories, the Charsadda Durranis have a heroine: Piari Bibi, daughter of Bahadur Sadullah Khan Durrani. Born in 1890, she was tutored to fourth-grade level. Piari Bibi was married at fifteen as the second wife of a rich nawab, but she did not abandon her interest in education. In 1908, she started a school for girls in her house, teaching only home economics and *Islamiat* (study of the Koran). Each student was accompanied by a servant who escorted her to and from school. Even this modest program caused criticism in the community. In 1912, the government offered to build a school on land belonging to Piari Bibi and her husband. The irate locals tore it down. Piari rebuilt the school at her own expense, though it was destroyed by a flood five years later. Three times, the government rebuilt the school. The girls liked studying so much that they refused to take vacations and completed a ten-year course in five.

Piari Bibi's husband died in 1918. She had worn colorful clothes before his death, but afterward, she dressed only in simple white shalwar kameez. Childless but with a stepson, she managed the land deeded to her as *mehr*, or dowry, so successfully that she was able to purchase more land. It is said that Piari Bibi knew how to do everything without having been taught. She used her money to help the poor, to provide scholarships to future doctors and engineers, to finance the first hospital in the town, and to build a guest house for visiting officials. She was modest but did not observe purdah. She gave lectures in public, consulted with officials, and prayed in the mosque. Every family in Charsadda benefitted from her knowledge and charity. I met one of her nieces, Begum Habibullah Khan Durrani, Principal of a girls' middle school. She and her three sisters were raised by Piari Bibi when their mother died. Begum Habibullah told me how people admired Piari Bibi, reporting that she washed wounded people and even treated smallpox victims. Her tomb is regarded as a holy place, and she is a considered a saint.

My plan was to administer at least two hundred fifty interview surveys during my time in Pakistan. By mid-April, two hundred seventy were completed.

An article in the newspaper said that the road to Hunza in the Karakoram mountains was open to foreign tourists. The mountaineer aspect of my personality took over from the scholar. I rushed to finish up my work and bought a ticket to fly to Gilgit on April 18. The last time I had been in Gilgit was ten years before when Eric was an infant. Then, no foreigners were allowed to go north to Hunza, and the road was very primitive. The small plane to Gilgit flew close to the shoulder of Nanga Parbat Mountain again. In Gilgit, I stayed in the government tourist hotel with other foreign tourists. I purchased a seat in a jeep that would leave the next day for Hunza.

As a guest and a woman, I was allowed to sit in the front seat, but two men squeezed in between me and the side of the jeep. At least eight more climbed on the back, on top of the baggage. The road was spectacular. It was a narrow shelf, barely wider than a single vehicle, high above the raging river. Passing oncoming traffic required one vehicle to reverse to a wide spot. Hunza is the small kingdom that is said to be the Shangri-la of fables. It was then ruled by the Mir, a hereditary and benevolent leader. On the west side of the river, for several miles, houses and farms utilize every inch of level ground for wheat, vegetables, and apricot orchards. Precisely engineered channels bring water from glaciers miles above the village. The people of Hunza are

Ismaili Muslims, followers of the Aga Khan. Their society is more egalitarian, and their attitudes are more modern than those in other areas of Pakistan. The schools are coeducational; women do not cover their faces; people are friendly to visitors. The jeep driver told me I should stay in the Mir's guest house. It was a small building with four rooms, each with a balcony facing the soaring peaks of the Karakoram. I was thrilled to be amid such mountain beauty. Rock spires and peaks up to 24,000 feet high, with glittering glaciers surrounding the village. I sat on the balcony, watching the sunset turn the mountains pink. Dinner was a delicious spinach curry, bread, and tea brought down from the palace kitchen on the hill above by a polite servant. It was so cold I put quilts over my sleeping bag. That was a change from Peshawar, where the temperature was over a hundred degrees in April. There were two friendly French tourists in one of the other rooms. This was my first visit to Hunza, but it would not be the last. I was sorry to take the jeep back down to Gilgit, but I had a flight back to the U.S. on April 25. The weather had deteriorated, so for two days, there were no flights to or from Gilgit. Each day, we tourists went to the airport to wait in vain. When the officials confirmed no plane was coming, the Frenchmen and I hired a taxi and a Pakistani tour guide to take us to several Buddhist carvings in the valley. I enjoyed mixing French, Urdu, and English in the same conversation. Finally, on April 24, a small plane arrived. The French tourists and I were already at the airport and were the first to board. The next day, I got my flight to New York, arriving in the evening after twenty-three hours of travel. I called Gene, then collapsed at the apartment of my friends Cecile and David. The next morning, after a run in Central Park (enjoying the freedom to wear shorts), I flew to California and found my family in good condition. During my absence, Eric had come home with chicken pox, which infected the caregivers, Richard and Kathy. Gene had a household of sick people for a few days, but with the help of friends, he muddled through. My research trip to Pakistan was the third of our separations in less than a year. The first had been my return to Colorado after our exploratory visit to California in the summer of 1973. The second was Gene's assignment in Bangladesh for two months. When we were reunited, we looked forward to enjoying each other's company and our children's progress.

Doing the research was a turning point in my life. Professionally, it was an essential step toward writing my dissertation and earning a Ph.D. I proved to myself that I could accomplish complicated tasks in a challenging location. I confirmed my language skills. My absence from my family for two months confirmed to me that I needed to be with them.

Chapter 16 Towards A Career

I was determined to complete my dissertation and receive my Ph.D. as soon as possible since I was already thirty-six years old. My plan was to run seven miles a day and write seven pages. Richard, who had stayed with my family when I was away, helped me process my data using UC Berkeley computers. The results of each interview were entered on punch cards that could be fed into the computer for statistical analysis, regressions, and graphs. By December 1974, I had submitted a draft of my dissertation, so when schools closed for Christmas vacation, we packed the children in the car and drove to Colorado. I had an appointment to meet with my thesis advisors who had reviewed my draft. We stayed two nights with Gene's mother, Stella, and her new husband, Tom. Then, without warning, Tom said his son was coming and we would have to move. It was stressful for me to gather up all our stuff, including ski equipment for five, and hastily move to my mother's crowded little house in Conifer while preparing for the very important meeting with my academic advisors. Tom did not take women's academic accomplishments or work seriously. Fortunately, my advisers were pleased with my work and had only minor suggestions for revision and expansion. We were able to ski in the woods around Mother's house and have an enjoyable, though crowded, visit with my siblings, their spouses and children.

During the spring of 1975, I made the recommended revisions to my dissertation and gave it to a typist. I was able to submit the finished document in time to be awarded a Ph.D. in June 1975. I did not travel to Denver for the graduation ceremony. I am not sure why I thought it acceptable to travel thousands of miles to climb mountains but not to take a three-hour flight to receive my highest academic degree. That summer, my father and stepmother invited me to bring the children to Connecticut for two weeks. It was enjoyable seeing old friends and cousins with their children, but I would rather have been in California camping in the mountains with Gene. In New England, there is a tradition of mothers and children going to country properties for the summer while the working fathers commute from New York or Boston. We were fitting that pattern, except that Gene was working in San Francisco and not coming for weekends.

"You can't train for a marathon because you have three small children and a job."

Mountaineering has been a part of my life since 1955. I started running in 1969 to get in shape for climbing Huascaran in the Andes. Gene and I ran every day until 2003, (except we did not run on the days we were climbing a mountain, taking a long bike ride, or skiing.) In the 1970s in California, running was very popular, and we started racing frequently. I discovered I could be a competitive runner, especially at longer distances and on trails; when I finished among the first women in a nine-mile race in the Oakland hills, a tall blond woman congratulated me and invited me to join her team, West Valley Track Club. She was Dr. Joan Ullyot, a well-known promoter of women's running and author of "*Women Running*." She was assembling a team of women over thirty-five to compete in the Masters division in national competitions. I was honored to be invited and participated in many races wearing the WVTC shirt.

In the early 70s, no women's running clothes were available. Men's shorts were not cut for women's hips. The T-shirts were baggy and chafed. A friend and I bought a soft cotton jersey to sew shorts and good-fitting shirts, using those sewing skills I learned in eighth grade. She went on to establish a successful women's running clothing company.

We joined the Dolphin South End Running Club in San Francisco. It held races every weekend in San Francisco and nearby areas. The leader and guru of the club was the legendary Walt Stack, a man who had been incarcerated at Alcatraz (for "communist" labor agitation) and later swam there and back. Walt seemed a curmudgeon, but he was not. He told off-color jokes when he had the microphone, encouraged slow runners, and was particularly supportive of women runners. He called the women who ran the Pike's Peak marathon "Peak Busters" and printed special T-shirts for them. He kissed the women who received first, second, or third place ribbons, whether it was Sister Marion Irvine, the running nun, or Margo St. James, founder of the prostitute's organization COYOTE. (Call Off Your Tired Old Ethics).

In most races, I finished in first or second place in my age category, fast enough! I enjoyed the competition, the comradeship, and the discipline. Running often seemed meditative and a time to refine complicated ideas for work or home. In Dr. Peter Glasser's book *"Positive Addiction"*, I am cited as an example. (The bunion on my left foot is cited in podiatrist Steve Sobotnik's book *"The Running Foot Doctor"*.) My fame spread through running as well as mountaineering.

Chapter 17   Marathons, Mountains, Indonesia

In 1976, our daily training enabled us to run the San Francisco marathon fast enough to meet the qualifying times for the Boston Marathon. A group of Bay Area runners flew together to Boston for the April race. My father and Stepmother took us to dinner in Boston. They were puzzled by the effort and expense we were devoting to a running competition with no monetary reward. Women had been permitted to join the race only a few years before, so Radcliff students and women spectators cheered every woman who ran. I finished ten minutes ahead of Gene because he did not adjust well to the heat; it had been 100 degrees at the start and stayed hot throughout the day.

Later in April, Gene's employer, International Engineering, offered him a two-year assignment in Indonesia. It seemed like it would be a good family adventure. Before departing, we planned one more Peru adventure. Instead of a big group like the Iowa Mountaineers in 1969, we were a small group of seven California friends and one from Alaska, three women, and four men. We made our own plans and bought our own supplies. We left Eric at Boy Scout camp in California and flew to Denver with Laura and Greg so they could stay with their cousins, aunts, and my mother there. On July 9, we flew to Lima. We caught a *collectivo* taxi for Huaraz, arriving at 3 a.m. Other passengers included the owners of a small hotel, where we slept for a few hours. Our friends had arrived a day before us and were staying at the home of an American. We discovered they had started off at 6 a.m. for the Quebrada Ishinca, the approach valley to the peaks we sought, Ranrapalca and its neighbors. We scurried back to our hotel and found a taxi to take us to Colon, the last village in the Ishinca Valley, which we reached at 1 p.m. We heaved our heavy packs on our shoulders and started hiking. The trail was narrow and not always obvious. False side trails lured us into dense bushes several times. Exhausted, at 5:30, we ate a cold dinner of cheese and crackers, unrolled our sleeping bags, and slept on the trail until it began to rain. Sleepy and damp, we struggled to erect our little tent in the dark. It was not an auspicious beginning.

In the morning, we joined our friends, who had set up base camp in a meadow at about 13,500 ft. To add to his lifetime list of peaks over 14,000 ft, Gene jogged 500 feet up a nearby moraine after dinner several evenings. There were beautiful peaks on all sides, with the fluted snow ridges typical of the Andes. We started with the ascents of Yanaraju and Nevado Ishinca, another modest snow peak. Then we moved camp up to a ridge below the face of Ranrapalka. At that high camp, one member of the team got symptoms of pulmonary edema, so he self-evacuated in the morning, promising to meet us in Huaraz. Above our camp, the route became progressively steeper and more dangerous. Dealing with complex snow formations and crevasses exhausted our supply of ice-climbing pickets and pitons, so we turned back.

We had to rappel (descend on the rope) from an ice bollard that we cut into the slope. The next day, we traversed a ridge from that high camp to a lesser peak, a beautiful snow summit with no danger or difficulties, and then descended to base camp. We had a few extra days. So, after joining our pal (and his new Peruvian girlfriend) in Huaras, we flew to Cuzco, where we marveled at the massive stone architecture of city walls and foundations. Then we took the train to Machu Picchu. We hiked from the train station up to the ruins. It rained in the evening, so we crawled into our sleeping bags under the veranda of the hotel and woke to sunrise over Machu Picchu. We spent a day exploring the ruins and hiking up the steep mountain that overlooks them. By July 27, we were back in Colorado in time for the Pike's Peak Marathon.

We went to my mother's house in Conifer to pick up Laura and Greg. We met Eric when he flew in from California, having completed his Boy Scout camp. After visiting Gene's mother and stepfather, we went to Colorado Springs for the Pikes Peak Marathon. I was the second woman to reach the top, but three women passed me on the descent. The race is 28 miles and 7,000 ft of climbing and descending. The altitude didn't bother me since we had been camping in Peru above 13,000 ft, but I got tired from the distance on the grueling downhill miles. We returned to California for our departure from Indonesia three days later.

1976 was a busy year; in addition to running in the San Francisco, Boston, and Pikes Peak marathons and climbing in Peru, I was teaching at San Francisco State and working two afternoons a week at Mountain Travel in Berkeley. I had one article published in a feminist journal, a chapter that had been accepted to appear in a book about women in the Muslim world, and prospects for more writing assignments. On winter weekends, the whole family went skiing in the Sierra. In other seasons, it was climbing and hiking. I was helping my friend Arlene Blum with research and fundraising for the 1978 women's expedition to Annapurna in Nepal. Our good friends from Chamonix, Harvey and Suzy, had exchanged their home in France for one in nearby Walnut Creek for a year, assuming we would be in the area.

Gene was enthusiastic about the job. It was part of a nationwide effort to increase food production by repairing and extending irrigation systems so that rice could be grown during the dry, sunny season when yields are higher. Gene would be working in the four provinces of Sulawesi, as well as southeast Borneo, the Moluccas, Sumba, and Sumbawa. He would travel to these provinces regularly. There would be lots of fieldwork and little paperwork. He had told me years before that he studied civil engineering so he could work outside, not in an office. This assignment fulfilled that hope. Two Taiwanese engineers, in addition to the staff of the Indonesian Public Works Department, would be working with him.

However, considering all our positive activities in America, I wonder why I agreed to move to Indonesia for two years. I would need to teach my children at home as there were no suitable schools in Sulawesi. There would be no snow for skiing. The mountains were jungle-covered volcanos. It would be impossible for me to teach at the university level. At ages six, eight, and twelve, my children did not have strong opinions about the move; perhaps they did not really comprehend it. Eric had been looking forward to starting middle school. He and Greg were a bit reluctant to leave their friends and the Boy Scouts, but they shared our sense of adventure. Laura was happy to go along with whatever we planned.

In preparation, we were required to have long-term visas and a series of inoculations, including cholera, typhoid, yellow fever, and smallpox. The government of Indonesia required the renewal of these shots every year. The kids certainly did not enjoy the inoculations. When we went for annual renewals in Ujung Pandang, we found a health department officer who would stamp our forms without doing the injections in return for a modest bribe.

As we boarded the plane that would take our family of five to Indonesia, I realized how little we knew about the country, culture, or language. I had used statistics about Indonesia in my comparative study of Muslim societies but had not read much about the country. My concept of Asia had been the area from the Caspian Sea to the Indian Ocean.

China and Japan were the Far East, or the Orient, to me. Southeast Asia seemed remote, though we had stopped in Bangkok for two days in 1966 on our home leave trip. Moving to Indonesia as a family of five would certainly be a challenge, with a new culture to observe, a new climate, and a new language to learn. I had a book for learning the language in my purse, so we started reciting words on the plane. Numbers: *satu, dua, tiga, umpat, lima*. Only the *dua* for "two" resembled other languages with which we were familiar. Also, *tiga* shared the T sound for "three" with French, Spanish, Italian, and Urdu. The Indonesian language (*Bahasa Indonesia*) is a Malay language, the lingua franca of the trading people of the archipelago. When the country won independence from the Dutch, President Sukarno wisely selected *Bahasa Indonesia* as the national language and the European alphabet for the writing system. The common language united the country, whereas choosing the Javanese or other local language would have alienated citizens from other parts of the country.

Until that point in my life, I had studied Indo-European languages: English, Spanish, French, Pushto, and Urdu. These all have verbs that conjugate to indicate time and person. Indonesian does not have verb tenses. Adjectives come after nouns; instead of prepositions, there are postpositions. The plural of nouns is made by repeating the noun. For example, one child is "anak," and several children are "anak-anak", written "anak 2.

In addition to suitcases, we packed our things in four large duffle bags. Eric and Greg carried their skateboards. When we transferred through airports, the boys piled the duffle bags on their skateboards and pushed them through the corridors. Other travelers jumped away as these apparently self-propelled missiles rolled along. Eric and Greg were invisible, both being shorter than the piles of baggage on the skateboards.

We stopped for a week in New Zealand, wanting to see the famous Mount Cook on the South Island. The weather was cloudy, so we only saw the glacier at the foot of Mount Cook. The scenery was beautiful anyway, and the people of New Zealand were very friendly. In Auckland, we stayed for a night with a couple who had met Gene's mother on a teachers' tour in Asia. They welcomed all five of us and our bulky luggage. The rolling green hills near their home were ideal for morning runs. New Zealand is an agricultural country, with more sheep than people. We were surprised to find milk was free in the motels where we stopped.

On our one day in Sydney, we saw a big running race, like Bay to Breakers, on the street. If we had known in advance, Gene and I would have entered it.

I learned more about the history of Indonesia while I lived in Sulawesi for two years and, a decade later, in Jakarta. Indonesia is an archipelago of over ten thousand islands, spreading across a distance wider than the continental United States. The peoples, cultures, and religions of South and Southeast Asia have migrated to it over the centuries. It had been a Hindu empire, then Buddhist. The largest Buddhist stupa in the world is in Java, not far from a vast complex of Hindu temples and tombs. The population gradually converted to Islam through the influence of traders and missionaries. The island of Bali remained Hindu despite the pressure of Buddhism and later Islam. The more primitive areas of Borneo, Sumatra, and Irian Jaya (West Papua) remained animist or were converted to Christianity by missionaries. Indonesia is the largest Muslim majority country in the world.

On arrival, we stayed in Jakarta for several days. In contrast to Pakistan, there were many women visible in public. The women were short and graceful. Some wore the traditional sarong and *kebaya* (blouse), but most wore Western-style clothing. I saw no women covering their faces or wearing the all-encompassing burka of Pakistan. The men had dark eyes and black hair but were smaller and more calm-appearing than the tall, hawk-nosed, bearded, gun-carrying men we had known in Pakistan. Only the policemen were armed.

The appearance of calm hid a surprisingly violent recent history. In 1957, a rebellion began in several areas of Indonesia. The rebels were unhappy with the autocratic government of President Sukarno, who had led the country since independence in 1945. The rebels included several dissident army groups. Because Indonesia was a leader of

183

the non-aligned movement of nations, it was considered Communist by some U.S. authorities. Since the rebels were opposing the "communist" government, they received clandestine support from the C.I.A. Sukarno was trying, unsuccessfully, to balance the Communist Party (PKI), the army, and the rebels.

In 1966, rebels kidnapped and killed six generals. The retribution was swift and severe. Sukarno capitulated, and General Suharto managed to take over leadership of the army. There followed a purge of suspected Communists throughout the country. Not all killings were the act of the military. Many individuals took advantage of the chaos to settle old disputes. The Chinese minority were resented for their apparent wealth, so Chinese businesses and homes were looted and destroyed as ordinary Indonesians took out their frustration and anger against the minority.

When we moved to Sulawesi, the memory of the time of violence was still fresh for some people. Neighborhood children mentioned relatives who had been in hiding for a decade, "returning from the forest." The rebellion simmered longer in Sulawesi than in other areas, evolving into a call for a more conservative Islamic regime. (The film *The Year of Living Dangerously* and the documentary *Act of Killing* illustrate this period of violence.)

On August 19, we flew to Ujung Pandang, Sulawesi (formerly known as Makassar, The Celebes), which was to be our home for two years. As the plane circled for landing, we could see an old fort, a port full of local schooners and small fishing boats, and the tile roofs of houses among palm trees. The tallest structure was a grain elevator at the port. It was not "just like San Francisco," as Gene's colleagues in California had told us.

A Public Works Department official met us. We drove through dusty streets to the Grand Hotel, a colonial-style place with high ceilings and sleeping rooms separated by floor-to-ceiling screens rather than walls. It had air-conditioning, as well as fans that turned slowly. Dinner in the hotel was not bad: rice with chicken and spicy vegetables. However, breakfast was awful. The toast and fried eggs were cold. The cereal was stale, and the milk was hot. There was no jam for the toast, only margarine and chocolate sprinkles, a Dutch treat, we were told. We bravely set out to visit the fort and museum, where someone directed us to a dock, suggesting a trip to a nearby island. In fifteen minutes, we were on Kayangan Island. There, we found a group of Canadian, Dutch, and Austrian women with their children on the beach. They would become our friends and help us adjust to Ujung Pandang. These expats recommended Dr. Hermann Meyer, a man of German origin, for health care. Like the doctor in Lahore, we never knew if Dr. Meyer was a professionally trained physician. Nor did I know whether he fled to remote Sulawesi because he was Jewish or because he was a Nazi. He was a bachelor and very friendly but did not speak about his personal history. He joined us for drinks or dinner from time to time and became our family doctor.

In the evening, we were taken to see the house intended for us. As in Pakistan, the government department constructed a housing complex instead of renting existing homes for the foreign experts. Every aspect of building a housing complex has opportunities for graft. The land is purchased from a favored politician or friend; every sack of cement and every window or door can be overpriced to provide a profit for the contractor, which he then splits with the officials in charge of the project. (Gene was told on a job in Pakistan that "the district engineer gets five percent, and the provincial engineer gets ten percent.)

The six-house compound was ten kilometers south of town, near a row of very tall palm trees known as *Tala Selapan*, or nine palms, in the local Makassar language. The trees were thought to be haunted. The houses were constructed on concrete slabs in a former rice field. The houses in nearby villages were on stilts to avoid flooding, snakes, and frogs and to provide storage and parking space below. Our house was almost finished but lacked screens and wiring for fans. It would have been so much nicer to rent a house in the town of Ujung Pandang, where we could walk to friends' houses and shops.

Rents in Indonesia were surprisingly high and often required extended advance payment. (When I was director of the Asia Foundation office in Jakarta and renewed the lease for my office in 1986, I had to pay for three years in advance directly to the landlord's son, who was studying in America.)

Accepting the project house meant that we would be following the terms of Gene's contract and saving money. There was no telephone. Since we had lived five and a half years in Pakistan without a phone, this did not surprise or worry me much. There were limited phone lines in Ujung Pandang, so getting a phone would take months and cost over a thousand dollars in fees and bribes. We had only one vehicle, Gene's official jeep. For some reason, our visas did not permit the purchase of a personal car. As I looked at this tiny cement-floored house, I wondered what we had gotten into. Living in project housing, along with lowered income-tax obligation, makes working overseas economically appealing. If we had tried to rent a better house, it might have absorbed all the savings we had anticipated. The bathroom contained a toilet, a huge bathtub, and an instant hot gas water heater. The builder had assumed that foreigners need bathtubs, not showers or the traditional Indonesian tank of water (*mandi*) from which one scoops water to pour over head and body. The only sink in the house was in the corner of the dining room. There was a utility sink in the kitchen courtyard. Behind the kitchen was a small room for servants and a little washroom.

When we moved into the house, a wall of brown faces pressed against every window. We looked in our dictionary for the word "go": *pergi*. We repeated the word with emphasis, only to have the boys outside mock us by imitating our accents. When we hung curtains, we were no longer a novelty show for the neighbors. Then, some of the boys came by after their school with a soccer ball to ask Eric and Greg, *"Main bola?"* (play ball?). Within a week, they were kicking the ball around and flying kites together. A few days later, the little sister of one of the boys, Ira, came along to play with Laura. They became close friends, exchanging dolls, toys, and head lice for two years. We got the building contractor to make a covered enclosure around the kitchen sink area, effectively doubling the size of the kitchen. We gave Eric and Greg the largest bedroom because they needed to have desks and bookshelves for their studies. Gene and I took the other regular-size bedroom, and Laura got a tiny room, large enough for her bed and a wardrobe.

A Canadian I met at Kayangan island on our first day lived with her husband and little daughter two kilometers closer to the town than we did. It was easy to walk to her house, so I consulted with her about life on the outskirts of Ujung Pandang. She found a servant for us, Siti, a young woman from the Toraja area of Sulawesi. Siti brought along a friend, also from Toraja, Rini. They were Christians. As in Pakistan, house servants in this part of Indonesia are often Christians. (Muslims try to avoid jobs that involve cleaning bathrooms, dealing with human waste, or washing underwear.) Most nurses are Christian because they must deal with bodily needs, while doctors are likely to be Muslim. We had learned in Pakistan that in the Indian subcontinent, the lowest castes and untouchables were the most likely to convert to Christianity. They often continued to do the "untouchable" sort of jobs.

The Toraja people resisted conversion to Islam, but eventually, some converted from animism to Christianity. The rough, aggressive Muslim people of the Ujung Pandang area raided Toraja for slaves. The tradition of the Toraja people as servants has continued. For two years, Siti and Rini washed all our clothes in buckets, cleaned the house, boiled and filtered all the water, and did a lot of the cooking.

We experienced the rough behavior of the South Sulawesi Makassar and Bugis people when we went shopping in the town. Men and women would try to pinch the children or pull their blond hair. I had to hold my purse carefully to ward off pickpockets. The Bugis are famed as sailors and pirates but are also known for traditional transvestites who perform in harvest and planting ceremonies. In Singapore, there is a Bugis Street in the rough port area, famous for bars and transvestite shows.

In the Indonesian language, *kassar* means rude. Makassar would, therefore, be interpreted as "most rude." It often seemed true. The Javanese people of Indonesia are more refined and gentler than the Sulawesi people.

On the highway by the palm trees, there was a steady stream of traffic. Many bicycles passed, some carrying huge bunches of bananas. Bicycle rickshaws came slowly, overloaded with passengers or freight. I once saw a couch and two armchairs on a bicycle rickshaw. For public transportation, there were *bejaks,* scooters with a passenger seat for two or three, and *bemos,* small pickup trucks. These had a roof over the truck bed and benches on each side. About eight people could ride in a *bemo.* As soon as we learned some basic Indonesian, we could stand by the road and wave for a vehicle to stop and take us to town.

Feeding my family in Ujung Pandang was a challenge at first. There were no grocery stores with refrigeration beyond small freezers for popsicles. There were no dairy products because there were no cows, and no one milked the ubiquitous water buffalos. There was one small shop, *Toko Lima Lima* (Store 55), which was favored by the expats. It was stocked with a wide variety of canned and dry foods, and wine, beer, and liquor, as well as the powdered milk and canned butter we relied upon for two years. Fortunately, there were daily open-air markets for fresh vegetables and fruit. There was also a market for poultry, beef, and goat, plus, once a week, a small pork market serving the Christian and Chinese minority populations. Muslims do not eat pork. Fresh fish could be found at the waterfront every day. I got a yogurt starter from a Swiss friend and taught Siti to make yogurt with powdered milk. All the packaged bread was white, sweet, and soggy. I was determined to bake better bread. The Chinese couple who owned the grain elevator were members of our evening tennis group. They offered me wheat bran and fresh flour, so I was able to make a decent crusty loaf of bread. I taught Siti and Rini how to make bread. They baked almost daily, keeping us well supplied with whole wheat, raisin, and herb bread. (When we departed after two years, Gene's replacement, a bachelor, moved into the house and kept the servants. Siti and Rini continued to bake bread. He sent a frantic telegram to Gene, asking how to stop this endless bread supply!)

Running in Indonesia through the rice fields could be problematic. Very hot during the dry season, but when the rains came, the berms became slippery, and the paddies were eighteen inches deep with muddy water. Frogs and snakes sought the drier ground on the berms, increasing the hazards. Frogs were so ubiquitous in the wet season that I had to shake them out of my shoes before I went running. Once, I found a tiny frog compressed beneath my plastic arch support.

Gene made a significant discovery in Indonesia: Coffee. Raised by Christian Science parents, he had never drunk coffee. He was not tempted by my mother's percolated coffee, which was a bitter, thin brew; in Pakistan, where we lived for five and a half years, there was only powdered Nescafé. Early in our stay in Ujung Pandang, at a tiny cafe on the waterfront, Gene saw a man pouring boiling water through a cloth tube or "coffee sock." He bought a cup. The coffee was fresh ground, strong, hot, and mixed with condensed milk. It was a revelation to him. He was hooked. On a work trip to the highlands of Sulawesi, he bought raw beans at a coffee farm. Siti roasted them in a wok and pounded them with a mortar and pestle. From that day forward, he would only drink coffee from Indonesia. Working later in Pakistan or West Africa, he mail-ordered Sulawesi coffee beans from Peet's coffee store in Berkeley. In 1989, the embassy mail staff in Pakistan complained of the coffee smell in the diplomatic pouch, so we had to put coffee shipments in the DHL service I used for Asia Foundation. Gene was not good at cooking, but coffee was his ritual. When camping, he would crouch outside the tent in sunshine or in snow to make the morning brew. When breakfasting in hotel restaurants, he would order a pot of boiling water and pull out a cone, filter paper, and bag of coffee. If the Mongolian, Chinese, Indian, or Kirghiz waiter did not understand his request, he would barge into the kitchen and locate the boiling water. Frequently, the coffee overran the cone, cup, or teapot and spread on the tablecloth, horrified waiters observed.

Indonesian food was a new experience for us. While the Pakistani food we had eaten in the 1960s was heavy with animal fat and butter, Indonesian food is lighter. It is equally spicey. Indonesia is a rice culture. People believe, "If you have not eaten rice, you have not eaten." Just as the Arctic people have many words for snow, Indonesians have many words for rice. Seeds are *biji*; in the field, it is *padi*; when harvested, it is *beras*; when it is cooked, it becomes *nasi*. Neighbors in the villages around us in Sulawesi cooked a large pot of rice in the morning and covered it with a netting umbrella. Throughout the day, family members would come, fill a plate with rice, and add a few vegetables and dried fermented fish, and very hot pickle or fish sauce. In the evenings, the family would cook vegetables and fresh fish or chicken with hot spices. There were no set times for midday eating except on special holidays or feast days.

In Indonesia, there was *nasi goreng*, fried rice, instead of the *pulau* of Pakistan. For special occasions, there was *nasi kuning*, yellow rice colored with turmeric and slightly sweetened. Raisins and nuts were stirred in, and the rice was served in a cone shape. An honored guest would be invited to slice off the tip of the cone.

In rural Sulawesi, a popular snack was fried slices of casava, *ubi kayu*. On our first trip to Bali, we discovered our favorite dishes: *gado-gado*, a peanut-based sauce served over steamed and raw vegetables, and *Sate,* Chicken, shrimp, and lamb (and pork on Bali, a largely Hindu province) cut in small cubes, marinated, threaded on bamboo skewers, and cooked over an open fire. Beef did not appear often in Indonesian meals, except as *rendang*, reconstituted dried beef, which is usually stringy. This led my children to say Indonesian food consisted of "cold rice and stringy meat."

However, they still love Indonesian food and prepare *gado-gado* and chicken or shrimp sate for parties at home. There was a vast array of tropical fruits and vegetables in Indonesia, and snack food was available along the streets. Food merchants came through our neighborhood on bicycle-powered carts selling noodle soup, fried noodles, skewers of barbecued chicken or fish, cooked vegetables, or fruit drinks. Each cart had a distinctive bell or whistle so customers would know what was coming. We called it "Meals on Wheels." The foods kept hot over charcoal were safe to eat, but I was wary of the cold drinks.

I found dishes that I liked in both Pakistan and Indonesia. Since they are Muslim-majority countries, wine is not served with meals, just tea or water. My travels have immersed me in other cuisines. In Asia, Thai and Vietnamese cuisines are excellent. However, in my opinion, the foods of France and Italy, enhanced by appropriate wine, cannot be surpassed.

A serious problem in the first six weeks was the absence of our schoolbooks. I had sent them by air freight, assuming they might arrive before us, but they hadn't. I had three bored children in a tiny house. We studied the Indonesian language together, though they were learning faster during afternoon play with the village kids. I taught them to play bridge, usually bidding, so that Laura could be a "dummy." At six, she was a bit young for the complexity of bridge. We played checkers, and I also tried to teach them embroidery and some cooking. We put up a badminton net and found a couple of places where we could play tennis. We took excursions, when we could use the jeep, to different beaches and islands.

Finally, on October 4th, the air freight with all the books and lessons arrived. It had been sitting for weeks at the customs office of the Jakarta airport. The director of Gene's project had not sent anyone to the airport with the required funds (legal customs fees and illegal bribes) to get it. I was really annoyed that they had not been more concerned about the family of an employee in a remote location.

The materials from the Calvert School in Maryland were very comprehensive and included textbooks, workbooks, and assignments. I set up a schedule. Gene and I would run as soon as it was light, from 5:30 to 6:30 a.m. Then we would wake the children and have breakfast. Gene would leave for the office in town before 8, but he could send the jeep and driver back if he had no errands to run in town. Then, I would get the studies started. Eric and Greg, in grades seven and three, had straightforward lessons, which I could help explain or supplement with my knowledge or library books. Laura, grade one, was more problematic. I had never taught someone to read because Eric and Greg had learned spontaneously. I had taught middle school, tutored high school students, and taught university courses, but never elementary school. I failed to teach Laura well. She was clever enough to fool me into thinking she had mastered a lesson even when she had not. The children would study until noon or one, and then we would have lunch and plan an excursion, experiment, or art project. They often played with local children in the afternoon, so their Indonesian language skills continued to improve. At least once a week, we arranged play dates with expatriate children. A Dutch friend invited Laura to join her daughter's traditional Balinese dance lessons. On Fridays, we went swimming at Kayangan Island, and on Sundays, we occasionally hired a boat to go to more distant, pristine, uninhabited islands for snorkeling and swimming. Government departments, including the one to which Gene reported, followed a weekly schedule of Friday afternoon holidays for prayers and Sunday holidays for rest. The Sunday holiday was a holdover from Dutch colonial times. I found tennis lessons for Eric and Greg and a group of Indonesian ladies for me to play with once a week early in the morning. A couple of evenings a week, Gene and I joined some other couples to play tennis at lighted courts. Life was busy, if not always easy.

Our mail arrived sporadically. Magazines were often censored. Any criticism of the Indonesian government was blacked out, as were photos of women in bathing suits or shorts. Many people must have been employed rolling black ink over pages in *Time*, *Newsweek*, or the *Far Eastern Economic Review*. The post office was a large colonial building. It closed between noon and 3 p.m. During that lunch break, the employees played badminton in the entry hall. The lines for the court were painted on the floor. Any mail larger than a standard envelope went to a shed behind the building. When I suspected a magazine or parcel was overdue, I would insist on being allowed to walk to the shed. I would sort through the stack of foreign mail to find my mail. This was especially important when I was expecting the corrected homework from the children's school.

Eric's village friends gave him some baby chicks. With their help, he built a bamboo chicken coop behind the house. Those chicks soon produced eggs and chicks. One chick hatched with a twisted foot. The hens tried to destroy it. They do not like handicapped offspring. Eric rescued this chick and fed it by hand. After that, "Chakin," as he called it, followed him around the house as though he was the hen.

Laura was interested in cats, so she brought two kittens home from the village. Of course, they grew into cats and had kittens, which we had to give away. The cats killed mice and frogs, but sometimes, they brought snakes home to play with on the porch. Siti, our maid, said one of those snakes was a "two-step," meaning that when it bites you, you die after taking two steps. Greg did not want any animals of his own, though he helped with the chickens and enjoyed the cats. When we wanted to catch a chicken to eat, Eric and Greg would gather some local boys to chase it around the outside of the house. They insisted upon taking the captured chicken to their village so it could be killed in proper Halal Muslim technique. They thought we should not eat meat that was butchered by our Christian maids.

Living on the equator was a new experience. We knew that Indonesia was near the equator, but we had not really thought how that would affect us. The days and nights were always the same length, twelve hours, all year long. The seasons were dry and wet, not the hot and cold of temperate climates. It was not as hot as Pakistan in the summer, but it never got cold! For cool temperatures, we had to go to higher altitudes. There was a small "hill station" called Malino at an altitude of 3,500 ft, an hour and a half drive from Ujung Pandang. It was a wonderful respite from the steady ninety-degree heat with 90 percent humidity at sea level. We went there for weekends throughout the year. There were ponies for the children to ride, a cold freshwater swimming pool, trails through the jungle to higher points, and rabbits, orchids, and exotic fruits to buy.

When we arrived in Sulawesi, it was the dry season. In November, the rains began. The water poured out of the sky as if from a bucket. Frogs appeared spontaneously everywhere. They came up the drain in the bathroom and pooped on the floor. We had to be sure to keep the bathroom door closed to keep the frogs out of the other rooms of the house. The water rose almost to the level of our porch and doorways. During the first heavy deluge, young boys from the villages raced outdoors in their underpants to stand and jump around in the torrents of water that poured off every roof. Our running became a contest of balancing on the slippery berms between rice paddies or sinking into deep mud. More snakes appeared on the berms, escaping from the water. I would shriek and jump in the air when a snake crossed my path. The rains stopped as suddenly as they started, so we could continue our tennis games some evenings.

Bali was our best change of scenery. Gene's field trips to different islands often involved changing planes in Bali. All the expats we met were enthusiastic about Bali, so we seized the opportunity to go there in December 1976. We flew together; after three days, Gene continued to Jakarta with one of his Taiwanese colleagues. Bali seemed a paradise after the somewhat rude people of Sulawesi; the Hindu Balinese seemed gentle and calm. No one wanted to pinch the cheek or pull the hair of a blond child. We found inexpensive lodging near the beach in Kuta, great restaurants, and bicycles to rent, and we easily traveled around the island to visit temples and attend dance and drama performances. In the highlands of Bali, we hiked in the forest with monkeys. The children loved the cultural atmosphere and the surf. I loved being able to run long distances on the beaches. I was amused by Gene's Taiwanese colleague who walked on the beach in a dark suit, pretending not to look at the buxom topless Dutch tourists playing volleyball. After a week, the children and I returned to Ujung Pandang, refreshed by the relaxing cultural interlude. Gene returned the next day after intense meetings with his team in Jakarta.

The Toraja culture of the highlands of South Sulawesi was the focus of some anthropologists Gene met on a field trip. They invited us to come for the funeral ceremony of an important person. We had read about the unique customs the Toraja maintained despite their supposed conversion to Christianity. For this ceremony, the family of the deceased had waited several years to accumulate enough money for the ceremony. On the first day, the corpse, wrapped in bright batiks and gold cloth, was brought to the center of the village. We were not close enough to know if it smelled. A spiritual leader proceeded to construct a life-size effigy known as a *tautau*. On the final day of the ceremony, this would be placed in a niche carved in a rock face. Several hours of recitation, the burning of incense, and processions of family members continued into the evening. The next day, a dozen water buffalo were brought to the central grass square of the village. Hundreds of people walked from their villages and farms to attend. A priest recited the history of the dead man's life. Then, a burly man with a large, curved knife came to the center; another man pulled a buffalo toward him, forced his head to the ground, and twisted it upward. With one slash, the butcher slit the buffalo's neck. Small boys holding hollow bamboo containers rushed up to catch the blood. This performance was repeated until all the buffalo were dead and the grass was red with blood. Butchers came forward to skin the animals and divide the meat. Then, the villagers paraded past the butchers, each departing with a dripping chunk of meat. It was quite a spectacle. The following morning, a procession carried the *tau tau* and the body to the final location on a rock balcony.

A tall young American, a member of Volunteers in Asia, was working in Toraja making bamboo pumps to raise water from channels to fields. His enthusiasm was contagious, and his language skills were impressive. Nine years later, when I was director of the Asia Foundation in Jakarta, I hired him to work on similar projects in remote island provinces.

My father visited us in March 1977. He loved to travel, but his enthusiasm was dimmed by the death of his wife, Mary, the year before. After a day or two in Ujung Pandang, we went to Bali, where he enjoyed the dance performances and the beach scene. We took a ferry to Surabaya, in East Java. It has a wonderful zoo containing about twenty Komodo dragons, the largest lizards on earth. Then we took the train to Jogjakarta. My father had always loved trains, so this was a treat for him. On this trip, he seemed to be drinking and smoking more than ever, which worried me. As we arrived in Jogjakarta, he insisted on finding a store where he could buy a bottle of gin before we went to our hotel to wash off the dust of hours on the train. I did not realize when we watched his plane leave that I would never see him again. He died in August of that year at his home in Connecticut.

The telegram informing me of his death was sent to the headquarters of Gene's company in Jakarta, so I did not learn of it until a week later when someone called Gene and read the telegram. This was another example of how the head office in Jakarta ignored the employees in distant field offices.

Chapter 18   Fourth Pakistan: Trek Leader

"It is irresponsible to leave your three children with their father and servants while you lead a trek in the Hindu Kush."

Before leaving Berkeley for Indonesia in 1976, I worked part-time for Mountain Travel, an adventure travel company. I had discussed leading a trek in Pakistan. Early in 1977, the possibility became a reality. The previous year, a woman participant had complained that the trek leader had been more concerned about his photographic equipment than the comfort and enjoyment of the clients. To reduce complaints in the future, Mountain Travel's directors thought it would be best to have a woman and a man as co-leaders. With my language skills and experience in the mountains of Pakistan, I was a good choice. My co-leader was Ray Jewell, an experienced mountaineer and trek leader. I do not remember feeling anxious about leaving Gene with the children and servants for three weeks. He planned to take the children to Jakarta for a week while he worked there. They could stay with the family of a coworker who had three children about the same ages. They could go to the American Club every day to enjoy the pool, snack bar, and game rooms. I assumed they would do minimal schoolwork the rest of the time but continue language study, tennis lessons for the boys, dance lessons for Laura, and visits to our European and Canadian friends in Ujung Pandang. I must have been a little worried, but it did not stop me from undertaking this challenging job.

I lived in Pakistan from 1962 to 1964 as a Peace Corps Volunteer, from 1964 to 1967 as a memsahib, mother, and housewife, and again as an academic research scholar in 1974. Now, in 1977, I returned as a trek leader. I left Ujung Pandang on July 27, waving goodbye to my family with anticipation of an adventure. I stopped for a day in Jakarta to get a gamma globulin shot and stay with friends. My flights from there went through Singapore and Karachi, and I finally arrived in Islamabad at 6:30 a.m. on July 29.

Mountain Travel had booked a room for me at the Intercontinental Hotel, the best in Islamabad. It took a few hours to find my co-leader, Ray since there were no room-to-room telephones. Ray introduced me to two essential members of our staff, the cook, Hasan, and a Pakistan Tourism Department employee, Asif Khan, nephew of the Mir (hereditary ruler) of Hunza, the area where we would begin our trek. Asif was only twenty-four, but he was respected throughout the region we would visit due to his family. His knowledge of the local languages was extremely helpful also. Hasan had been a chef at the Embassy of Pakistan in Washington, D.C. He was an excellent cook, spoke English, and was at ease with Americans. We spent the next few days getting permits, buying food, and meeting our fifteen clients as they arrived. At 39, I was younger than most of them. There were two couples, and the rest were single men and women. A divorcee from Idaho brought her beautiful eighteen-year-old daughter, Tara. She was a distraction for all the Pakistani men! By the end of the trip, Asif was smitten.

One day, while we waited for our permits, I took the group to the nearby archeological site and museum in Taxila. Founded in 516 B.C., it became the capital of the eastern province of the Persian Achaemenid Empire. During the next hundred years, it was a great center of learning with the largest university in the Indian subcontinent. The writing system of Sanskrit was developed there. The Buddhist Emperor Ashoka made Taxila one of his capitals and built a stupa for some of the ashes of Buddha there. Fortunately, the museum at Taxila is outstanding and air-conditioned. The ruins are more difficult to appreciate as many are just the remnants of brick walls in the grass.

In the hotel lobby, I saw the baggage of several mountaineering expeditions. I felt a pang of envy. I was leading a group of tourists over trails instead of pursuing a challenging mountaineering route. Among them was Jay Hellman, leader of a recently completed American Nanga Parbat expedition. A tanned, muscular young man, he was a contrast to the pale, middle-aged clients on my trip. I would have liked to spend more time with him, but our clients were my priority. He joined us for dinner in Islamabad. He thrilled and horrified the clients with stories of his expedition's triumph and tragedy, the death of a climber.

We flew to Gilgit on August 6. In Gilgit, we made final purchases of kerosene, kitchen equipment, and rations for our porters. Jeeps took us several miles west to the village of Yasin, where we would start the trek. The Raja of Yasin welcomed us with a tour of his house and garden. His wife, the Rani, was gracious, intelligent, and a firm believer in education for all her children, boys and girls. We camped in their apricot orchard and were entertained by the local men dancing. In Yasin, we purchased a sheep and a few chickens. The sheep would walk with us for several days until Hasan butchered it. The chickens produced a few fresh eggs and, eventually, chicken stew. The next day, we hiked almost twelve miles to the village of Harph, where we camped in another apricot orchard. We were walking up a steadily rising valley with towering granite peaks on both sides. One client, a woman from New York, complained that she had trained by running five miles a day in Central Park, but she did not realize we would be hiking uphill! The trip was described as "Passes in the Hindu Kush," so one should assume there would be some hills.

I watched closely to be sure that Hasan treated all our water appropriately. We had two large bottles of iodine to treat all our water. The water tastes strange, but the parasites are killed. We wanted to avoid dysentery and parasites, but boiling the quantity of water needed for a group this size would have required a huge amount of fuel, all of which would have had to have been carried by men or donkeys.

Ray and I worked out a system to start the days smoothly. After Hasan's excellent breakfast of tea, eggs, oatmeal, fresh chapatis, and jam, we would count the duffels and packs and weigh each so that all donkey loads were equal. We would write in our notebook which animal was carrying which load. The highest priority was the locked duffle that contained our money. The porters and donkey owners had to be paid in cash. They did not like large bills because there were no banks in their villages to change for smaller bills. Each man expected fifteen dollars a day for the trek out and half pay for returning. There were sixteen to eighteen men or donkeys for sixteen days. We had about seven thousand dollars in fifty-rupee notes. It was a hefty bag. Ray would start hiking with the clients while I made sure every bag and donkey was on the way. Then, I would hike at a brisk pace, overtaking the clients and reaching the campsite to welcome them. I enjoyed the challenges of interfacing between the porters and the staff in Urdu and Pushto. By the third day, we were beyond the villages, camping near a glacier. We had to pay the men from Yasin and hire a new set of men and animals from Shotaling in the next valley. The villages in each valley are competitive and hostile. They do not welcome men from other areas who are passing through and earning money by working for foreign visitors. During our sixteen-day trek, we had four different sets of porters. We went over two high passes and camped near them. Ray and I, and the most active clients, Tara, Asif, and Hassan, climbed a 15,500 ft peak above each of the two passes. The trip gave me summits to challenge Gene's lifetime list of

14,000 ft peaks. These rugged, rocky hikes were a great change from the jungles of Indonesia.

There was only one serious problem during the trek. A bridge had washed out at a small but turbulent river. Two porters forded the river on their donkeys, carrying a rope that became the foundation of a precarious bridge for the hikers. The rope was strung across the river. Two strands supported some logs that the men cut, then placed across them, covering the surface with sticks and flat rocks. The other two strands were the handrails. It took half a day to complete this bridge. We lounged in the sunshine, taking photographs while the donkey men worked. It was an unplanned rest day for us. The clients tiptoed across this rickety construction while the other donkeys reluctantly swam across.

I wore Nike Waffle Trainer shoes on the trails, saving my rugged leather climbing boots for the passes and rougher hikes. The clients said they could easily follow my distinctive waffle-pattern tracks. In the villages, we saw quantities of marijuana and opium poppies growing. One evening, we made tea with opium poppy seeds. It was mildly soporific. The marijuana was pleasant for a gentle smoke after dinner. The weather was good, and the group was congenial. I found it a bit tiring being always alert for problems, constantly cheerful, and ready for conversation. I missed Gene and the children, too, especially when I saw happy children playing in the villages.

When we arrived at the end of the trek, the town of Chitral, we were told the flights from there to Islamabad were canceled due to bad weather. The road out of Chitral crosses Lowari Top, a pass that is clear of snow for only a few weeks a year. Several clients and I had flights to catch in Islamabad, so we hired a jeep to go by road. The rest of the group would wait until a flight was available. The road was passable for the jeep, but authorities on the other side of the pass insisted we hire a minibus there. Fortunately, I had taken a good supply of the group's cash for these transportation challenges. We arrived at the major highway, the Grand Trunk Road, at Nowshera at 3:00 in the morning. There, we would catch a bus to Islamabad/Rawalpindi. Fortunately, it was Ramadan. The tea shops at the intersection were preparing the early morning food for people who were fasting from dawn to dusk. We enjoyed hot sweet tea and fresh chapatis while we waited for the bus, watching the steady parade of bullock carts and camels on the road. At 5 a.m., we were on the bus, arriving in time for lunch at the Intercontinental Hotel and our evening flights to Karachi. These final days of road transportation were as exciting as the mountain trek for the five clients who were with me! Ray and the rest of the group managed to get a flight out of Chitral two days later.

Home in Indonesia, after one day fulfilling Gene's shopping list of camera accessories in Singapore, I was happy to be with my family and back into our routine. I had escaped domestic duties and homeschooling for a few weeks and had my skills and knowledge appreciated by a group of adults. It was good to be back interacting with the kids and Gene instead of the forced friendliness with Trek clients.

Two students joined our home school classes in the fall of 1977. One was a Chinese-Canadian second-grader, John. He was using Canadian distance learning materials, similar to our Calvert school lessons. The other was a Vietnamese American boy, Robert, who was twelve. He had little prior schooling. In spite of his age, he was at the fourth-grade level of nine-year-old Greg. I adapted Greg's lessons for him. The presence of these boys made studying more interesting for Greg and Eric and even for Laura. The local boys of the nearby villages were fascinated by these exotic newcomers. At the end of our lessons, as the local school let out, they would come by and call out, "John, you play?" Hoping that John and Robert would stay to join their afternoon soccer and kite flying.

Chapter 19 Annapurna Sanctuary Family Trek

I continued to correspond with Arlene Blum about the women's Annapurna expedition. Gene and I discussed going to Nepal to see Annapurna before I made a final decision about going on the expedition. We decided to take the children to Nepal in November for a trek to the Annapurna sanctuary on the south side of the mountain. Two friends from Colorado, siblings Charlie and Mel Grant, agreed to join us. In early November, the five of us flew from Ujung Pandang to Jakarta, Bangkok, and Kathmandu. From the plane, there were spectacular views of Everest and neighboring Makalu Mountain. In Kathmandu, we met our friends and went to the Mountain Travel Office, where a high-school classmate of mine, Al Read, was in charge. He recommended a Sherpa, Pasang, to lead our trek. Pasang and I went to the bazaar to buy food and cooking equipment. I enjoyed figuring out menus based on the limited available foods. Meanwhile, Gene and the children rented bikes to tour around Kathmandu. There were so few cars it was quite safe for children to bicycle.

A family and friends trip was more relaxed than leading a Mountain Travel trek. Pasang hired ten porters. One was assigned to walk near Laura in case she got tired and needed to be carried, but she never needed help. (Porters in Nepal carry passengers in bamboo baskets on their backs for many miles since there are no roads to most villages.) On the third day of our trek, by chance we met our friends, California climbers Galen Rowell and Kim Schmidt, for afternoon tea in a village. On the trail, we met one of Gene's fraternity brothers from Dartmouth. Some French hikers we chatted with knew our friends Harvey and Suzy from Chamonix, demonstrating how small the population of trekkers was in 1977. Laura, seven, Greg, nine, and Eric, thirteen, were enthusiastic and capable hikers. We did not need to slow down for them. Family trekkers were unusual in those days, so Nepalese in the villages were fascinated by the children.

On the sixth day, we arrived at the basecamp south of Annapurna. The vast south face, a wall of vertical ice and rock, loomed 12,000 ft above us. It had been climbed in 1970 by a British expedition, and one climber died in an avalanche. We planned to camp for three days so we could try to climb a minor peak. Eric, Gene, Charlie, and I ascended to 15,200 ft towards Tent Peak, while Greg and Laura stayed with Mel Grant and the porters in the base camp. Eric and Charlie felt weak from the altitude, so in the morning, Gene and I headed up a rocky slope to a snow dome 2,000 feet higher. We could not discern the route to Tent Peak and were both having mild altitude headaches, so we declared our location a "summit" and descended to our camp, packed our gear, and hiked down to the base camp where Laura, Greg, and Mel were waiting with the porters.

The trek back to Pokhara was very enjoyable. Each day, we camped in fields near villages where Diwali, an important Hindu holiday, was being celebrated with crude

Ferris wheels and swings for kids, markets, and garlands of marigolds on all the animals. Laura was the focus of gentle attention in the villages. No one had seen a little American girl before! In Nepal, there are no level trails, so descending from the Annapurna base camp to Pokhora, we went uphill at least 40 percent of the time. Typically, each day would start with breakfast near a village, then descent for some miles to a river crossing, where Pasang would meet us and cook lunch, then back up the other side of the river to another village. At the end of this trek, we all felt strong, though our friend Mel had a sore knee.

We wanted to show the children a little of India on the way back to Ujung Pandang, so we flew to Delhi, which has ancient and colonial monuments and a wonderful zoo featuring white tigers and other exotic animals. We visited Agra and the Taj Mahal for a day. The air pollution and traffic had increased since 1963, when we first visited. However, the children loved the Agra Fort, where they ran around on different levels and pretended to ward off enemies. They giggled as they slid in stocking feet on the polished marble of the Taj Mahal. I gazed in awe at the white domes, the inlaid stone, and the minarets of this tomb built in 1628 in memory of the wife of the emperor of India. We saw across the river, the smaller tomb of an aunt of the emperor, designed by the same architect, Ustad Ahmad Lahori.

Then we stopped in Madras (now Chennai), on the southeast coast of India. The guidebooks said it had the longest beach in India. It was a very long beach, but it was also a very long morning latrine for the city. One had to step carefully on the beach until the tide swept it clean. When the kids were building sandcastles, they were quickly surrounded by crowds of curious Indians, making the experience claustrophobic.

Madras was then a "dry" state. To get a cold beer in the evening, Gene had to complete a three-page form, submit it to the hotel clerk, and wait for an unmarked package to arrive at our room; by then, the beer was quite warm. Hardly worth the trouble. I found the Hindu architecture and rituals at the temples interesting and a great contrast to the mosques of northern India and Pakistan.

Our final stop was Singapore, where we shopped for camera equipment for Gene and toys for the children. I took advantage of the fact that flights from Singapore to Ujung Pandang stopped in Bali. We had a couple of days to swim and enjoy some dance and music performances after the hectic trip. When we arrived back at our little house, it seemed small and boring after our experiences in Nepal, India, Singapore, and Bali. Since it was already early December, we were happy to remind ourselves that we would be going home in six or seven months.

We plunged back into the schooling. I wanted to accomplish something scholarly to bring back from two years in Indonesia. I revived the survey I had used in Pakistan to explore variations in restrictions on women and their attitudes toward education, family planning, and work. I conducted over a hundred interviews in villages near our house. My thesis had been that restrictions on women impede social, economic, and political development. My research on the modernization of Islamic laws affecting women in Muslim-majority nations revealed a correlation between the legal changes and the education of women, population growth rate, and participation of women in the labor force. The survey tested this relationship in individual women's lives, considering variations in economic class, age, and rural or urban settings.

To determine the economic status of my subjects, I used my observation and checklist, as I had in Pakistan. I noted the type of house construction (was it mud/adobe, wood, or cement), whether the woman had a sewing machine, whether she cooked with a wood or dung fire, whether there was a gas or electric stove, whether transportation by members of the household was by foot, bicycle, motorcycle, or automobile. In Pakistan, most of the village homes were made of mud bricks, and the cooking was done with a fire of wood or dung. In Indonesian villages, most of the houses were made of bamboo or wood. A few of the wealthiest families had cement homes. All homes had kerosene or propane stoves. The standard of living was higher.

I enjoyed meeting the women, some of whom were mothers of boys who played games and went fishing with my sons. Children running from village to village announced my presence. Most village houses were raised on stilts to provide ventilation and protect the homes from snakes, frogs, and vermin. Bicycles, motorcycles, harvested crops, chicken coops, and sometimes a large loom would be stored beneath the raised home. In the afternoon, women and girls would sit on the steps, each one picking the nits from the head of the woman or girl below. In contrast to Pakistan, where the literacy rate for adult women was 10 percent in the rural areas when I conducted my survey, 75 percent of the rural women in Indonesia were literate, having attended at least 5 years of coeducational school. In Pakistan and other countries where schools are segregated, fewer educational opportunities are available for girls.

Most of the older women had "arranged" marriages when they were under 20. They assumed that their children would select their own spouses, with the approval of their parents, and marry later, in their mid to late twenties. The women I interviewed were observant Muslims but had never worn a face-covering veil. They had a term for face coverings–*Sakit Malayu*, or the Malaysian sickness, because some ultraconservative groups in Malaysia were promoting face coverings for all Muslim women. For religious services on the important Muslim holidays, the women wore white sarongs and blouses and a head covering, but not a face covering. Going on pilgrimage to Mecca, they could be seen at airports wearing the required modest clothing but without face covering. Most families observed fasting during Ramadan and prayed daily. Women attended services at the mosques, in a section reserved for women. In daily life, there was little gender segregation. Women dominated the vegetable and fruit markets and worked in government and commercial offices.

Rice farming is labor intensive and requires both women and men to work in the fields. This is a more egalitarian food production system than the wheat and meat agriculture of Pakistan, where men plow, plant, and harvest wheat and herd large animals while women stay close to home, tending chickens and vegetable gardens. The value of women's work is recognized in Southeast Asia if it is not compensated monetarily. In their spare time, women weave, sew, and prepare snack foods for sale in the market. These activities add to family income. South Sulawesi women weave beautiful silk sarongs. Some of the brightest are intended for men to wear for special occasions. It was startling to see a group of men walking to a wedding, each clad in a pink or aqua sarong topped by a somber suit jacket.

Although most of the women had three or more children, they were all aware of Indonesia's national family-planning campaign slogan, "Two is enough." Indonesian coins are stamped with the image of an ideal family: father, mother, son, and daughter. Posters proclaiming the ideal family were on display in every village. I wrote an article based on my findings and presented it at a conference of the Association of Asian Studies on the West Coast in 1979.

When we traveled to remote areas of Sulawesi, crowds would form around us in an almost threatening manner. I remember staying in a government guest house in a port town where a French family and I went to see a traditional boat building. Local men and boys stood on each other's shoulders to peer in every window, jeering in a hostile way, commenting on our appearance, and probably hoping to see us undress. We felt threatened and trapped. The mother of the French family and I were increasingly worried and the children were frightened. Finally, after 10 p.m., the night watchman and police came by. They shooed away the crowd so we could have some peace and quiet. Then they asked, "You were having some trouble?"

During our last few weeks in Indonesia, Laura became very ill. She had a high fever and cough. With Dr. Meyer's help, she was tested for typhoid, diphtheria, and various kinds of dysentery. Dr. Meyer determined from an X-ray that she had either tuberculosis or pneumonia. He prescribed Rifampin, an antibiotic used to treat TB. She took the pills for several weeks and recovered.

Gene's boss and the USAID officials wanted him to extend his contract for two more years. We were not enthusiastic. We said we might consider it if we could be in Jakarta, where there was an excellent international school and were provided a proper house, not a tiny project house in an inconvenient neighborhood. In the end, we decided two years was enough. I was eager to get the children back into normal schools and to push ahead with my career. We had given up the opportunites of California, with schools for the children, university-level teaching opportunities for me, and an office job for Gene, but we gained some unique experiences as a family and as individuals.

The two years in Sulawesi were positive for our family despite intestinal parasites, snakes, lice, and jungle thorns. It gave our blue-eyed children, Eric, Greg, and Laura, the experience of being a minority. Everyone else in Indonesia had black hair and dark eyes. Sometimes, they suffered from excessive attention, such as when being photographed by Japanese tourists on the beach in Bali, surrounded by curious Indians in Madras, or having their blond hair touched and cheeks pinched in the Sulawesi market. But that gave them a sense of the world and their place in it. As adults, each of them has returned to Asia several times. Homeschooling was a challenge, but we all learned from it. I had led a trek in Pakistan, and the whole family made an impressive trek in Nepal.

Gene's work was challenging; he had to balance local interests with the directives of his company and USAID, as well as Indonesian officials at provincial and local levels. His project was part of a nationwide effort to improve irrigation so that rice could be grown in the sunny, dry season. In a few years, Indonesia achieved self-sufficiency in rice production. His job involved extensive travel over the eastern half of the Indonesian archipelago. Opportunities to observe varied cultures and purchase handicrafts and textiles in remote areas were a bonus for him.

All five of us had acquired functional fluency in the Indonesian language. Eric, the oldest, acquired some slang and curse words in the local Makassar language also. Four years later, he studied the Indonesian language formally at the University of California, Santa Cruz. He achieved sufficient mastery to play Scrabble with Indonesians. My familiarity with Indonesia and the language made it possible for me to become the director of the Asia Foundation Indonesia office in 1985. Greg and Laura's language fluency exceeded that of most of their classmates when they attended the International School in Jakarta in the 1980s. They could lead others in interactions with Indonesians. Their accents were perfect, and their vocabulary was at the level of younger children. They could not converse about politics and economics, but they knew the vocabulary of sports, games, and friendship. For years, as a family, we used Indonesian expressions, such as *panas-di!* (it's hot).

We had missed artichokes and asparagus, cheese, and skiing for two years, but later, I found myself missing the papayas that grew in our garden and snorkeling in the sparkling warm water of the sea. I experienced reverse culture shock again, as I had when we returned from living in Pakistan. In America, there was so much advertising and so much choice of products, from cereals to automobiles, far more than even in Europe. *Ikut saja* means "I am just the accompanying family." In Sulawesi, I was *ikut saja*, but in Jakarta in 1985, Gene would become the *ikut saja* spouse.

Chapter 20   Return To USA: Chamonix

Rather than flying directly home, I flew to France with the children in July. We stayed in Paris for a few days, visiting as many sites, museums, and zoos as possible. Then we took the train to Chamonix, where we could stay in the home of our friends Harvey and Suzy while they were away on a trip. I ran every day with Marie, a French woman I had met in Berkeley. We went on hikes in the forest, where we picked wild raspberries and *myrtles* (like huckleberries) and enjoyed the recreation center's huge swimming pool with water slides. Though it was summer, the temperature was lower than it ever was in Indonesia. To be surrounded by the snow-capped, rocky spears of the Alps was heaven for me. Two weeks later, when Gene arrived, he and I, with Eric and Greg, climbed the Aiguille du Tour, an 11,600 ft peak at the head of Chamonix Valley, approached from a refuge at 8,800 ft, where we spent the night. At 6 a.m., we tied on our rope and hiked across a glacier for a few hours to the rocky summit. The fog rolled in, making the rock slippery. Greg (age ten) was a little scared. He told me later, "Dad said I could do it, so I did." Laura stayed with Marie, my French running partner, and her parents while we were on the peaks. Then, with our American friends, Gene, Eric, and I climbed the quite significant Aiguille de Chardonnet, 11,700 ft by the classic Forbes Ridge route. The ridge is a narrow, airy snow traverse above glaciers on both sides. Topping off the mountaineering, Gene, Eric, and our American friends climbed Mont Blanc, 15,771 ft, the highest peak in Europe. Quite an accomplishment for a boy not quite fourteen. On the final days in Chamonix, our hosts, the Edwards, returned with their teenage sons, so we had a happy social time. With them, we did a three-day hike above the Val Ferret on the Italian side of the Mont Blanc massif; camping in meadows in view of the high peaks and sharing cheese we bought from shepherds tending cows in the high pastures. All too soon, it was time to take the train to Paris and fly home.

Laura, Greg, and I made a stop in Scotland to visit my sister Louise, who had recently moved there with her second husband, an Engishman. We met her husband's teenage sons who took Laura and Greg fishing in a small stream near the house. Greg remembers vividly how those boys stood in the water and "tickled" the trout. They cautiously slipped a hand under the resting trout, stroked it until it relaxed, and then they pulled it out of the water. They brought home three lovely big trout. This method of catching fish is mentioned in Shakespeare's *Twelfth Night*, used by poachers and now outlawed in the United Kingdom. Gene and Eric flew via Missouri to visit Gene's father and stepmother. We all arrived in California the same day in September 1978, and we moved back into our house in Berkeley. Gene returned to the San Francisco office of International Engineering where he was quickly put to work writing proposals for more water resource jobs in Asia. Before the end of the year, he had traveled to Thailand, Malaysia, and Nepal to discuss proposals with government officials and funding agencies.

A checkup with our family doctor was an important aspect of returning to America. We all had stool tests and TB tests. All were negative for TB, meaning Laura's diagnosis of TB was incorrect. She also had no intestinal parasites; the TB drug she had been taking had cleared them out. Gene, Eric, Greg, and I had an assortment of worms and amoebas in our intestines. Our doctor told us, "Your stool samples crawled off the slides."

Our Berkeley house seemed large and luxurious, though it was in need of a few changes. We had been discussing bathroom remodeling but opted instead a redwood hot tub in the backyard. The boys ripped up the green shag carpet in the living and dining rooms, revealing beautiful oak floors perfect for Gene's growing collection of carpets.

I entered a ten-mile hilly race in Angwin, California. I crossed the finish line first in my new "over 40" age category. A woman crossed the line after me and said, "If I knew you were over forty, I would have passed you." I doubt she could have passed me! She became a friend and continued to compete with me as we entered each succeeding age category. When I was running the San Francisco Marathon, at about mile twenty, I passed two men. As I pulled ahead, I heard one say, "Why did you let that broad pass us?" No one "let" me pass them; I was just faster. Since I love hills and trails, the Dipsea Race was always my favorite. It is America's second-oldest footrace, started in 1905. The course begins on steps in Mill Valley and continues over the shoulder of Mount Tamalpais to Stinson Beach. There are over two thousand feet of ascent and descent in the seven-and-a-half miles. In 1979, I finished in thirteenth place overall and received the thirteenth-place shirt. In 1980, I was twelfth and received another shirt. I treasure those T-shirts. They cannot be purchased; they must be earned. The 1983 Dipsea was scheduled for my forty-fifth birthday. There were qualifications for entering the race, but I knew the organizers and got permission for my whole family to enter. We all finished in respectable times and had a big birthday picnic at the finish. Gene and I held the couple's record for several years. Once, I won first place for women in the Double Dipsea, which goes from Stinson Beach to Mill Valley and back.

The children went back to Berkeley schools. Greg was happy to find some of his old friends at King Middle School. Eric went to Berkeley High, joining a class of 700 after middle school in Indonesia on the dining room table with his siblings. The boys had no apparent adjustment problems. Laura was supposed to go into third grade at Thousand Oaks Elementary, but testing indicated she needed to repeat second grade. The correspondence materials and testing methods made it possible for her to appear to have advanced in reading more than she had. I was not an effective early elementary level teacher.

Chapter 21   Towards a Career

"A course on women in developing countries won't appeal to American students."

I returned as an adjunct professor at San Francisco State, teaching "Women in the World." It was fully enrolled with enthusiastic upper division and graduate students. I enjoyed teaching but was frustrated that I could not get a full-time or permanent teaching position. Each semester, I had to re-apply for the courses that I was qualified to teach, including a "History of India" and "Islamic Civilization." Adjunct or temporary professors are paid much less than regular employees. My salary was $1000 per course, while friends who taught at the University of California got over $20,000 a year for only three or four courses. One semester, I also taught a course on Middle East History for Chapman College on the Alameda Naval Base. One student asked if we would spend "most of the time on the Israel/Palestine conflict?" I replied, "We might not even get to the 20th century." My interests were more in the ancient empires of Mesopotamia, the Persians, the advent and spread of Islam, and the Turkish empire. At Golden Gate University, I taught a course on doing business in the Muslim world.

To supplement the teaching, I marketed myself as a consultant on development and women's roles in South and Southeast Asia. One fascinating assignment I obtained was a three-day workshop hosted by USAID in Washington. The goal was to define terms and indicators for measuring the impact of development projects on women. The Percy Amendment to the Foreign Assistance Act of 1973 stated that all U.S.-funded projects should be reviewed for their impact on women.

Then, in May 1979, the State Department issued a statement that a "Key objective of U.S. foreign policy is the worldwide advancement of the status and condition of women." Federal agencies were struggling to meet that goal, so a group of scholars and activists like me were gathered at an estate in Maryland for three days of lively discussion. Most of the criteria we outlined were adopted but not always utilized by administrators who approved projects. For example, engineers designing river diversions might ignore the places along a river where women have always gathered to wash laundry and socialize. Livestock programs designed to teach men methods of improving their stock might ignore the fact that women and children are responsible for the care of poultry and smaller animals. Road construction might block the path women need to a water source. A school for girls might be built without a toilet and be too distant from a village to be considered safe for the students.

I searched in the San Francisco phone book for organizations with "Asia" in their names and mailed numerous copies of my resume. To my surprise, I received an answer from The Asia Foundation in August of 1979. The Bangladesh office of the foundation had requested a consultant to advise Women for Women Bangladesh, a group of highly qualified women scholars, to expand their research and increase its impact on Bangladesh society. They had considered some of the "big names" in women's studies, such as Ester Boserup, Hanna Papanek, or Nadia Youssef, but I was more available and had the appropriate geographical focus. After a pleasant interview at the Foundation office in San Francisco, I was offered a contract for a two-week consultancy in Bangladesh. During my interview, I was pleased to meet Edith Coliver, who was departing for Manila to become the first woman to direct a country program for the Foundation. She had been an interpreter at the Nuremberg trials at the age of twenty-three and joined the Asia Foundation in the late 1950s.

In a reversal of roles, I went to Bangladesh as an expert consultant. In 1973, Gene had an assignment in Bangladesh while I settled the children in California and struggled to work on my dissertation and train for running races. This time, I was going to Bangladesh, and he was staying in Berkeley with the children and a job. My contract was much shorter than his. I arranged for friends to invite the family for dinner when I was gone, made a list of sitters, and enrolled the children in numerous after-school activities. A 4-foot-long piece of butcher paper taped to the back of the kitchen door listed everything from tutoring and play dates for Laura, orthodontist appointments, and Boy Scout meetings for Greg to major homework assignments and track team training sessions for Eric. Gene and the kids and friends went camping and hiking for two weekends, so the time went quickly for them, and there were no major crises.

In Dhaka, I stayed at the Ford Foundation guest house, a rambling old house in a leafy residential neighborhood. It was a much better choice than a sterile modern hotel downtown. The area was safe for my early morning runs (modestly dressed, of course). I often saw Bangladeshis and a few foreigners out for morning walks. The other guests were interesting. Most impressive among them was Merle Goldberg, founder of the National Women's Health Coalition. She received a medal from the President of Bangladesh in recognition of her creation of an organization to assist the thousands of women and girls who had been raped during the war for independence from Pakistan. She had organized training for health workers to provide safe abortions and social workers to help women and girls be reintegrated into their communities.

After a day of recuperating from jet lag, I began my meetings with Women for Women. It was an interesting and enthusiastic group. Already, they had published some articles and a book on women and education, funded by The Asia Foundation. Though they were highly educated and professional, the constraints of a traditional Muslim society prevented them from conducting fieldwork in rural areas or far from their homes. They relied upon the results of foreign scholars or official reports and statistics. They felt that I was very brave to have visited villages in Pakistan to collect data for my dissertation. To ensure the sustainability of the organization, I helped them develop a plan to do commissioned research and consultancies for foundations and corporations that needed assessments of the impact of their projects on women. We had some lively discussions of topics they could consider for subsequent research and publication. They took me to visit some community development projects and vocational training centers in and near the city. It was at Women for Women that I met Rounaq Jehan, a truly inspiring scholar and international activist. A 1970 Ph.D. graduate of Harvard, she had fellowships in Norway and Chicago. Her subsequent career took her to several posts at the United Nations, the International Labor Organization, and Columbia University. I followed the trajectory of her career with awe.

While I was in Dhaka, I contacted one of Gene's colleagues, whom I had met in Pakistan in the 1960s. He and his wife invited me for dinner. They and the other American guests spoke disparagingly about the food, the climate, and Bangladeshi people, even when English-speaking servants were in the room. None of them had tried to learn the language in Bangladesh or in other countries where they had worked. They had no interest in local culture or history. Having spent my day on a field trip with sophisticated Bangladeshi women who had Ph.D.s from Harvard and Oxford, I was uncomfortable with the evening company of complaining Americans and glad to retreat to the Ford

Foundation Guest house where my fellow guests were more culturally sensitive and interesting.

At the end of my brief consultancy, Women for Women members had developed greater confidence to investigate controversial topics, such as abortion, domestic violence, and child labor. They developed a plan to market their expertise to contractors and foreign aid agencies. I learned from this experience that people can gain confidence from having their work recognized as worthy of the attention of a foreign consultant, even if the impact is subtle. In my subsequent work, I applied this concept. For example, a struggling women's legal aid organization in Indonesia could benefit from a visit from a leader of the Korean Legal Aid group. More than technical advice, the visit would increase their courage to face restrictions and criticism.

I submitted my report to The Asia Foundation when I returned. Two weeks later, Mr. Andrews called to tell me that my report was much appreciated in San Francisco and Bangladesh. I was invited to interview again. Before the end of the year, I was hired to be the Advisor for Women and Development and Islam. It was a challenging prospect. The Foundation, established in 1954 as the Committee for Free Asia, had offices in 15 Asian countries. Its programs focused on the development of just and democratic societies. It provided funds for local nongovernmental organizations, training for diplomats, administrators, and legal professionals, and arranged conferences and experts responding to the needs in the different countries. Foundation leaders had to be very circumspect in their support of human rights and democracy since many of the Asian countries had autocratic governments.

In December 1979, I started commuting to San Francisco. Gene and I continued running for an hour before quickly fixing breakfast for the children and dressing for work. His day started at eight, so he took the 7:20 "G" bus while I could delay until the 7:40 bus. It was a hectic schedule. I had my own office with a window and an assistant! My responsibilities included reviewing project proposals, evaluating reports, and responding to requests from field offices for assistance and expertise. I was pleased to meet Edith Coliver, who was departing for Manila to become the first woman to direct a country program for the Foundation. She was an excellent manager and a champion of human rights and democracy. She managed to be accepted by the elites and the government while supporting nongovernmental organizations and journalists who were in opposition to the regime. She was an excellent linguist, learning Tagalog in the Philippines and Chinese, when she was director of the Taiwan program from 1988 to 1992. When I went to Jakarta in 1985 as a Representative of the Foundation, I became the second woman to direct a country program. Edith's capable leadership made it possible for other women to take on leadership roles in the organization.

Early in 1980, the Foundation sent me on a tour of four Asian countries, the Philippines, Malaysia, Sri Lanka, and Pakistan, to become familiar with projects focusing on women and Islam. In each country, I was introduced to the leaders of women's organizations and programs with a focus on women, some Muslim and some not. The economic and social structures of these countries were, and still are, very different.

In the Philippines, Edith Coliver, the Foundation Representative, was providing financial and technical support to many organizations throughout the country. She was particularly proud of supporting Christian and Muslim groups working together for peace and prosperity in Mindanao, where there had been an active Muslim independence movement, the Moro Liberation Front, for decades. In 1980, dictator Ferdinand Marcos ruled the country, but the Foundation supported journalist groups and others who quietly argued for human rights and democracy. The Marcos regime was overturned in 1986 and replaced by a democratic government.

Malaysia was a far more prosperous country. The Asia Foundation had a long-established presence in the country. The Muslim Malay majority dominated the government but allowed the large Chinese and Indian minorities to practice their religions and customs. Each could follow their legal systems for domestic and family issues. There were women lawyers working for the rights of women within each legal system: Muslim, Christian, and Hindu.

In Sri Lanka, the Foundation reopened its office after its closure during the years of Sri Bandaranaike's rule. Sri Lanka is ruled by the Buddhist Sinhala majority, with a significant Tamil Hindu Minority and a smaller but important presence of Muslims, known as "Ceylon Moors." Each group has its own educational institutions, language, and system of personal law, though Sinhalese is the only official language. I met the leaders of several Sinhalese women's organizations and the Principal of a Muslim women's college, but no Tamils.

Karachi, Pakistan, was my final stop. In Manila and Kuala Lumpur, I stayed in the home of the Asia Foundation country director. In Sri Lanka, I stayed in a small guest house in a residential neighborhood. I far preferred these homey accommodations, in neighborhoods where I could safely do my morning run, to the impersonal hotel where I stayed in downtown Karachi. I was hosted by members of the All-Pakistan Women's Association (APWA) because the Foundation did not have a resident representative at that time. The APWA ladies took me to community development and informal education programs for poor, illiterate women for which they had received funds from The Asia Foundation. Evaluating these programs, I saw the funds had been used according to the contracts, but the projects were very top-down, providing no opportunity for the participants to modify the curriculum. APWA is the oldest women's organization in Pakistan. Its members are upper-class women who have time and resources to do charitable work.

The trip impressed upon me the multiplicities of cultures I would need to take into consideration in my role as Advisor for Women in Development at the Foundation. In view of the US foreign policy recognizing the importance of the role of women in developing economies, I undertook a survey of the past decade of Asia Foundation grants to determine what percentage of Foundation funding benefitted women. The Foundation President, Ambassador Haydn Williams, objected, saying, "We don't identify our projects by gender, but the Foundation has always considered women in its programming." I insisted that having some solid data would help the Foundation compete for grants. The annual reports for each country program did not specify which grants might have been most beneficial for women. It was possible to identify women's organizations and grants made to enable women to attend conferences and participate in study tours, seminars, or advanced academic training. I found that more than one-fourth of Asia Foundation grants were made to women's organizations. Also, women constituted over 20 percent of the individuals participating in conferences and study tours. This was impressive compared to government programs and those of larger organizations, which tended to benefit institutions headed by men. I presented a paper based on this research at the Inaugural Conference of the

Association for Women in Development in 1983 in Washington, D.C.

During my years of work for the Asia Foundation, I had the opportunity and honor of meeting many inspiring Asian women of different nationalities and religions. Among them were some Muslim women whose accomplishments I found most impressive because they defied the traditional limitations imposed by their religion and societies. In Indonesia, the largest Muslim-majority country in the world, the attitudes towards women taking visible roles in society are more tolerant than in some other Muslim countries. For instance, in Pakistan, Afghanistan, Central Asia, and the Middle East, bazaars and markets are dominated by men. In Southeast Asia, including Muslim Indonesia, markets are the domain of women. Many schools, even religious schools, are coeducational. Nevertheless, women in Indonesia are often victims of domestic violence and economic injustice. Many are unaware of their rights in the context of Islamic or civil law. Mrs. Nani Yamin had studied law and was aware of the problems. She founded the Center for Consultation and Legal Aid for Women and Families. After consulting with experts in religious law, she opened the first center on the premises of the Al-Azhar Mosque in Jakarta. The location assured clients that the counseling they sought was approved by their religion. The staff included professional counselors, lawyers, and volunteers, all familiar with both secular and Islamic law as it applies to families. The program was so popular that soon, Ibu Nani opened branches in Aceh, Padang, and Bandung. Since the counseling addressed the problems of women factory workers and labor organizing, it was distrusted by the government, which denied it permission to accept assistance from the Ford Foundation. By 1985, however, the Center was able to accept support from the Asia Foundation so I could provide funding for expansion to other areas. I arranged for women from other Muslim countries to visit the centers to determine if the concept could be replicated in their countries. I enjoyed every time I had an opportunity to speak with Nani about her work or visit the sites. I admired Nani Yamin for her courage to address domestic violence and the problems of women workers in a country where such issues were kept out of the public eye.

In Pakistan in 1980, Asma Jehangir and her sister Hina Jilani, both of whom received their law degrees from Punjab University, established the nation's first woman-led law firm in Lahore. They also formed the Women's Action Forum (WAF) to campaign against the Hudood laws, legislation that made it virtually impossible for a victim of rape to prove her innocence. Asma Jehangir argued in the courts on the most difficult cases of rape, abuse, and blasphemy. In 1983, she defended Safia, a blind servant girl who was raped by her employers. According to the Hudood laws, her pregnancy was evidence of her guilt; she was charged with fornication and sentenced to twenty years in jail. Fifty members of the WAF, led by Asma, took to the streets, demonstrating against the injustice of this judicial decision. Each court appearance by Asma brought death threats. In public demonstrations, Asma was beaten and partially stripped by police officers, but she did not waver in her pursuit of justice. With other attorneys, she and her sister established the Punjab Women Lawyers Association. Asma was the U.N. Special Rapporteur on Freedom of Religion and chairperson of the Human Rights Commission of Pakistan later in her career. Nevertheless, she was among the five hundred lawyers and human rights activists who were put under house arrest for ninety days in 2007. Once, she participated in a mini-marathon run to publicize the problem of domestic violence. Both men and women runners were arrested and forced off the course by police! I admired her courage and dedication to protect the rights of women, children, the poor, and religious minorities. These women were all from upper-class families that encouraged education for both sons and daughters. They had the support of their families and were highly educated, but they had to overcome societal pressures and brave physical threats to pursue their ideals.

"Books for Asia" was an important program of the Foundation. Each year, it shipped thousands of American books to Asia for colleges and universities, public libraries, and government institutions. In countries where English was the medium of instruction in schools, elementary and secondary books were also included. The books were donated to the Foundation by bookstores, publishers, libraries, and individuals. Most books were new, though some older books were valued for historical significance. I enjoyed visiting the Books for Asia warehouse. It resembled a giant library. With the Director of the Books for Asia, I assembled collections of books that were "by, about, and for women." This included biographies and books about women's rights, women's roles in economic development, and political, social, and legal institutions. These special collections were welcomed by universities and research institutes in all the countries in which the Foundation had a presence.

I interrupted my first year of employment at The Asia Foundation to participate in a major mountaineering project we had planned prior to my accepting the job.

Chapter 22   Berkeley 1980, Makalu II Expedition

Gene's company won the bid to implement a project that Gene had presented to the Government of Nepal. It was intended to bring water to a dry valley south of Pokhara. It involved a tunnel and other construction. Gene was responsible for supervising the construction, so he had several month-long trips to Nepal. At the end of one of his trips in 1979, he convinced a couple of American friends to join him for an ambitious trek over a high pass and a climb of Island Peak (20,000+ ft) near Everest. They had such a good time on this trip that Armando, one of the friends, suggested applying for a permit for a peak 1000 meters higher than Huascaran, our highest summit in South America. It seemed an appropriate "next step."

"You should not go to the Himalayas again, starting a new job and leaving your children with a friend who has no experience with children."

Having opted out of the Annapurna women's expedition, I was heading for a lower, perhaps safer, Himalayan peak. Ours was a small, self-financed expedition. No fundraising or sponsorships. The goal was Makalu II or Kangchungste. 25,130 ft (Makalu I is 2,700 ft higher and far more difficult.) The team consisted of Gene and me, his brother Jim, and Armando Menocal, all over 40, and Michael Warburton, a recent CAL graduate. An outstanding climber, we hoped he could lead the most technical parts of the route. Along for the flight and hike to the base camp were two other friends, a doctor and her fiancé.

As my job was getting more interesting every day, I was a bit conflicted about going on the expedition. I wondered if I was putting my future career at risk, and of course, I was worried and felt guilty about leaving my children for a risky adventure again. I recruited a recently divorced friend to live in our house with the children during our absence. My brother Bill who was working for the San Francisco Opera, agreed to spend some time at our house to help. I arranged multiple after-school and weekend activities for Laura, Greg, and Eric. Greg, then 12, seemed the most worried about our absence. I overcame my misgivings and guilt sufficiently to get on the plane for Kathmandu on April 11, 1980. Mike's mother brought a bottle of champagne to the airport to celebrate our adventure. Arriving in Kathmandu, we gathered our whole team, starting with our "Sirdar" (leader of porters and Sherpas) Pasang. Pasang had been with us in 1977, trekking with our children, so he often called me "Mommy." He had also trekked with Gene and Armando in 1979. He was a friend as well as employee. We were also introduced to our required Liaison Officer, P.T. Ghimere. At our simple hotel, I bumped into Ray Jewell, the co-leader on my Pakistan trek in 1977. When we went for dinner at a nearby restaurant, we met Scott McBeth, another California climber. The mountaineering community is small.

Pasang and I finished the final food purchases. Some porters and heavier luggage, fuel, and stoves had already been taken by a truck for Tumlingtar in eastern Nepal. The American Ambassador welcomed us to a reception where we had a lively discussion about mountaineering in Nepal. Because Makalu II was an official "expedition" category of a mountain, rather than a "Trekking Peak," we had to pay a $1,500 fee to the government of Nepal and take a Liaison Officer assigned by the Government.

The Liaison Officer, P. T. Ghimere, had to be outfitted and provided a porter and an assistant. His cost was over $1,000, including new clothing and equipment, special food, and a large supply of local alcohol, Rakshi. He refused to use any of the excellent but slightly used clothing we had brought for him, even though we were all wearing well-worn clothing and equipment. In Nepal, Sherpas, high-altitude porters, and Liaison Officers expect to receive brand-new clothing and equipment each time they are hired. They promptly put the new items on sale on the market. The total cost of our expedition was $15,426, according to Armando's careful accounting. It would have been 40 percent less had we chosen a "Trekking" peak that did not require a permit or a Liaison Officer.

We had a tight schedule on this trip since the trek to the base of the mountain could take seven to ten days each way. Establishing camps and a route would require several days and could be delayed by weather and unexpected technical difficulties. Every delay could erase any chance of success. Our flight to Tumlingtar was scheduled for 7 a.m. on April 16 but was postponed until 3 p.m. At 1:30, we loaded everything on a bus in the courtyard of the hotel, only to have the bus get stuck in the doorway. Finally, at the airport, we were told that the plane had been delayed and would not arrive in time to take us to Tumlingtar. On the 17th, we were loaded up and at the airport at 7 a.m., only to be told the flight would go at 2:30 p.m. We spent the time sightseeing in the antique town of Bhaktapur. In the afternoon, strong wind and clouds gathered, obviously preventing any more flights to remote locations. We raised complaints at the airport and demanded to see the schedule for the next day. Nancy and I sat in the Airport Manager's office, refusing to leave until we saw our flight written on the blackboard. It listed a plane for us at nine in the morning.

At nine on April 18, a plane appeared at the airport, but other people's baggage was loaded on it. Nancy and I returned to the office of the airport manager and complained irately. Our baggage was moved over to another small plane, but the staff could not find a rope to tie down the baggage. The pilot finally appeared, questioning the amount of luggage. It had been weighed every day at the airport, but no one had informed the pilot. Finally, we took off for a one-hour flight to the grass landing strip at Tumlingtar. Grazing cows moved aside just before we landed. The entire village raced out to see us.

Our caravan was finally on its way. Seven Americans, 30 porters, including three women, a cook, two cook's helpers, the Liaison Officer P.T. Ghimere, and Pasang. The trail alternated between high ridges and deep river crossings. After three days of walking, the porters threatened to strike if they were not paid six days' wages. Negotiating with local employees is supposed to be a duty of the Liaison Officer P.T., but he was not helpful. After lots of shouting and dropping loads on the ground, everyone calmed down. P.T. complained, "Where is the goat?" He wanted meat for supper, though he insisted he was a Brahmin, so he should be vegetarian.

Beyond the last village, through rhododendron forests blooming pink, red, and white, we came to snow-covered Shipton pass (14,000 ft), where we finally could see Makalu, Everest, and the entire wall of the Himalayas. We were humbled by the scale of the mountains and the terrain to reach them. We descended steeply 2000 ft from the pass to the Barun Valley and turned northwest up the valley towards the site for our base camp. The porters wanted 11 day's wages for only 9 days of carrying, including two very short days. After some hassle and shouting, we paid them. I got too involved in these discussions; Armando advised I should step out of earshot when there were disputes about pay. We settled into our base camp at around 15,000 ft with P.T., Pasang, another Sherpa, Birbahadur, the cook, and two cook helpers. The following day, I stayed in camp organizing with Armando and Jim while Gene, Mike, Fred, and Nancy crossed the gravel-covered glacier and hiked up to where another expedition had its base camp. That group of four very strong climbers was attempting to make the second ascent of the very steep west ridge of Makalu. A French group made the first ascent of this route in 1971, using oxygen and a large team of Sherpas. The 1980 American team considered their climb notable because it would be without Sherpa's assistance or supplemental oxygen. They had already been at the mountain for a month, establishing their route and high camps. They had the best base camp cook in Nepal, waiting with their bored Liaison Officer.

Our trekking friends, Nancy and Fred, decided two hikes on gravel-covered glacier ice was enough. They would hike back to Tumlingtar and explore other parts of Nepal. They departed with one Sherpa and one cook's helper to carry their gear. They had not intended to go high on the mountain, anyway. When I saw them leave, I felt a pang of regret and homesickness, missing my children and wondering what I was doing on a major Himalayan peak.

My doubts disappeared in the sunshine and spectacular scenery, so I was eager to get up the mountain. We gradually moved up to camp at 17,000 ft, just below the other team's base. Each day, we carried loads beyond there for several hours, then returned to sleep lower down. The terrain was varied, and horizontal distances were longer than expected. One day, we went through endless scree and rock fields, and then we went to a section we called "serac alley" because we had to thread our way through 10- to 20-foot-high ice towers or seracs. Then, we trudged across a long snow field. We made a temporary camp where the snow field ended below steep walls of ice on one side and boulders ranging in size from shoe boxes to refrigerators on the other. On May 4, I felt especially guilty because it was Greg's birthday. However, the weather was beautiful, and we had plenty of food and fuel to move up for our attempt at the summit. After a couple of nights at intermediary camps, four of us, Gene, Jim, Mike, and I, struggled up steep boulders to a smooth glacier, which led to the pass between Makalu I and Makalu II. We put on our crampons and the rope because there were crevasses under the smooth surface of the glacier. Gene and I thought we were walking as slowly as possible in view of the altitude and our heavy packs. However, Jim and Mike were even slower. Some heavy snow fell just as we reached the spot where Jim and Gene had left some loads the day before at about 21,000 ft. We hurried to put up the tent and get inside. After tea and naps, the storm was over. In the last sunshine, the mountains glowed. We melted snow to fill our water bottles and cooked dinner. We had to wake Mike for each course. During the night, Mike breathed noisily and moved around a lot, waking us up frequently. In the morning, he was unconscious and appeared to be having a series of seizures. We knew that he had suffered a head injury climbing in Russia in 1976 and that he had experienced seizures after that, so we did not immediately assume that he had high-altitude cerebral edema. We tried to make him stand and walk unsuccessfully. We decided that Gene and Jim would walk with me to the edge of the glacier, roped for safety crossing the crevasses, and then they would return to try to wake Mike. I would hurry down to the other expedition's camp to consult with the Doctor. I worried as I watched them return up the glacier towards the tent. Would Mike be alive? Would he be able to walk? Quickly, I descended the steep big boulder slope, the snow plateau, serac alley, and endless scree fields, more than 4,000 vertical feet. I arrived at the camps mid-afternoon, delighted to find the doctor and three other climbers of the other expedition there. They knew Mike; in fact, one of them had climbed with him, so they shared my concern about his condition. Armando was also at our camp nearby. He offered to immediately dash down to our base camp to recruit whatever staff was there to assist in a rescue. The "expert" expedition invited me for dinner, lent me a radio, flag poles to make a stretcher, extra clothes for our porters, and gave me lots of advice. They did not volunteer to join in the rescue effort. I was shocked by their reluctance to help but too reticent to insist that they should. They chose to complete their climb rather than get involved in a rescue. I crawled into my sleeping bag, very worried.

In the morning, Armando returned with Pasang and three Nepalis: a porter and the two cooks' helpers. Only Pasang had experience on snow and ice. We outfitted them with our extra clothing and boots donated by the other expedition. A tall Sherpa from another expedition who was visiting the porters volunteered to come as well. He claimed he could carry anyone on his back. I started back up the mountain with five Nepalese. Armando had persistent problems with the altitude and was unable to go higher. He remained at the 17,000 ft camp to communicate and promised to recruit more help. I set off with this motley crew of Nepalis who boasted they could bring Mike down in a few hours.

Meanwhile, up at the high camp, Gene and Jim tried all night to get Mike to drink a little water and wake up. He was incoherent and repeatedly crawled out of his sleeping bag. They looked through his pack for medications and found that he had finished his supply of valium and had only three Dexedrine pills remaining. In the morning, they dressed Mike, gave him two Dexedrine pills, and put on his boots, but he could not stand, even with their support. They put him back in his sleeping bag with all his clothes, put water and food nearby, and left him.

Jim and Gene have been criticized for abandoning Mike, but they were unable to do anything to help him. Jim was feeling very anxious, cold, and helpless at 21,000 ft. The food and fuel were dwindling. Gene felt strong but could not let his brother descend alone across the crevassed glacier.

Leading my group up through the serac area, I saw two figures in the distance. I was sure a third figure would be following, but no. It was Gene and Jim coming down without him. They said Mike was alive but unconscious. I asked, "Are you going down?" They said "Yes." I said I would go on up whether they came or not. Gene and Jim promised they would return the next morning, and they did. I later told Mike's mother, "If that were my kid up there needing to be brought down, I would want everyone to go without hesitation." I did not doubt my decision, though I was disappointed with Gene and Jim. At that point, Jim could have descended alone, and Gene could have turned around and gone up with me. Caught up in the anxiety of the moment, I did not argue.

I stopped at an interim camp to melt snow and make tea for the Nepalis. At this point, one of the cook-helpers turned back and left the flag poles on a rock. With the remaining four, I led up through the boulder field to the glacier plateau. Every hour, I radioed to the doctor and Armando. The doctor insisted Mike must be brought down immediately, or he would die. I was doing all I could to make my reluctant team continue, using my fluency in Urdu (which shares many words with Hindi and Nepali) and my friendship with Pasang. Although the Nepalis might be reluctant to accept leadership from a woman, they respected my strength and determination and the fact that I was a married woman with children, thus worthy of respect. When we got to the glacier at about 4 p.m., clouds rolled in, reducing visibility. I pulled out the climbing rope and tied everyone to it. Those who had crampons put them on. My first step on the glacier one leg dropped into a crevasse. That was the low point of a very discouraging day. And the first time I felt fear. Pasang, tied on the rope just behind me, pulled me out. As clouds rolled in, Pasang worried we might not locate the tent. He suggested that we consider returning to the camp where I had made tea. Fortunately, two days before, we had placed bamboo wands on the glacier to mark the way to the campsite. We reached the big red tent at six. Mike was alive! I was surprised and happy to see him.

Pasang reached into Mike's pocket to take his little Swiss Army knife. I did not criticize this theft because I did not want to alienate any of my crucial helpers, and I was very tired, having descended from 21,000 ft to 17,000 ft the previous day and returned less than 30 hours later. All night, the Nepalis smoked and made tea to keep warm. The four had to share two sleeping bags. Mike tossed and turned. It was a very strange night in that smokey tent with Mike on one side, rolling and trying to get out of his sleeping bag. I managed to sleep a little. In the morning, Mike was still alive, though unresponsive. It was a beautiful sunny day. I was disappointed we were not going up the mountain. I had a very different challenge. I piled the sleeping mats on the tent fly and tied the edges together. We then put Mike in his sleeping bag on top. I put sunscreen on his face and glacier goggles over his eyes as he was facing up towards the sun. We gathered as much of the equipment as possible into two big backpacks, mine and Mike's. I had Pasang and two of the Nepalis tie their ropes in front of Mike and one with me in the back as we dragged Mike across the glacier. I cautioned the Nepalis to step in our footprints from the previous day to avoid falling in crevasses, but several times, one would veer off the steps and slip down to hip level.

We reached the edge of the glacier by noon and lowered Mike to some flat rocks. I got out of the stove to melt snow for tea and soup. Mike took a few sips. The big, tall Sherpa said, "Now I will carry him." He tried to carry him "piggyback" but could not lift him off the ground. Mike weighed about 200 pounds and was stiff and uncooperative. It was impossible for one man to carry him. I peered down the rocky slope and, with great relief, saw Gene and Jim.

Birbahadur of the kitchen crew was with them, carrying the flag poles to make a stretcher. When we met, I gave Gene the radio and turned downhill. I had done my job. It was time to let them struggle to create a stretcher using climbing rope, flag poles, and the tent fly. When I arrived at our camp one, 4,000 ft lower, I heard Gene asking on the radio for more porters. They found negotiating the rough terrain with a stretcher was exhausting. It required three people on each side. They did not make it to Camp One that night. They slept six in a tent designed for three. I spent the night at Camp One and left at 5:30 in the morning for our base camp.

As I picked my way slowly across the gravel-covered ice, I was delighted to meet eight men from Tesigown village coming up. These were our porters for the return journey; they had arrived a few days in advance of the planned departure date.

When I arrived at our base camp, I was welcomed by our liaison officer, P.T. Ghimere, and the cook, who prepared a nice breakfast for me. He also gave me a bowl of hot water so I could have a welcome sponge bath in my tent. Later, a porter ran down with a note from Armando stating that "the porters won't go higher than Camp I, and Jim and Gene vow they won't carry the stretcher anymore." I was upset but recovered after dinner when another porter brought a note saying Mike was at Camp I and on oxygen. They had found a bottle left by the French expedition. Mike regained consciousness in the morning, but he could not walk. He had been unconscious for four days due to high-altitude cerebral edema. The dehydration and immobility had caused a huge blood clot to develop in his leg. It was clear that he needed to get medical help as soon as possible, but P.T. Ghimere told us there were only three helicopters in Nepal and all were being used for political campaigns. Mike would have to be carried for a week to the airstrip at Tumlingtar. It took six porters to carry the stretcher every step of the way. P.T. insisted upon having a mail runner take a message to the nearest telephone that someone on our expedition had been rescued. This filtered through the international press but without the name of the injured climber. The news made our friends and our children at home very worried.

The weeklong trek was painful for Mike, exhausting for the stretcher carriers, and frustrating for us as discipline in the team dissolved. Too often, P.T. and Pasang paid more attention to Rakshi and pretty Sherpanis than to keeping our team's progress steady. Finally, on May 20, Mike crawled up the steps of a plane in Tumlingtar. An hour later, in Kathmandu, Armando and I took him to the American Embassy doctor, who quickly diagnosed thrombosis in his leg. He was admitted to the hospital for anticoagulation therapy. His private room would cost 150 rupees a day, about $5. The rest of us flew back to our jobs and families in America the next day, Mike came two weeks later.

After returning, I told my story to Andy Kaufman, one of the grand old men of American mountaineering. (He and his partners made the first ascent of Broad Peak in Karakoram, the first 8,000-meter ascent by an American team.) He was appalled that the other expedition had not postponed their summit plans and rushed to help Mike. He and the club leadership created the Sowles Award (named for David Sowles, a climber who made several rescues before his early death) to recognize climbers who came to the aid of others. For the first few years, the award was given to members of several notable historical rescues. Finally, eighteen years later in 1998, I received the award. I was the first woman recipient. My decision to continue up the mountain to get Mike, when none of the American men on our team or the other expedition would or could, was critical to his survival. However, my effort alone would not have been enough. The porters and everyone in our small expedition did what they could.

The recue is described in <u>Rock and Ice</u> magazine # 184, March 2010 "Rescue on Makalu, An Unlikely Story of Himalayan Heroism" by Alison Osius. Pg 54-61.

Chapter 23   Lessons Learned: Denali

On Makalu in 1980, we learned some lessons about the inconvenience and expense of climbing mountains that require permits, liaison officers, and porters. We also learned that we should monitor one another for signs of altitude sickness. So, in 1981, after a pleasant winter of family ski trips to the Sierra and running races, we decided to tackle the highest mountain in the USA, Denali. It is 20,320 feet in elevation, but at the high latitude of Alaska, the altitude effects on the human body are more pronounced because of the relative thinness of the atmosphere towards the poles. The altitude of Denali is equivalent to 24,000 ft at the equator, so we realized it would be challenging. We did practice ice climbing on Mount Dana in Yosemite. It was necessary to get a permit from the Forest Service, costing $20 per climber, but that was trivial compared with the permitting process in Nepal!

Our party consisted of Gene, our 17-year-old son Eric, me, Gene's brother Jim, and two friends, Eliot Goss and Cliff Jennings, both experienced climbers. We planned to ski, hauling bags of gear and food until we reached the 14,000 ft level. Above there, we would need to carry everything on our backs. We allowed ourselves two weeks, including travel, though the climb has been done in less. It involves 32 miles of travel over glaciers and rock and ascent from 6,000 to 20,000 feet.

I assumed responsibility for planning and buying the food since I had been doing this for mountain trips since I was a teenager in the Colorado Junior Mountain Club. On our climbs in Asia and South America, we could rely upon purchasing some supplies in villages on the way to the mountain, such as eggs and chickens, vegetables, and fruit. There were no villages on Denali. For a margin of safety, I planned food for six people for 16 days. The total was 96 breakfasts, lunches, and dinners! I prefer ordinary grocery store food to freeze dried, so I planned cereals, peanut butter, coffee, tea and powdered milk for breakfasts. Lunches contained high-calorie foods like cheese, canned fish, homemade beef jerky, crackers, cookies, dried fruit, and candy bars. For dinners, quick cooking rice, pasta, instant mashed potatoes and bulger, dried soups, pudding, jello, and more chocolate. For dinners it was necessary to add a few freeze-dried vegetables and meats. I found a store which sold bulk foods for survivalists who want to hold five years of food for emergencies. It was cheaper than fancy back-packing meals, but not as tastey. Packing the food required careful planning, so that I could quickly find the appropriate meal when needed. Using orange waterproof fabric, I sewed bags to hold food. Someone would ask, "Where is the oatmeal?" "In the orange bag." "Which orange bag?" was a frequent refrain!

Since every drop of water we needed would come from melting snow on our little stoves, determining the amount of fuel was critical. Gas cannot be carried on commercial airlines, so we had to purchase 2/3 cup per person per day after arrival in Alaska, depending upon the model of the stove, we were advised.

On June 13, we flew to Anchorage and hired a van to take us to the town of Talkeetna, the last town before Denali. I loved rustic Talkeetna. The few dirt streets were lined with log buildings. There were a couple of hotels and hostels, a bar or two, a cafe, a general store, and a post office. The activity of the town centered on the airstrip where small ski or float planes came and went regularly. Our first activity was to walk to the airport to check flying conditions. We had booked flights from Talkeetna to the "Kahiltna Glacier Base" at 6,900 ft. This is a glacier landing area, so the planes must have skis that can be released below the wheels that were used for take-off. The planes are small Cessnas with room for three passengers and some luggage. As a party of six, we needed two planes. We and our luggage had to be weighed and measured so the plane could be packed for balance and maximum use of the limited space. The plane had to clear several 14,000 ft ridges before landing on the glacier. Trudging uphill in the Alps, I had seen these glacier planes perform with envy. Now I was excited to be in one, with Gene and Eric. The flight was spectacular and the pilot, Kitty Banner, skilled. I was especially pleased to have a woman pilot. Since flat areas are rare on glaciers, the planes must land on an uphill slope. Passengers and gear were unloaded in minutes, new passengers jumped in, and the plane did a U turn to take off downhill, gaining speed and altitude over the descending glacier.

The second plane arrived within an hour, with the rest of our team, so we organized ourselves to ski down the glacier, turn right and start the long ascent of the main Kahiltna Glacier. We were on the West Buttress route, known to be the easiest. We were using our traditional wood cross country skis, wearing big packs, and pulling haul bags. The latter were manufactured for hauling rock climbers' loads up cliff faces. The fabric is extremely tough and waterproof. Nowadays, climbers use special alpine skis with climbing skins and put their luggage on small sleds. We discovered on the first gentle downhill that the haul bags had minds of their own about which direction to go. Carrying heavy packs and using cross country skis, we were trying to traverse the slope and make graceful turns. The heavy haul bags rolled straight down. Another complication was that I promised Eliot's wife that I would not let him ski on the glacier unroped. We had to manage with the rope between us dragging one direction while the haul bags pulled in another.

It was hot on the glacier until the sun set, then the temperature dropped 40 or more degrees in minutes. I would be skiing along in a light shirt, reveling in the spectacular scenery, my own strength and rhythm of the skis and poles. When we stopped to set up tents I knew to change immediately into a down jacket and wool hat. Fortunately, in Alaska summer, the days are very long. An even greater temperature differential occurs if one falls from the sunny surface of the glacier into a crevasse where the sun never penetrates. Death by hypothermia often occurs before a rescue can be completed.

Eric was full of youthful enthusiasm that spread to our whole group. He created shields out of duct tape to protect our noses from the sun, so we looked like a team of strange insects. There were other parties on the mountain whose tracks we could follow, but the challenge of avoiding the numerous deep crevasses remained. We usually stayed roped to one another.

As on other snow and ice climbs in Europe, the Himalaya, and South America, I found there was no place to be modest about defecating. Tied on a 120-foot rope between two men I would need to call out for them to stop, secure the rope, and turn away. Then I could look for a crevasse with a safe lip for squatting. High on the mountain in the cold, I wore a one-piece Gore-Tex suit with a drop seat. That simplified toilet stops somewhat.

The usual advice for adjusting to high altitude is to gain only 1,000 feet a day. With the excellent weather and our fitness, we proceeded much faster. On the third day we camped at 11,200 ft. There we paused to carry and leave loads at "Windy Corner", 2,000 ft higher. On the sixth day we camped at 14,000 ft and rested one day. At that last flat campsite there were several other parties camped, some descending, others going up. We left our skis there and switched to climbing boots and crampons. The next challenge was steep 900-foot icy wall draped with several fixed ropes on which we clipped our "jumars," metal clamps slide up the rope but do not slide down. I was nervous on the fixed ropes, depending upon a slender nylon rope instead of my own feet. Also, one of my crampon straps became loose part way up. I had to stop to tighten it, causing several climbers behind me to wait impatiently.

At the top of the fixed ropes, we continued on a narrow, rocky ridge which swept upwards, with steep drops on both sides to reach the 17,000 ft camp, the last before the summit. It was a gorgeous site, somewhat spoiled by the evidence of overuse. There were a dozen ice caves carved by climbers, some full of spilled food and garbage. Though ugly, the garbage was all solidly frozen, so it did not smell. We found an igloo that was a good location for cooking and eating dinner out of the wind. The sunset from that camp was gorgeous. To the west, we looked over a 3,000 ft cliff to the sunset on Mount Foraker.

Early the next morning, Jim and Eliot left for the summit and returned in the late afternoon. We were thrilled with their safe accomplishment. Gene, Eric, Cliff and I had decided to rest one day before attempting the summit. Alas, in the night, Cliff woke speaking nonsense, his eyes bulging. After our experience with Mike on Makalu, we knew he needed to descend as soon as possible before he became unconscious from high altitude cerebral edema. Gene and Jim tied Cliff on short ropes and steered him down the narrow ridge to the fixed ropes where they could lower him. Meanwhile, Eric and I gave up our hopes for the summit. With Eliot we packed up the gear and trudged down. When we reached the 14,000 ft camp, we found Cliff was recovering his usual mental capacities, so we closed our camp and continued down. Each foot of descent brought a decrease in the severity of Cliff's symptoms.

When we were within two hours of the airstrip, our progress was interrupted by a guide. One of his clients was unconscious with altitude sickness and was tied on a sled on the flat glacier. It was uphill from there to the airstrip. They needed more manpower. Of course, we agreed to help. Gene and Cliff set down their packs, unclipped from their haul bags and helped drag the client through the slushy lower glacier up to the airstrip.

Every summer, the Park Service hires someone to stay in a large tent at the airstrip to relay radio messages. In 1981, it was a formidable woman with braided hair. She played cello in the Anchorage symphony, when not camping on a glacier. She was clad bright in red long underwear from shoulder to foot; easy to see on the white glacier! Near her tent departing climbers left excess fuel and food for others. We asked her to radio K2 aviation for our flights. She warned us there was a major storm predicted to start the next day. We breathed a sigh of relief when we heard the plane approach. Three of us jumped in with our skis and packs, much lighter than on the incoming flight. Still there was room for only three passengers. The pilot wanted to take off quickly because snow on the glacier was soft with the weeks of sunshine. He dropped us in Talkeetna and went back for the rest of our party in spite of the snow conditions. Delayed by their rescue efforts, Gene and Cliff arrived just in time for the second flight. We later learned that a major storm had arrived so that no planes flew to the Kahiltna Glacier for two weeks. Our remaining food was enough for three or four days. We would have gotten hungry waiting for two weeks!

After one night in Talkeetna we took the bus to Anchorage airport to catch our homeward flights. Changing planes in Seattle, we ran into the guide and rescued client at a bar; they said hello but did not thank us as I expected! In recent years, the popularity of Denali among climbers of all nationalities has caused the National Park Service to create a more stringent registration process and to charge a fee which in 2020 was $375 for each climber. This only partially offsets the cost of multiple rescues, additional climbing rangers, and cleanup efforts.

Chapter 24   The Asia Foundation

My responsibilities at The Asia Foundation increased when I returned from Denali. I was Area Director, (the home-office manager) for Indonesia, Korea, Pakistan, Sri Lanka, and the Pacific Island program. There was no office in the Pacific Islands, so every year I visited Western Samoa, Tonga, Fiji, Vanuatu, the Solomon Islands, and Papua New Guinea. Our entree to these countries was the Books for Asia Program. Since English is spoken in most of the islands, American books were very popular. However, shipping was costly. I managed to get a few bulk shipments on US Navy ships to increase the number of books distributed. For the smaller countries, we relied upon the library of the University of the South Pacific, USP, in Fiji to distribute books to national libraries. I awarded a grant for advanced librarianship study in the U.S. to Esther Williams, an assistant Librarian at the USP. After this, she became the first native Fijian to be Head Librarian. (She was a favorite grantee of Ambassador Williams, the President of The Asia Foundation, due, in part to the shared surname).

For these trips, I would send letters and telegrams ahead to government officials and the National Librarians of each country I planned to visit. The island people were very friendly and egalitarian. For instance, in Tonga, I played badminton with the sister of the King. I hoped to increase programming with legal and human rights organizations throughout the area. I met with national and regional women's organizations addressing the problems of poverty and domestic violence. On each trip, I interviewed candidates for study programs in the U.S., including summer programs for diplomats at the Fletcher School of Diplomacy and for international conferences. These small countries had only a few attorneys and fewer judges. Each Supreme Court was headed by a judge from England or Australia. The Asia Foundation responded to requests for additional training to qualify local lawyers to become judges. We funded attendance at the National Judicial Academy in Reno for several attorneys.

We also provided funding for additional delegates to the annual South Pacific Judicial Conferences. Because the U.S. Ninth Circuit Court has jurisdiction over American Samoa and Guam, Justice Anthony Kennedy was a keynote speaker several times. I helped organize and attended the 8th such conference, held in Kauai in 1989.

The Foundation hosted a Pacific-U.S. Bilateral conference in Samoa. This included scholars, diplomats, and local leaders from throughout the region, including the independence movement leader of New Caledonia, Jean-Marie Tjibaou. (He was assassinated a year later.) Also in attendance was a British scholar whose goal was to prove The Asia Foundation was affiliated with the CIA. We stayed at the legendary Aggie Grey Hotel. I struck up an intense, intimate friendship with an Australian diplomat participant; he visited the U.S. a few months later, and we were able to continue this romance. Both of us remained committed to our marriages, so we kept this a secret and happy temporary diversion.

A highlight of my Pacific trips was the annual meeting of development organization leaders. The Peace Corps, Save the Children, Foster Parents Plan, and various Australian and New Zealand assistance organizations met to review and compare programs for better coordination and for avoiding duplication. The delegates were young and lively, and our discussions continued into the evenings, frankness and humor facilitated by beer. When I was the Director of the Foundation's Indonesia program, I activated a similar group of donors there, though most were older, and the meetings rarely included beer. Sharing methods of dealing with everything from corrupt customs officials to censorship proved helpful. It was also important to avoid duplicate funding of local organizations.

The Asia Foundation had USAID grants to support family planning programs in Bangladesh, but these funds could not be used for any organization that even mentioned abortion to clients, according to the "Mexico City Doctrine" of the U.S. government. I knew from my research and correspondence with field offices that there was a need for assistance that was not subject to those limitations. I decided to look for other sources of funding. I discovered a likely source nearby: The William and Flora Hewlett Foundation. With input from the field offices, I put together a proposal to present to the Hewlett Foundation. To assure approval within the Asia Foundation, I had to word the purpose of the grant carefully. I avoided the word abortion but referred to clinics "addressing contraceptive failure" and "full-service family planning and women's health programs." I succeeded in obtaining a multi-year, multi-country grant which proved useful in several countries.

Chapter 25   Fifth Pakistan: Mountaineering

In 1984, Gene was working in Sri Lanka. I was overseeing several country programs for The Asia Foundation in San Francisco. A mountaineer friend, Phil Trimbel, formerly Ambassador to Nepal, where he had hiked in many regions, asked us to join him in a remote area of either India or Pakistan. He suggested the Siachen Glacier in India or the far north of Pakistan, the Shimshal valley. There were rumblings of conflict near the Siachen where the cease-fire line between Pakistan and India is ill defined. Therefore, we opted for Pakistan. Gene joined us in Islamabad where we stayed a few days. My position in San Francisco made me the "boss" of my colleague, Frank, the head of the Pakistan office. Previously he had been my boss. I met the local staff in the office and had a very interesting afternoon with the Pakistani Women Lawyers Association, while Ambassador Phil gave a talk on diplomacy to the Strategic Studies Center.

Then we flew to Gilgit. Tourism Department Official, Asif Khan, the young man who had accompanied the Mountain Travel trek I led in 1977, met us. He said Shimshal was closed because some tourists had gone to the China border from there. We were determined, so we went to the office of the District Police Inspector. He was impressed with our credentials: a former Ambassador, an Asia Foundation officer, and an Engineer who had worked extensively in Pakistan. He gave us a special permit. We then hired a jeep to proceed north along the Hunza river on the under-construction Karakoram Highway. At Passu, we unloaded our baggage from the jeep onto the wide expanse of river rock, near a primitive stone hut. Some Austrian climbers appeared, returning from climbing a 7,000 meter peak. They recommended we hire their Shimshali porters, including their chief porter, Rajab Shah.

Four days of very rugged trekking followed. The 18-inch-wide path was carved in vertical rock or slippery scree on gravel slopes descending to a raging river. It incuded one glacier crossing, and bridges made of flat stones balanced on ropes. Finally, we welcomed the sight of an oasis of green fields and fruit trees, dotted with white-washed stone houses. This was Shimshal, surrounded by snowcapped peaks. As we entered the valley, we stopped at Rajab's house for tea with his wife and children. Other women of the village had taken yaks, sheep, and goats to graze in high altitude pastures. They would send yogurt and cheese to the village weekly. The village leader escorted us to a small guest house which had a water pump outside and an outhouse. We planned to spend one night and then move higher up towards the peaks either to the north or the south. Phil took the single bed; Gene and I spread our air mattress and zip-together sleeping bags on the floor.

The people of Shimshal are Ismaili Shia Muslims, as are the people of Hunza. Ismailis, followers of the Aga Khan, are very supportive of education for girls and boys and do not enforce veiling or strict segregation of women. The open society of Shimshal was a pleasant change from cities in Pakistan where all the women are veiled and hidden.

We wanted to hire three men to carry our gear higher, Rajab told us it was impossible due to the Aga Khan birthday celebration. He also told us we could not go north because it led to the China border. We had been intrigued by going north because so few outsiders had ever been there. However, the mountains to the south also looked appealing; we were frustrated that we could not start but pleased to observe the festivities in the village. We were allowed to take short hikes. Gene and I hiked past the upper village to find a route for our ascent. We tried to find a private spot to make love, but three small boys followed us. When the boys retreated, we stopped on a grassy field that seemed ideal for a tryst, until the canal above started gushing water to irrigate it. We did succeed in picking some wild lettuce for dinner. Food was scarce in these mountain valleys in July. Vegetables were not quite ready to harvest; the apricots and peaches were small and green. Meat, flour, and yogurt were available, also eggs and chickens.

Brightly colored tents had been erected around a field by the mosque, with chairs for the important men and guests, refreshments of tea, bread, yogurt, butter, and old meat. Women and children gathered at the other side of the field, looking over a low wall. I went to the women's celebration to take photos. Everyone was dressed in bright new clothes.

Men and boys danced, schoolgirls presented two dramas, and everyone cheered for a tug of war between the teachers and the "volunteer corps," the local constabulary. Gene had a long discussion with the head of the village, the Lambardar, about our plans. He insisted we pay porter wages for the days we were delayed in the village! Later he came to our veranda to continue the discussion. With reluctance he agreed we could go to the high valley to the south.

Our friend Phil was sick in the night with violent diarrhea, probably caused by the food at the celebration. He stayed at the guest house while Gene and I, with Rajab and three porters, ascended to 13,000 feet to establish a camp. We sent the porters back, with full two day's pay. Rajab stayed with us. At midnight, my stomach had the same trouble as Phil's. Gene and Rajab carried some of our gear up another 2,000 feet while I lay in the tent clutching my stomach. Phil arrived at noon, completely recovered. I was relieved to see it was a 24-hour food poisoning attack, not a long-term illness. I dosed myself with paregoric and empirin with codeine. The next day we moved up to camp at 15,000 ft and enjoyed two days of ascents of four unknown, unnamed peaks over 17,000 ft. Recovered from the intestinal woes, I led the way up the steep snow and glaciers, carefully stepping over the few crevasses. The views were spectacular, but we could see there were no other peaks sufficiently near or safe for our small party to tackle. We decided to descend and have two extra days to hike in the Hunza region. We arrived back in Shimshal the next afternoon. An initial warm welcome was followed by a huge argument with the Lambardar and his deputies. For three hours they invented additional fees. Each time we would agree to something, the demands increased. Phil and I started our little stove to cook dinner, but the heated discussion continued. Finally, they left us alone. We insisted we would pay the porters and Rajab in Passu after conferring with authorities there. We threatened to carry all our own stuff and leave.

The melting glaciers upstream caused the Shimshal river to rise four feet during the day, so it is important to start early. Starting each day at 6 a.m., we completed the four day hike in three. On the first morning, the porters threatened to strike. They insisted we should hire a young boy who was walking down the valley on his own errand. Away from the greedy Lambardar, the porters accepted the wages we offered: full pay for three days, half pay for returning days. Rajab begged to be given Phil's down jacket, but Phil had worn it on Everest, so it had sentimental as well as monetary value. He would not part with it. Our trip had been a success in terms of scenery and culture but marred by arguments about pay.

Rajab became one of Pakistan's leading mountaineers. In 1989 he climbed Nanga Parbat; he was the first Pakistani to climb all five of the nation's 8,000-meter peaks. He started a mountaineering school in Shimshal, teaching young men and women technical skills so they could be mountaineers, not just porters. Samina Baig, graduate of that program, climbed Everest in 2013 and the "seven summits." (The highest points on each continent). She said to reporters, "I am doing mountain climbing to empower women," and "In my Ismaili community women are as important as men and they are playing an equal role in society. The nation needs to recognize women's capacity to contribute to development." Rajab had watched me leading up those steep mountains in 1984. Perhaps my example helped influence him to include women in the mountaineering school.

Chapter 26   Second Indonesia: The Asia Foundation

"A woman with children can't be a country director for a major foundation."

In late 1984, The Asia Foundation needed to replace the Representative (country director) in Indonesia. I met with the President, Ambassador Williams, to discuss my qualifications. I pointed out that I had lived in Indonesia two years; had a working knowledge of the language and familiarity with the cultures. Holding a Ph.D. in international development, I was as qualified as the person I would replace. I would be the second woman to direct a country program, and the first married woman with children to have that responsibility. It seemed a good time for another family adventure. Gene was getting frustrated with the hierarchy at the firm where he worked. Our son Eric had transferred from UC Santa Cruz to UC Davis and seemed to be more on track for his education. The younger son, Greg, was getting distracted at Berkeley High. Our daughter Laura had some undesirable friends who were making her skip school and run away from home. I accepted the job in November. It took eight weeks for our visas to be approved. In early January, Gene and Laura flew to Hong Kong, to remove her from bad influences. Greg had to finish semester exams, so he and I left a week later, met them in Hong Kong, and flew together to Jakarta.

In Jakarta, my assistant Julie and her husband met us with two cars and took us to a hotel near the Foundation office in a residential neighborhood. In the next two days, Greg and Laura were enrolled in the Jakarta International School. No more correspondence courses! With help of the office staff, I looked for houses to rent. No more cheap project housing! I knew we needed to rent a house with a functioning telephone line, a garden, and sufficient space for official entertaining. My predecessor had lived in a small house without enough room for a family of four – increasing to five when Eric visited. Within a week we found the ideal house. It was walking distance from my office. It had a telephone, four bedrooms, three baths, a large garage, and a three-room servant quarter. There were fruit trees in the garden, and a large lawn. It was surrounded by a high, white-washed wall topped with broken glass, typical of Jakarta. The widow who owned the house asked us to keep the resident servant, Musur. We were happy to have him and his wife. They did most of the cooking, boiling, and filtering water, cleaning, and gardening. The Foundation provided a night watchman who dozed on a chair in the driveway.

Gene became the *ikut saja*, or accompanying spouse. He quit his job at International Engineering and became an independent consultant. He found part time work with Development Alternatives International, (DAI) a small firm which had offices in Washington D.C. and Sacramento. He found working with a small group more congenial than a large firm. He wrote proposals, reviewed project documents, and went on short term assignments in Pakistan, West

Africa, and Irian Jaya while I worked in the Foundation's Jakarta office and traveled around the country to monitor projects that the Foundation supported.

My job in Indonesia was wonderful. On my staff were two American assistants Julie and Jim, and 18 Indonesians. Another American, Craig, (whom we had met when living in Sulawesi a decade before) worked on outlying islands. The office was a colonial two story house. My assistant Julie and her husband Paul lived in the second-floor apartment. Offices occupied the main floor, and the full basement was dedicated to book sorting and distribution. The staff included men and women, mostly Muslim, but also three Christians. They were very respectful; some called me "Doctor Elizabeth" while others called me "Ibu White." *Ibu* means mother in Indonesian and is the honorific title for a woman. Laura and Greg were very fond of our driver, Harsono. He loved the overtime pay he could earn driving them on the weekends. The Foundation supplied an official car, and we bought a used VW bus for private travel.

The Foundation supported projects from Aceh in the north of Sumatra to Irian Jaya, in the western half of New Guinea. I visited almost all the provinces in the country during my two and a half-year tenure. Unlike the self-funded Ford Foundation, The Asia Foundation had to raise funds to support its work. The core of our budget was an annual grant from Congress. About a third of the budget was a USAID grant to support community development organizations and another third was funding from Mobil Oil.

The Oil company had large operations in Sumatra and was required by the Government of Indonesia to invest in the welfare of the area. The Foundation had been chosen by Mobil Oil to design and implement programs to strengthen the universities in Aceh. Indonesia has a dual education system, Islamic and secular, institutions from elementary though university. In Aceh, the Islamic university campus was next to the government university campus. They shared a library in which some of the Mobil funds were invested. We identified advanced study programs for professors of both universities and contracted consultants to help create departments of business, agricultural economics, and English as a foreign language. Mobil hoped to recruit trained Acehnese staff instead of bringing in Javanese who would be resented.

We also utilized some of the Hewlett Foundation grant to support innovative family planning and women's health projects. I submitted proposals for funding of various projects to members of the American Chamber of Commerce in Jakarta and was successful in obtaining small grants. Every year we arranged and monitored the placement of two or three Luce Scholars. Their program was funded by The Henry Luce Foundation. The Luce Foundation also supported a multi-year program to encourage cooperation among non-governmental organizations in the Association of Southeast Asian Nations, (ASEAN) region. These varied sources of support made a dynamic and varied program possible. However, each of the funding sources had different substantive and financial reporting requirements.

My job involved meeting with the leaders of Indonesian organizations, coordinating with other donors, large and small, reporting to funders, and maintaining communication with the U.S. diplomatic community. At a dinner party I might find myself seated with the former Indonesian Ambassador to Canada; David Newsom, former U.S. Ambassador to Indonesia; the current U.S. Ambassador to Indonesia, John Holdridge and the Commander of the Pacific Fleet.

Indonesia requires foreign people working in the country to have an exit/reentry visa to leave the country. These can take several days (and bribes) to obtain. It was my policy that the American staff and dependents always have a valid exit visa in their passports in case they had to leave in an emergency. Our passports soon required extended pages because these visas required half a page of space.

The years in Jakarta were busy and the work challenging. As in America, Gene and I ran in the early morning when it was still dark and cool. We found others to join us, a French woman, a Canadian diplomat, and a British couple. I saw the Canadian at a reception and told him it was the first time I had seen him in clothes! On our early morning runs he wore only running shorts and shoes.

After our runs we would have breakfast with Greg and Laura, and send them off to school with the driver. Then I would walk over to the office. Gene would either go downtown to the DAI office or lounge on the porch, reading. Some days we would have a language teacher visit. After work we joined the weekly group runs of the local Hash House Harriers club. A year after we arrived, Musur and his wife had a baby. A woman from their village came to help with the baby. Our household expanded with a servant for our servants.

We brought our good bicycles to Jakarta but the traffic most of the time was daunting. Sundays some major roads were closed to cars and available to bikes and pedestrians only. Some weekends we rented a cottage in the cool highlands south of Jakarta. Perched on the side of a volcano, the small town was surrounded by tea plantations, and had spring water swimming pools. This was good respite from the heat and pollution of Jakarta, one of the world's largest cities. Other weekends we joined a group of snorkelers and divers who rented boats to visit the islands north of Jakarta Bay. We usually spent one night on an island. The water was warm, the sand white, and the fish and corals brilliant. The farther one went from Jakarta, the clearer the water became.

Greg and Laura adjusted to the International School well. The classes were small and the student body very diverse. At an assembly introducing new students Greg distinguished himself by wearing converse high top sneakers, red on his left foot, green on the right. He announced he had come to Jakarta because of his mother's job. (Most expat families moved because of the father's job.) He built a small skateboard ramp in our garage and soon acquired an avid group of skater friends. Laura joined the swim team, played trombone in the band, and became friends with girls from Australia, New Zealand, and Holland. In Berkeley marijuana was interfering with Greg's studying; in Jakarta beer was the distraction. The school conducted random drug tests on Monday mornings; use of drugs could bring a jail sentence or expulsion from the country. No one under 18 was allowed to drive, so the teenagers who were drinking were not driving. They either used taxis or had their parents' driver take them home.

During the summer of 1985, Greg's girlfriend from Berkeley came for a visit as did one of Laura's best friends. They travelled by train through Java to Bali, where Gene and I joined them for a few days. I was proud of how well Greg and Laura could use their language and cultural knowledge to help their friends enjoy Indonesia. In June 1986, Greg graduated from the International High School. Another friend came to visit during the summer, traveling around Indonesia until they left together for UC Santa Cruz. Eric was at UC Davis, so both my sons were in California. I felt lonely in the big Jakarta house with only one child, Laura, and Gene frequently absent for short term assignments in Pakistan and west Africa.

The interior of Irian Jaya seemed a stone age culture in 1987. For a month Gene was working there, the easternmost province of Indonesia, now called West Papua. His job was another effort to rehabilitate old irrigation structures, funded by the Asian Development Bank. Irian Jaya is the western half of the island of New Guinea, inhabited by Melanesian people, governed by Indonesians from Java. The other half of the island is the independent country, Papua New Guinea. Germans had first explored the northern coasts of Papua New Guinea. At the end of World War I the Dutch gained trusteeship for the western half of the island; the Australians controlled the east. In its struggle for independence after World War II, Indonesia gained control of the Dutch area. Australia granted independence to Papua New Guinea in 1975.

Gene had a challenging job in the roadless jungle province. He flew in tiny missionary planes to remote sites where old Dutch irrigation and drainage systems needed upgrading. He was able to indulge his love of shopping. His hotel room was full of spears, shields, elaborate wood carvings, knotless netting bags and penis gourds. Gene and I planned a trek, since he was already in Irian and I needed to follow up on several human rights and environmental projects which had received support from The Asia Foundation.

I had been to Irian Jaya before, to meet with faculty of the University in Jayapura and to review projects of nongovernmental organizations. This visit would be different. We were going to the interior highlands hoping to climb the second highest peak, Mount Trikora, 15,584 ft. It was impossible to get a permit for the highest peak, Carstensz, (16,024 ft) because it is near a huge copper and gold mine that is unpopular with the indigenous people and environmentalists. For many years a rebel movement has objected to the mine and sought autonomy for the province. The residents know that the mineral wealth generated by the mining goes to Jakarta while the locals pay the price in polluted rivers, damaged soils, and forests. The government did not want Americans observing the devastation caused by an open pit mine, especially not someone from a foundation supporting human rights and environmental organizations. Gene and I were joined by Chris, a Luce Foundation scholar then interning at the hospital in Sulawesi, and Gerd, an Austrian aid worker and mountaineer whom we met as we boarded the small plane for the interior highlands. (The people of the highlands of New Guinea were not in contact with the outside world until 1930. (Look at the Oscar winning documentary, "First Contact," produced in 1984, which includes interviews with the Australian explorers and some of the local people.)

We needed to hire a few porters to carry our food, fuel, and gear for ten days. At the edge of the airstrip, men were waiting to help the arriving tourists. One man spoke a little English and Bahasa Indonesia so we could communicate with him where we wanted to go. Within an hour he returned with five men, wearing nothing but penis gourds, and two women wearing grass skirts. One woman picked up my large backpack and confidently put the shoulder strap across her forehead. The farther we hiked, the more primitive the villages became. We camped in villages where the women and children sheltered in long low grass huts, the roof no more than four feet high, with a fire in the center filling the space with smoke. They cooked by simply putting the sweet potatoes and cassava (or meat when available) right in the hot coals. They had no cooking pots or pans. They brought water from a river or spring in a gourd. The men and adolescent boys slept on a raised platform, under a high roof that allowed them to stand. If it was cold, they could build a fire below. Traditionally, when an important man died, a finger would be cut off the hand of a small girl to confirm the tribe's sorrow. Among the older women missing fingers were common. A man's wealth was measured by how many pigs he had. Pigs seemed more valuable than women; we saw women suckling piglets. Several times on the trail, we encountered a tall man, decorated with boar's tusks and feathers, walking along with a spear while behind him several women were bent low bearing the weight of string bags loaded with pigs, vegetables, and babies. I was shocked by the miserable status of women.

By the third night we were camping above 9,000 ft and it was cold. Sleet was falling. We found a cave-like overhang for shelter, rather than putting up our tents in the wet. We gave the shivering porters big black plastic bags which we had brought to keep our packs dry. Their penis gourds poked out in front. The terrain was steep and the mud deep in places. After establishing a camp 3,000 ft higher, we went for the summit, finally hiking on rock. An afternoon storm of sleet blew in, so Chris and I decided to wait under a sheltering rock while Gene and Gerd went the final few yards to the summit.

For three days we hiked back through the jungles to the airstrip and a semblance of civilization. Flying down to Jayapura, we were able to take hot showers and buy cold beer at the Asian Development Bank guest house. The Indonesian government does not allow alcohol to be sold to the public in Irian Jaya. Across the border in Papua New Guinea beer has contributed to social and economic problems. Men with salaries spend much of their income on beer, neglecting the needs of their families. I was told in Port Moresby (capital of PNG) not to go out alone on Friday. It was payday and the streets would be crowded with drunk and feisty men.

Our adventure in the Stone Age of West Papua completed, we returned to Jakarta. My office was a busy place with a steady stream of written proposals and reports to review, interviews with Indonesian project leaders or participants, evaluations of completed projects and fund raising. My fluency in Indonesia was sufficient for conversation and interviews, but I usually asked the staff to translate documents into English. In my annual program plans I wrote that a focus of my work was to enable women, minorities, the disabled, and people of remote areas to participate in and benefit from the nation's development. I made this a purpose of the Afghan program when I directed it a few years later.

I particularly enjoyed working with women's organizations, such as The National Businesswomen's organization. It had branches in all major cities. In addition to promoting member-owned businesses, the group in Jakarta wanted to strengthen the smaller city affiliates and to help women's market cooperatives. We found that providing professional auditors for the cooperatives was very helpful. These market cooperatives served as savings banks and lenders for their members who might not have sufficient capital or confidence to deal with commercial banks. We made some small grants to enable businesswomen from remote towns to attend the regional and national meetings of women entrepreneurs. Other grants supported mentoring women new to business by experienced entrepreneurs.

Another program was designed to strengthen the faculties of law in remote provincial universities. We provided funds for men and women law professors to attend conferences and to pursue advanced study in Jakarta and overseas. These and other projects required that I travel frequently to different provinces of Indonesia.

We had a busy social life also. We ran with friends in the early morning, attended social dinner parties and official receptions. We went to the International School to attend athletic events, theatre productions and band performances. Friends visited, including a family from Colorado. One visitor, an 11-year-old boy, wanted cereal for breakfast, so I asked Musur to bring Cheerios or Cornflakes. As the boy shook some cornflakes into his bowl, a gecko jumped out of the box. We were all surprised and he decided on toast, instead of cereal.

Gene was working for the consulting firm, DAI in Jakarta, and going to other countries on contract jobs. He worked in Pakistan, and Mauritania and Senegal in west Africa, where his French language fluency was important. I found telephoning from Jakarta to Nouakchott, Mauritania difficult. The Jakarta operator spoke Indonesian and English but was not familiar with the city or the country. The Mauritanian operator spoke French and Arabic. I had to try to speak over the Indonesian operator in French to the Mauritanian to ask for Gene's hotel. These calls were frustrating and expensive, so we did not call often.

Gene spent many weeks preparing a proposal for DAI to compete for a three-year project of irrigation systems management in Indonesia. This was a continuation and expansion of the work he had done in Sulawesi in the 1970's. He was listed as Team Leader on the proposal. They won the bid, but the Indonesian Public Works Department objected to Gene as Team Leader. They provided no justification for this. I think it had something to do with his strictness in pointing out shoddy work in 1976-78 or perhaps his unwillingness to pay for "entertainment" for the Indonesian engineers accompanying him on field trips. I was shocked that the USAID officials did not insist upon specific reasons for the objection. After all, he was an experienced engineer, he spoke the language and had travelled widely in the archipelago. Even the staff of DAI did not come to his defense. I felt this was unfair. It made me doubt the integrity of the Indonesian and American officials. When The Asia Foundation asked me to continue for another two years in Jakarta, I decided to give up the job that I loved because Gene would continue to work on contracts in other countries and I would be left with just my daughter in our big house.

The Foundation selected a replacement for the Indonesia office and welcomed me back to San Francisco. Leaving my loyal staff and challenging job in Jakarta was not easy. I believe I had been an effective director of the Asia Foundation's program. I had found some new sources of funding and had initiated innovative programming. By providing support to environmental organizations and consumer groups I had indirectly supported protection of human rights. No small achievement in a political atmosphere of repression. My final weeks in the country were punctuated with farewell parties hosted by think tanks, government offices and nongovernmental organizations.

Most of Gene's work had been outside Indonesia or in remote Irian Jaya. However, he had gained experience as a part of a small consulting firm, writing, editing proposals, and preparing reports and evaluations. He would continue to use these skills for the next 15 years.

We stopped in Pakistan for a family trek on the way home, joined by another American family from Jakarta whose two sons were classmates of Laura and Greg. We flew to Gilgit and hired jeeps to take us north to Hunza. Then we crossed the river to Nagar village and drove to the end of the road. We hired some porters to carry our food and equipment onto the Hispar glacier and up a side valley, the Kinyiang Chish glacier. We made camp on a meadow behind the moraine of the glacier. It was a scenic site with Kinyiang Chish mountain, then the highest unclimbed mountain in the Himalaya, shining thousands of feet above us. Our camp was situated to avoid avalanches, though some came close enough for us to be sprayed with ice crystals. We did hikes up several of the smaller peaks above our camp. We would have liked to move camp farther up the valley, but the amount of cash we brought was not enough for more porter days.

After this brief Karakoram adventure, we flew to Paris where our son Greg was to meet us at Hotel de la Paix, on Rue du Gros Caillou. He had stayed there before. He can speak French as well as Indonesian. However, linguistic confusion ensued: *Caillou* means stone in French, but *"kayu"* means wood in Indonesian. The words are pronounced the same. Greg repeated *"bois"* (wood in French) to the taxi driver, pointing to the trees. After some detours, he made it to the hotel. We were reunited and continued our journey to Dijon. There we rented bicycles to spend five days riding through the vineyards of Burgundy. Then on to our favorite place, Chamonix. We did some hiking and mountain biking in unsettled weather. Finally on a clear day we were able to climb Mont Blanc de Tacul, 14,008 ft, the third summit of Mont Blanc. It was a joy to share the summit with Gene and two of our children.

Returning from my assignment in Indonesia, in 1987, I was given new responsibilities in the home office in San Francisco. Asked to write a final report for the Luce Foundation of the six-year grant for promoting linkages among non-governmental organizations in the Association of Southeast Asian Nations (ASEAN) region, I insisted on having a computer, rather than a typewriter. This was the beginning of a big change for the Foundation. Gradually all offices acquired computers. We thought, mistakenly, that having computers and using email instead of memos with three carbons, would reduce the amount of paper generated daily. It did not; most people printed their emails and writings anyway. The number of assistants did decline. It was hard to justify having a personal secretary when we were writing on our own computers.

I was happy to resume responsibility for the program in the Pacific Island nations and serving as Area Director overseeing six Asian field offices. Outside of work, I was running competitively and looking forward to turning 50 in 1988. Then I would be at the young end of a new age group for competition. Laura enrolled in Berkeley High for her final two years; Greg was at UC Santa Cruz, and Eric was in Philadelphia pursuing an MBA. Gene continued his consulting jobs for DAI, requiring some overseas travel. He had jobs for several weeks each in Mauritania, Senegal, Sri Lanka, and Pakistan. He always returned with bags of textiles and rugs to keep or sell or give away to our friends.

I was not so happy with his frequent absences, but I was much less lonely than I would have been in Indonesia. In California I had lots of friends and companions with whom to pursue my interests, whether athletic or cultural. Laura was living at home and Greg was nearby. My mother and most siblings were in Colorado so I could visit them more easily. My job also required some international travel. Gene and I tried to coordinate our travel so our paths would cross in Asia. I visited him when he was working in Pakistan and Albania. I did not make it to west Africa, though that area fascinates me.

In the spring of 1989, Laura was ready to graduate from Berkeley High except for lacking some Physical Education credits. For the final month of the year, she was required to be at school at 7:30 a.m. to run laps around the track. Every morning, I would return from my run at 6:45 to make sure she was on the bus at 7:15.

Gene was working in Sri Lanka, in the Mahaweli region where the civil war was raging. The minority Tamil people were fighting for autonomy from the majority Sinhalese. Religious, linguistic, and economic inequality had fanned the flames of a civil war that lasted over ten years. He and his team changed the color of their vehicles each week so they would not be recognized as belonging to the government. The fenceposts near their accommodations were sometimes decorated with human heads. Gene called me frequently to ask if Laura was going to graduate. He worried that he could not get home in time. He flew back to California a day before the graduation. It was a 24-hour flight. We were happy to be a united family for her big day.

Chapter 27   Sixth Pakistan: Afghan Program Director

"A woman should not be the director of a program for Afghans."

As an older, respected professional woman, I could meet both Afghan men and women to discuss project ideas. A man might be limited to discussions with men because Afghan women would be hesitant to meet with a man. An added advantage for a foreign woman is being in a different category than local woman. She becomes a neutral person, as I had experienced before, being able to visit both sides of segregated gatherings.

In 1989 the Afghan Mujahidin, with arms and training provided by America and other countries, channeled through the Pakistani Intelligence Service, had defeated the Soviet troops who had invaded in 1979. About three million Afghans had taken refuge in Pakistan; two million in Iran. They fled during the decade of conflict with the USSR. As most fighting men stayed in Afghanistan, the refugee camp populations were largely women, children and old or disabled men. In Peshawar, at least three men were competing to become president of free Afghanistan.

American policy shifted from supporting military action to assistance for Afghanistan's social and economic recovery. Already scholarships were being awarded to Afghans for study at universities in America. The Asia

Foundation cooperated with that effort by providing the services of Carla Grissman to interview candidates and provide orientation to study in America. Carla had been my friend since we met in Sri Lanka in 1980. She had worked in Afghanistan in the 1970's and could speak Dari, one of Afghanistan's main languages. USAID announced the creation of a budget for Afghanistan reconstruction. Agencies and non profits like The Asia Foundation would compete to implement programs supported by that budget. The Foundation was a good candidate, having had an active program and office in Kabul from 1954 to 1979. The Foundation established an Afghan office, located in Peshawar, distinct from the Foundation's Pakistan office, in Islamabad. The Afghan program would have its own budget and personnel. As soon as Afghanistan was diplomatically certified and safe for the return of Americans, the office would move from Peshawar to Kabul.

Meanwhile, Gene's consulting firm won a contract to modernize the irrigation department management in Pakistan. Gene was named Director of the North West Frontier Province. His office would be in Peshawar. It was a great contract that included a house, hardship pay, air travel for the family, and a generous shipping allowance. It included access to the U.S. Commissary in Islamabad and use of the diplomatic pouch for mail. He flew to Pakistan in November 1989 to start the job and returned for a Christmas visit. I asked the President of The Asia Foundation if I could become the Director of the Foundation's Afghan program. I could speak and understand Pushto, one of the two major languages of Afghanistan. Carla, who spoke Dari, would be my assistant. A perfect team. I would be a low-cost program director for the Foundation because my housing would be provided by Gene's contract. By January 1990, the proposal I submitted to USAID for a block grant to support Afghan organizations was accepted. I wrote that the central purpose of the program was to assure that women, minorities, and the disabled participated in and benefitted from the postwar recovery and development of Afghanistan. I became the Director of the Afghan program.

I flew to join Gene in late January. The travel coordinator at the Foundation was Miss Mimi Tripp – very appropriate name. She wrote all air tickets. She tried to get me the most direct flights to Peshawar. She chose a flight with a short connecting time in Islamabad but it had one stop. The stop was in Swat, the once independent mountain kingdom north of Peshawar. When the small plane landed in Swat, all the other passengers deplaned, and it started to snow. The pilot and co-pilot invited me to join them for lunch at the grand old Swat hotel, formerly the palace of the *Wali,* ruler, of Swat. They were not sure when it would be possible to take off for Peshawar. I tried to call both my new office in Peshawar and Gene to say that the flight was delayed. Pakistan's telephone system defeated my efforts. Finally, three hours late, we landed in Peshawar. I did not see any driver with my name on a card, so I took a taxi. Gene had told me the house number, 24, Civil Officer's Lines, but he had not given me a street name. It was a neighborhood of houses assigned to civil servants and judges. The taxi cruised around several streets until I saw the number on a gate. Each house was surrounded by white walls, topped with broken glass. A guard stood at the gate and welcomed me. A cheerful man introduced himself as Bashir, our cook and all-round household servant. He told me Gene had gone on a field trip to Quetta and would return soon. I was impressed by the house. Living room, dining room and two bedrooms with baths on the ground floor, and two bedrooms with baths and an open terrace upstairs. Outside there was a driveway, garage, and servant quarters. There were terrazzo floors and air conditioners in several rooms. The furniture was standard USAID issue, but the house glowed with the rugs and embroidered pillows that Gene had collected. I went upstairs, bathed, and took a nap until Gene arrived.

We were happy to be united again in a place we knew well and to both have interesting, responsible jobs. We were living only a few blocks from where we had lived as Peace Corps Volunteers 28 years before, but this time in palatial splendor. We had a big house, a cook, a gardener, and 24-hour security guards. Gene had two big cars, land cruiser type, with drivers; I had one car and a driver, and an office and staff. Gene's office was in the provincial Irrigation Department.

Gene had hired one Afghan driver, Ghazi because he thought we could learn some Dari (Afghan Persian) language from him. His other driver was Pakistani. We had hoped that we could eventually work in Afghanistan. We had visited Afghanistan three times in the 1960s. It seemed to be a country that we could appreciate, enjoy, and apply our expertise.

Peshawar was no longer the sleepy old city we knew in the 1960's. The population had expanded in numbers and variety. "Twice as many people, twice as many guns, and half as many trees," I would answer people who asked us if we had seen changes. There were over a million Afghans in refugee camps west and south of the city. There were volunteers who had come to join the fight against the godless Soviets. They included disgruntled Muslim groups from many countries, ranging from the Polisario group from Western Sahara to the Moro Liberation Front from the southern Philippines. Especially annoying were the Arabs who occupied a large compound across the street from my office. They looked dirty and arrogant. They were rude to all women, sometimes tossing a stone or spitting at women (foreign or Pakistani) walking by. Osama Bin Laden was probably among them, though I never saw an Arab as tall as he. There were also numerous international organizations supporting the refugees.

My driver picked me up every morning to go to my office. It was a small house in University Town, a city that had developed between the university and the Peshawar cantonment, spreading out over the flat desert terrain. Carla Grissman, my Foundation colleague and friend, had set up the office. The staff consisted of two Afghan men and three Pakistani men, smaller than my team in Jakarta, but all hard-working and friendly. We had a small "Books for Asia" program and funding to support Afghan initiatives. Some former mujahidin fighting groups transformed themselves overnight into reconstruction "NGO"s. They submitted proposals for road building, *karez* (underground water channel) cleaning, and school building in their local districts. Unfortunately, the U.S. government did not allow Americans to go into Afghanistan. This made it difficult to evaluate projects. Some of these had "food for work" support, so at least food was getting across the border, even if some of the cash was not utilized as planned.

It was in Peshawar that I got the name I use for my email address. An Afghan commander had heard that The Asia Foundation director was "Dr. Elizabeth." I received an envelope addressed to Dr. Ali Zabet. He was sure I was a man. It contained a project proposal and a plea for funding. From that day onward, Carla called me "Zabet." When I later established an email account, I used zabetwhite for my name.

Projects I supported ranged from grants to the Association of Professors of Afghanistan Universities and the Afghan Lawyer's Association to basic literacy programs for women in the refugee camps. All the beneficiaries were Afghan, though most of the activities took place in Pakistan. One significant project was the Afghan Women's University, located in a large rented house at the edge of one refugee camp. Afghan girls were allowed to attend some schools in Pakistan, but not the colleges and universities. With the sponsorship of one of the fiercest Mujahidin Commanders, a group of educated women had organized a university. The 150 students were enthusiastic, although they did not know from semester to semester if the institution would continue. These students hoped to become doctors, teachers, and leaders in a future, peaceful Afghanistan. I despaired that one of the largest items in the Women's University budget was for transportation. The conservative commander said it was not safe for the students to travel in regular buses, taxis, or motor rickshaws. They had to travel in rented buses, curtains hiding them from curious eyes. I pointed out that I had seen some of the Afghan women students shopping in the Cantonment, on foot or traveling by motor rickshaw. The commander replied that two or three young women, veiled, would be anonymous, while a large group on the way to advanced education would be a vulnerable target for extreme fundamentalists.

I tried to help Afghans renew contacts with their counterparts in other Asian countries after the isolation of a decade of war. For instance, we made a grant to enable an Afghan woman judge to attend a LAWASIA conference in

Malaysia; she made a presentation on family law in Afghanistan. Several of the professors conferred with their counterparts in India and Bangladesh. We provided funding for conferences hosted by Afghan organizations and recruited participants from neighboring countries.

Among the Afghan NGOs focused on the disabled, I particularly admired Afghan Amputee Bicycle Messengers, founded by a triple amputee, Nasir. He helped Afghan amputees build and repair bicycles and use them to earn money running errands. I contacted the bicycle messenger organization in San Francisco; they held a benefit race for the Afghan Amputee Bicycle Messengers. I made a small grant to enable Nasir to attend a Disability International meeting in Indonesia, where he met Ralf Hotchkiss of San Francisco State University, founder of Whirlwind Wheelchair International (WWI) and MacArthur Award winner. WWI has set up a network of factories in 20 countries where disabled people assemble wheelchairs and hand cycles using inexpensive local components. A few years later, Whirlwind established a workshop in Afghanistan.

While directing the Afghan Program, I met many brave men and women who had risked their lives to support their country. Among them was Dr. Sima Samar, a widow of the Hazara minority who established medical and social services for women and children in a huge refugee camp in Quetta, Baluchistan, Pakistan. She expanded her activities to include a hospital in Ghazni province in Afghanistan. She braved armed road stops and bandits to travel to and from this hospital. Later, she became the director of Women's Affairs and the commissioner of human rights for the Afghan government's Independent Human Rights Commission. Dr. Samar was nominated for the Nobel Peace Prize in 2009. Her courage and determination in the face of danger were inspirational. All the women whom I found inspiring were married and had children. The Asian Muslim women were from upper-class families that encouraged education for both sons and daughters. They had the support of their families and were highly educated, but they had to overcome societal pressures and brave physical threats to pursue their ideals.

I made a grant to support the work of another brave Afghan woman, Patuni, a poultry expert. Accompanied by a driver and one other woman, she would cross the border to villages in Afghanistan to distribute baby chicks. She trained women in poultry raising, recognizing poultry disease and how to treat it. These poultry projects could help families improve their diets and earn money from the sale of eggs and chickens. A decade of war had disrupted agricultural production, so the people of Afghanistan were hungry.

I funded and organized an American tour for a group of seven Afghan women. They were teachers, professors, and leaders of women's organizations. The Foundation offices in Washington and San Francisco planned the itinerary to include urban and rural areas where they met with their

American counterparts. Two days before the end of the tour, one of the young women disappeared from the hotel where they were staying. A year later, we learned that she had married a distant cousin who lived in Texas. I was shocked at her defection, but I admired her courage to break the rules to assure herself a safer life in America.

The Secretary-Treasurer of the Association of Professors of the Universities of Afghanistan (APUA) was a historian and a poet, Hakim Taniwal. He prepared excellent proposals and reports for the APUA programs that were supported by the Asia Foundation. After years of effort, he found asylum for his wife and children in Australia and a teaching position for himself at an Australian university. However, in 2002, President Karzai of Afghanistan asked him to return to be Governor of Khost Province. Three years later, he transferred to Paktia Province. In 2006, he was killed by a suicide bomber, probably the Taliban. It is tragic that many educated, skilled, and patriotic Afghans have been killed in the continuing conflict in their country.

Instead of the staid old British Peshawar Club, the center of social activity for expats was the International Club. It had a typical American menu and was the only place to buy alcohol in Peshawar. One Saturday evening, two tall pretty, English women came in the door, announcing they were British Air flight attendants who had taken a flight from Islamabad, having been told that the Peshawar Club was "the liveliest place to be on Saturday night in Pakistan."

They were welcomed warmly and whisked onto the dance floor. The Club hosted parties and held aerobic classes on the roof. When curious neighbors peering from rooftops saw us jumping around, they complained about "immoral activities." (In spite of the fact that all the women in the aerobics class wore long pants and modest shirts. Some of the men wore shorts and could have been the source of the immoral accusation.) The club then installed a tall canvas wall around the roof.

There were many interesting young men and women working with American, European, and Australian aid organizations. Gene was quick to recruit the more athletic ones to join us on mountain excursions. Every holiday and many weekends, we would fill his big cars with camping and climbing gear, food, and friends and head north to the mountains of Swat and Chitral. When we returned, we had the luxury of just walking into our house to take showers and read our mail while the drivers and Bashir dealt with unpacking and washing the mud off the cars and our boots.

In Pakistan, Bangladesh, and India, I had to wear very modest clothes for running, pants below the knee and baggy long-sleeved shirts. Nevertheless, the sight of a foreign woman running inspired negative comments and actions, including stone or stick throwing. After a boy threw a rock at me in Pakistan, Gene picked him up and dropped him in a nearby irrigation canal. The boy was startled, not injured. That boy didn't throw things at us again.

Stray dogs were another hazard. In some places, there were packs of them wandering on the roads. Since we ran before dawn, we sometimes didn't see the dogs until they were quite close. These strays certainly did not have vaccinations, and they were hostile! We understood why Pakistani men on their morning walks carried sticks—not for use as canes, but to ward off aggressive dogs. The list of municipal officials in Peshawar included "Dog Shooter" for good reason.

I was called back to California for a staff conference in June, making it possible to attend Greg's graduation at UC Santa Cruz. Then, I went back to my job in Pakistan. Late in the summer, Laura, Greg, and Eric came to join us on a ten day mountain trek. I selected Gondogoro mountain, a non-technical 18,500 ft peak in Baltistan, northern Pakistan. Frank, an American doctor working in Peshawar, joined us. Eric and Greg brought a snowboard after determining from photographs that the summit area had smooth snow slopes appropriate for snowboarding.

When we camped in the first village, Laura woke with a terrible nightmare and felt ill and disoriented. She remained unsteady for another day, so Gene and I decided to take her home, reversing our jeep journey. Gene flew with her to Karachi to make sure she got a direct flight home. Greg, Eric, and Frank remained to climb Gondogoro Peak with the local porters. The boys had a glorious time taking turns snowboarding the high slopes.

Gene and I came back to Berkeley for a two-week Christmas visit. Then the Gulf War erupted. The U.S. government warned all Americans working in Muslim countries to stay away until further notice. Our visit was extended to two months. Gene commuted to Chicago to work in the headquarters of the firm that was the main contractor on his project. I returned to taking the express bus to the Foundation office in San Francisco. Fortunately, the arrangements at our home in Berkeley allowed us to move back into our bedroom and share the kitchen with Laura and the two graduate students living with her. We could also access our ski equipment and bikes in the basement.

"The Sierra backcountry is not safe in mid-winter." On a weekend trip to Mount Lyell in Yosemite with a friend, Gus, we had an unplanned adventure. We camped in a forest clearing with a view of two distinctive peaks, Ritter and Banner. The next day, we skied over Donahue Pass and up the Lyell Valley. A heavy snowstorm began just after Gene and Gus descended from the summit to the rock where I was waiting for them. (I decided they could make a faster ascent with just two people on the rope, so did not go up the final pitch.) The swirling snow made it impossible to find our tracks over the open slopes of the pass, so we skied down the valley until we reached the forest. We found a fallen tree with a cave-like trench beneath. While the guys dug out more snow from under the tree, I collected dead wood from trees nearby. We were able to sit inside, keeping our feet warm in our backpacks. Our fire sputtered and extinguished itself on the snow regularly, but it kept us warm psychologically, if not physically. Our biggest problem was water. Our water bottles were plastic; we had nothing in which to melt snow.

By morning, we had finished our water. The sky had cleared, so we crawled out of our shelter to start skiing up the valley and over the pass. Then we saw only five skis! One of Gus' skis was missing from the cluster we had thrust vertically into the snow. We probed with our poles and dug with our ice axes to no avail. So, Gene and I left, assuring Gus that one of us would return with an extra ski after we had found the way over Donahue pass to our camp. Two feet of new snow had fallen, so there were no tracks to follow, but the geography was clear to go up the valley and over the wide, treeless slopes of the pass. We managed to melt a few sips of snow that we packed in our water bottles and held under our jackets, but it was not enough. We hurried down the far side of the pass. Our tent had been flattened by the snow, but fortunately, I recognized the view of Ritter and Banner peaks and saw a rectangular undulation in the snow. With joy, we pulled up the tent, grabbed the stove and pot, and started melting snow before setting up the tent properly.

Just as we drank as much as possible and filled two water bottles, we heard a shout! It was Gus. He had tied his ice axe on his boot and followed our tracks. We packed up our gear and skied back to our car, Gus limping along on the ice axe the whole way. Six months later, a ranger found his ski. From this trip, I learned to carry a metal "Sierra Club Cup" for melting water and a zip lock bag that holds matches and candle ends whenever I go on a long hike or ski tour. At the end of February, we had permission to return to Pakistan.

A detour through the "Stans" was proposed for me in 1992 after I had returned to the U.S.A. for a conference. Instead of flying directly back to Pakistan, I traveled through Russia to the newly independent states of Kazakhstan, Kyrgyzstan, and Uzbekistan to explore opportunities for the Foundation and identify candidates for training programs and conferences. ("*Stan*" means land of, so Afghanistan is land of the Afghans. Uzbekistan, the land of the Uzbeks, etc. Pakistan is the land of the pure *"pak."* Since I am from a foreign country, I have been asked, "How are things in *Ferengistan?"* (land of the *Ferengi* or foreigners)

An assistant, Emily, went with me. After a day in Moscow, we flew to Alma Ata on Aeroflot. We had to drag our luggage across the tarmac to the plane, toss it into a yawning door at ground level, and then climb the stairs inside the plane to the passenger compartment. The service was miserable. The stewardess wheeled a cart holding a bucket of grey greasy soup down the aisle. I refrained from eating anything. As we descended towards Alma Ata, then the capital of Kazakhstan, I was delighted to see snow-capped mountains surrounding the small city. We stayed in an apartment in one of a dozen identical grey cement four-story Soviet-style apartment buildings. When I went out to run in the morning, I glanced at our building to remember it, but when I returned, I was lost. Every building looked the same. Finally, I spotted a distinctive tree and found my accommodation. It was harder to find than that tent flattened under the snow in the Sierra. On this trip, Emily and I met dissident journalists, political leaders, women's organization leaders, and academics. An American scholar helped set up appointments, as did the local U.S. diplomats.

One early morning in Kyrgyzstan, I jogged up a hill near our hotel. It was covered with bright green grass, accented with scarlet poppies. Suddenly, a man mounted on a white horse came over the horizon, wearing the traditional Kyrghyz embroidered domed felt hat. He had a large falcon on his wrist. We exchanged "Salaams" and went our separate ways. It was an enchanting way to start the day.

These countries were emerging from 70 years of Russian Soviet rule. The Soviets brought universal literacy and a subway to each capital city but discouraged ethnic and religious traditions. Celebration of Muslim holidays was forbidden. Only a limited number of carefully selected elderly people were allowed to make the pilgrimage to Mecca. Polygamy was banned, but domestic abuse and gender inequality were rife.

South of the Oxus River in Afghanistan, every village has a bazaar of small open-front shops, while in the Soviet-dominated "Stans," the only shops were state-owned, with closed doors and white tile walls and counters. Most of the shelves were empty. The empty shelves did not affect us because our hosts in each city were extremely hospitable, wining and dining us lavishly. For example, one evening in Kyrgyzstan, a group of scholars took us into a beautiful mountain valley where they produced a picnic of salads, cold cuts, caviar, and fruit washed down with champagne. A few years later, the streets and monuments were lined with tiny shops and stands, the men and women entrepreneurs selling everything from soft drinks to antique carpets. Since my visit, I have followed the political developments in these countries. Only Kyrgyzstan has had regular elections. Uzbekistan, Kazakhstan, and Turkmenistan continue to be ruled by the former Soviet strongmen or their handpicked successors. Several of the outspoken journalists we met have been arrested or killed.

The Mogul monuments of Samarkand and Bokhara were stunning but in need of some repair after years of neglect. The huge mosques and madrassas (academies) were empty. During my early morning runs, I could visit the monuments undisturbed. These monuments were created by the dynasties of Genghis Khan and Tamerlane. They imported craftsmen from Persia and throughout Central Asia. Their descendants, the Moguls, ruled the Indian subcontinent for more than 200 years.

Back in Peshawar, I was happy to resume my work on the Afghan program. We planned another big mountain trip for the summer. We would trek along the Biafo Glacier (40 miles) and Hispar Glacier (30 miles), crossing the 16,824 ft Hispar pass. These two glaciers, with their huge junction, "Snow Lake," and the nearby Baltoro glacier constitute the largest glacial expanse outside the polar regions. An added appeal of this trek for me was that in 1899, Fanny Workman, one of America's early women mountaineers, had camped on the Biafo glacier, viewed Snow Lake, and climbed a nearby peak. She and her husband were the first Americans to explore this part of the Himalayas. Permits had to be obtained from the government because the area was close to the Siachen glacier, where Indian and Pakistani troops were battling. Nazir Sabir, one of Pakistan's leading mountaineers (who had arranged several previous trips for us), helped obtain the permits and hired a man named Ghulam to lead us and coordinate our porters. Our son Greg flew out from California with two friends; the son of one of Gene's colleagues in Islamabad also joined the group. At the last moment, Brian, a volunteer with the International Rescue Committee, asked to come. He and I drove from Peshawar to Islamabad after work to meet the rest of the team, which now consisted of Gene, me, and five 24-year-old men. The following morning, we flew to Skardu, the last big town in Pakistan-controlled Kashmir. We stayed in the Skardu Hotel with a multinational collection of mountaineers. Some were starting expeditions with bright new gear and enthusiasm;

another was returning, glum, after the death of one member of the team.

After a dusty jeep ride to the last village, Askole, we began hiking. Gene dealt with the complexity paying porters on a traverse. The government regulates a set fee per porter-day or "stage" and requires half pay per day for the return journey. Our 17-day trek was considered officially 25 "stages" by the porters. Though it was possible to return from the end in Hunza to the start near Skardu in two days by bus, the porters wanted 17 half-days to pay for their return journey.

In addition to our food, stoves, and fuel, and camping gear, the porters had to carry their own food, fuel and stoves and tents. We would not pass through any villages where we could buy food. We started with 18 porters but were able to send two back after four days, and another two on day eight. The loads were reduced by the consumption of food and fuel. As we hiked up the Biafo we were stunned by the dramatic granite spires on both sides of the glacier. Most afternoons, the young men would climb a nearby snow slope with their two snowboards and take turns gliding down. Gene and I would hike to an attractive small peak or viewpoint, adding to our lifetime list of summits. We crossed the white expanse of Snow Lake in brilliant sunshine and spent one night on Hispar pass. The porters camped lower. During the day on the pass, Gene and I climbed a snowy peak with Brian, while the other four young men built jumps for their snowboards.

The photos and memories from this day at 17,000 ft are spectacular. Descending the Hispar glacier, we were on the rocky sides of the glacier more than on the ice. In all we spent seven days and eight nights above the altitude of Denali.

When planning the food, I had not known that Brian would be joining us at the last moment. I also underestimated the appetites of young men! Fortunately, the porters were happy to share the chapattis they made every evening. On the final day we were walking down on a dusty jeep track. One porter had run ahead to locate vehicles at the first village. It was hot. We sat beside the trail and looked in our packs for lunch. I had a packet of crackers. Gene had a can of tuna, Greg had a chocolate bar. The seven of us carefully divided it: One teaspoon of tuna on a cracker for each, followed by a square of cholocate! At the first village, peach and apricot trees were in fruit. The first peach was the best I had ever eaten. We each ate several. Later after hot showers and a warm dinner in Karimabad, Hunza, we sat in the garden of the inn, looking back up the glacier valley to the sunset glowing on the peaks. It was one of our best trips.

After our wonderful glacier trek, I returned to my office in Peshawar. It was a hectic time for the Afghan community. Attempts were being made to form an interim government, but there was fierce competition between various commanders and their Mujahidin followers. At least three men were claiming to be the rightful president. I continued to work with and support those organizations and individuals who seemed most likely to make a positive contribution to the future of Afghanistan. The needs of the refugees and the people who had remained in the country throughout the Soviet war were huge. The agricultural base of the economy was nearly destroyed. Farmers had joined the fight, and many were killed. Most of the refugees were women and children, displaced from their traditional social structures, mostly illiterate, dependent upon strangers to help them get ration cards and access to the food, fuel and medical services provided by the UN. Back in their Afghan villages, these women had identity and status from their tribal affiliation, their skills at gardening, sewing, and housekeeping. In the refugee camps they became anonymous, without village social structures. My program provided financial support for some basic literacy and numeracy training for women. I visited the classrooms to observe the progress of the refugees in gaining the ability to sign their names, read simple texts and math, such as ration card allowances. Twice a year, a woman official from USAID would accompany me, but most of them preferred to stay in their air-conditioned offices in Islamabad. The refugee camps were vast, dirty, dusty, or muddy depending upon the season. Once I was joined by the tall blond wife of the American Ambassador. She wore her "Muj Suit" a khaki safari suit with pants that I considered too tight for a woman to wear in public, with no scarf for her shoulders or head. She was not following Gene's fashion advice for Pakistan: "No humps no bumps, no elbows no knees." I always wore my shalwar-camise with a proper dupatta across my shoulders. I saw rolled eyes, but the people with us knew she was the Ambassador's wife and above reproach.

Religious schools, (madrassahs), often funded by very conservative Arabs, offered clothing, food, and housing for boys. Many poor widows in the refugee camps were happy to send their boys to a place where they would be fed and housed. The education in these schools consisted of learning to read and recite the Koran. These madrassahs also preached extremism and became recruitment centers for the Taliban.

One encounter I had with the ultraconservative educators happened when an Afghan chemistry professor came to my office to request science books for a boys' college. After shaking hands and the obligatory cup of tea, we looked over the collection of Books for Asia books in my office and selected three boxes of books. I suggested I should present them at the college. The college had been established with funding from Saudi Arabia. It was ten miles from Peshawar. When I arrived at the starkly modern building, I was greeted by the Afghan professor and the Principal, but both kept at a distance; neither would shake my hand, even though I was dressed in shalwar camise and had a scarf over my head, very proper and modest, and gray-haired. My driver unloaded the books and handed them over. I was not invited inside the college building. As we drove away, my Afghan driver, said it was not proper for the recipients of a valuable collection of books to send me away without even a cup of tea. Afghans are usually very warm and friendly. Women kiss on each cheek when they meet. Most men would greet an older, respected, foreign women with a warm handshake. Every meeting must include several cups of tea. The Wahhabi-Saudi mentality had erased that friendliness.

Another time, paying my respects, on behalf of The Asia Foundation, to one of the competing Presidents in Exile of Afghanistan, I was ushered into a walled compound and then into a building. Rows of Kalashnikovs and dusty shoes were lined up outside the President's office. He remained behind a huge desk and never looked me in the eye. Fortunately, I can read upside down so I amused myself by reading some of the correspondence on his desk while his voice droned on describing how his party would repair and rule the country. He was under the influence of foreign ultra conservative Islam. It was not a gracious way to interact with a respectable person who represented a possible source of funding.

We spent the holidays in India and Nepal. Gene's contract provided a round-trip ticket for our daughter, Laura to visit us in Pakistan during her college Christmas vacation. We went skiing at a hill station near Islamabad, Laura using a snowboard her brother had left from the summer trip. Then we flew to Delhi and continued by train to Khajuraho. We rented bikes and rode through the green fields to visit the more than twenty temples covered with amazing erotic carvings. Three friendly Canadian college students were staying in the same little hotel. They joined us on a train to Benares, the holy city on the Ganges. As we walked from our modest hotel towards the banks of the Ganges, the crowd was increasingly dense. I became claustrophobic. I hid my face in Gene's back so he could plow a path through the human flood. At dawn, Laura and the Canadians took a boat to an island in the river and immersed themselves in the holy polluted river. It was December so the water was cold as well as polluted. Laura escaped with only a slight cold. Gene and I opted to be rowed across the river in the morning sun, observing the burning ghats and the ceremonial bathing of hundreds of people.

From Benares we flew to Kathmandu. In our favorite bookstore, as Gene searched for missing issues of the *Himalayan Journal* for his library, we saw our friend Arlene. She was leading her annual winter trek for families. We asked for ideas for trekking. She recommended a five-day trek from Gorkha to Trisuli Bazaar in central Nepal. She also suggested a trekking company to take us. The views of the snowcapped peaks were inspiring. There were no other tourists on the trails. However, it was quite cold in the evenings and the days were short. One day the porters wandered off trail and were late, making us wait several long cold hours for our sleeping bags. Nevertheless, it was a pleasant trek. It was nice for Gene and me to have this extended trip with Laura alone. She felt more at ease in

Hindu/Buddhist Nepal than in Muslim Pakistan, where foreign women attract unwanted attention.

The political situation in Afghanistan was chaotic in 1992. The Soviet-appointed President Najibullah was killed in the spring. Mojeddedi was declared President for two months, then President Rabbani took over for nine years, but his "Islamic State of Afghanistan" controlled only ten percent of the territory. In the countryside, commanders who had led the fight against the Soviets competed for control. Bandits roamed, strongmen collected fees at every bridge and road intersection, so commerce and transportation were dangerous and expensive. The Taliban came into this power vacuum promising to eliminate crime and enforce discipline, so they were welcomed in many communities. *Talib* means student. The Taliban were graduates of the conservative religious schools, the madrassahs, many of them funded by Saudi Arabia, teaching the strict Wahabi version of Islam.

Pakistan was no longer needed as a conduit for arms to fight the Russians. The U.S. Financial Assistance Act required annual certification that Pakistan was not developing atomic weapons. Pakistan already had produced and tested atomic weapons; therefore U.S. financial assistance was cut off. Gene's project would end by the fall of 1992. U.S. policy towards Pakistan swung from supportive to distrustful as it had over the decades. The funds for Afghanistan were decreased as well, so my job would be ending. The Asia Foundation continued to support a few

Afghan organizations from headquarters until 2002, when it was possible to open an office in Kabul. Gene's Afghan driver disappeared with the big car just before we were to leave. He drove it to Afghanistan. Rumors of his establishing a taxi business reached us a few weeks later. I hope he and his family survived the chaos that has continued in Afghanistan.

We were sorry to have our time in Peshawar come to an end. We had two challenging jobs. We had a good house, and household help. We had identified several relatively safe routes for our early morning runs and bike rides. We had found a group of people who shared our interest in the mountains. Our life had been comfortable despite power outages, air pollution, and the need to boil and filter our water.

Assessing what I had accomplished was not simple. I felt my work supporting Afghan organizations and individuals would contribute in a small way to the reconstruction of the country. The grants for professionals to meet with their colleagues in other Asian countries had expanded their horizons and increased their awareness of possibilities for a peaceful Afghanistan. Dozens of Afghan women refugees had acquired basic literacy and numeracy through classes and 50 young women had begun their post-secondary education at the Afghan women's university. Handicapped Afghans gained self-confidence and respect as their skills expanded. A small program like The Asia Foundation's could only benefit a few of the three million refugees. Those who participated in programs we funded could lead the way for others, I hoped. Of course, I could not anticipate that Afghanistan would be plunged into another two decades of war after 2001.

Gene's accomplishments were easier to quantify. He knew exactly how many district irrigation offices had installed new monitoring and record keeping systems and received training in using them. He had inspected all the equipment used to maintain the canal system and he had personally inspected most of the channels. The project was about two thirds completed. He returned in 1994 to take up a similar project in the Punjab, with funding from the World Bank rather than USAID.

In October the movers come to pack up all the rugs, embroideries, copper and brass, and stone carvings that Gene had bought. We managed to fill a "lift van" a plywood box that would half fill a shipping container. I had hoped to take Gene on an extended trip home through the "Stans" of Central Asia, but The Asia Foundation wanted me to return by November to become the Director of a new Environmental Fellowship Program.

A trek in Ladakh, India fit into our journey home. One of our Peshawar friends, Pippa, and another from California, Val, joined us in New Delhi October 10. We flew from there to Leh, the capitol of Ladakh. Ladakh is the northernmost area of India, geographically part of the Tibetan plateau. Leh is over 11,000 ft altitude. The culture is Tibetan Buddhist, evident in the beautiful temples and the faces of the inhabitants. We went to a hotel owned by a Tibetan friend of my colleague Carla. He assured us he could find a capable guide and donkey team for us while we visited the city. The monasteries and temples in Ladakh were beautiful. The bright colored images of birds and plants and dragons glowed in the sun. The temples are in stark contrast to the arid countryside. We set off the next day with two men and four donkeys, to trek through this starkly beautiful country. On the second day we walked over Stok La, a 15,300 ft pass then descended to camp near a tiny village. Every second day that we trekked, we went over a pass that was higher than any point in the Rockies or the Sierra. The rocks were shades of red and yellow; there were no trees; the shrubs were bare in the fall. In the villages, people were harvesting wheat and barley, winnowing the grain with yaks walking in a circle. They were friendly but obviously very poor with nothing to share with passing trekkers. Our final camp was near a village. We put some plastic bags outside our tent. The donkey men said we should put them inside so people would not steal them. We told him it was just trash we intended to take back to Leh for disposal. He threw the bags in the river. I was shocked but realized if we had carried it back to Leh the bags would probably have been thrown in the river there, as well.

At the end of the trek, we returned to Leh. Pippa flew back to her job in Pakistan. Gene, Val, and I planned to leave by road to see more of this extreme north of India, though the road was supposed to close for the winter in the next few days. While Val and I shopped and bathed, Gene went to the taxi area to select a sturdy car to hire. He kicked tires, looked at engines, and spoke with drivers before choosing a taxi. In the morning we jumped in a jeep and were on our way to cross the world's highest paved road (made by the Indian military to ward off Chinese invasion). At its highest the road is 17,580 ft above sea level. Unfortunately, Gene had neglected to inspect a critical feature of the car: the heater. There was none. Luckily, we had our down sleeping bags and jackets. We huddled in those, dressed for arctic temperatures until we descended to Manali, a popular vacation spot. It was in a wooded valley, famous for apples and pears. Here we visited Hindu temples and enjoyed a soak in hot springs.

We continued by road to Chandigarh, the city designed by the French architect, Le Corbusier, to be the capital of Punjab and Haryana states. The cast concrete buildings and parks of the municipal center were elegant, but the surrounding city was a typical chaotic jumble of building styles; then by train to Delhi and an evening flight to Geneva. Gene and I had to have the requisite "decompression" visit to Chamonix for three days before returning to America, but we arrived home in time to vote for Clinton! We were so excited that there might be a president really committed to environmental protection, access to health care for all, and justice.

Chapter 28 New Career Directions

In November 1992, after working in Pakistan as Director of the Afghan program for almost three years, I became Director of the U.S.-Asia Environmental Fellowship Program (USAEP) at The Asia Foundation. I had a lovely corner office, two Program Officers and a Secretary for assistance. It was a three-year contract to arrange observation tours in the U.S. for Asian industrialists and environmental activists and for Americans to go to appropriate sites in Asia to observe and advise people working in their specific industries or fields. The program emphasis was on industry and commerce. One of our first Fellows, for example, was the vice president of a cement company in India, identified by USAID in New Delhi. We arranged for him to visit several leading cement firms in America, and some chemical experts who were developing manufacturing methods that minimized air and water pollution. In exchange, we sent an American cement company executive to India where he discovered some of the factories were more effectively reducing pollution than those in the U.S.

Each Fellowship itinerary had to be submitted for approval from the USAEP hierarchy in Washington and the Asian country USAID office. The Asia Foundation's network of offices in Asia were essential to the implementation of this program. I had to travel to Asia two or three times a year. Since the Foundation did not have an office in India at that time, it was particularly important that I visit India to confer with the USAID officials and environmental experts there. I enjoyed the opportunity to travel to Delhi, Bombay, and Calcutta. The industries involved ranged from wool and carpet dying in Nepal, to tofu processing in Indonesia, livestock management in Mongolia, and medical waste disposal in Bangladesh. The Thailand hotel industry took the lead for tourism by creating a certification program for "green hotels" which minimized water and power use and utilized local sources for food and decoration. In three years, we created programs for over a hundred individuals. We established an advisory board of Asians and Americans, businessmen and scientists. I enjoyed putting to use my experience and familiarity with different Asian countries and my life-long concern about the deteriorating environment.

Gene continued to work with DAI at their Sacramento office and overseas. He returned to Pakistan, Nepal, and west Africa for a few weeks each year. He limited those absences to four weeks at a time..

Our busy careers and travel schedules did not stop our running or mountain adventures, required for our mental and physical health. In the winter of 1993, Gene and two friends did a long ski tour in Canada, from hut to hut on the Columbia ice field. This inspired him to return to Canada annually to ski at different remote huts. I found these trips very enjoyable. With 10 or 12 friends we could fill a hut, plan our meals, and take turns with the cooking and dish washing. The greatest expense was helicopter transport to the hut. In contrast to the huts of the Sierra Club in California, the Canadian huts were more like European refuges. They had bedding, saunas, showers, hot water, and fully equipped kitchens. Some had composting toilets, some had outhouses. Each day we would put climbing skins on our skis and explore the hills around the hut for untracked powder snow to perfect our turns. We did Canada ski trips every year until 2007.

In the summer of 1993 Gene and I and son Greg went to the Tetons to climb and bike. After those years in Pakistan paying little federal income tax, we had put away some savings. We decided to invest in property near the Tetons, so we would no longer be camping or staying on our friends' couches. The prices in Jackson, Wyoming, were out of our budget, but on the Idaho side of the range we found a small house in the final stages of construction. It had a view of the Grand Teton, almost three acres of land and a double garage which is a necessity in the harsh winters. We paid $112,000. This turned out to be an excellent investment. Our immediate family used it both in winter for skiing and in summer for hiking, biking, and climbing. After I retired in 2000, Gene and I spent two months in the winter and two in the summer, every year, returning to California in the mud seasons.

The Environmental Fellowship Program ended in 1995, so I took responsibility for the Henry Luce Scholars Program at the Foundation. Every year, through a competitive process, 18 to 20 scholars, college graduates under 30 years old, were selected to spend a year in Asia working in their respective fields. I was familiar with the program from my time in Jakarta when I would arrange and supervise placements for two or three Luce scholars each year. Among them were two artists in Bali, a medical student in South Sulawesi, a geologist in north Sulawesi, a law student clerking at the Supreme Court and an economist working with market women's cooperatives.

Placements for Journalists was easy because the editor of the *Far Eastern Economic Review* welcomed a Luce Scholar every year. FEER in Hong Kong was the Asian equivalent of the <u>*Economist*</u> magazine. Most of those Scholars went on to distinguished journalistic careers. It was more difficult to arrange successful experiences for business and technical graduates because these young people thought themselves experts, while in many Asian organizations, age and experience tend to be valued over fresh educational accomplishment. I remember one of the most respected and effective of our fellow Peace Corps Volunteers in Pakistan in the 1960s was Ralph Cole, a 70-year-old agricultural engineer from Texas. He did not rush around on field trips, but devoted hours to discussions with farmers and Agriculture Department staff.

An exciting aspect of the Luce Scholars program was participating in the end-of-year gathering of the Scholars.

Immediately after taking on the job, I travelled to Korea for such a meeting. Henry Luce Jr. attended. The Ambassador hosted us since he was a friend of the Luce family. We visited important historical sites and cultural events. Each scholar presented a report on his or her year in Asia, usually accompanied with slides, photographs, costumes or music. In subsequent years the meetings were held in Mongolia, Central Asia, Bali, and Japan. I brought Gene along to the meetings in Mongolia and Central Asia.

The Mongolia meeting began with two days of sightseeing in Beijing. In addition to the palaces and Tiananmen square, the Scholars wanted to visit Silk Alley. This is a warren of tiny shops behind the high-rise hotels. There one can find discounted manufactured goods from the factories. The salespeople insist they have tiny flaws so cannot be sold retail; they may be illegal copies. Every Scholar walked back to the hotel with a "genuine" North Face or Patagonia jacket, while I was content with a small backpack.

A short flight took us to Ulan Bator, the capital of Mongolia. A nephew of Henry Luce was the Asia Foundation Representative. He designed a very enjoyable week for us, including observing the annual Naadam festival of cross-country horse racing, wrestling matches, and archery. After the Scholars departed, Gene and I took an antique Russian helicopter west to a monastery called Karakorum. During 70 years of Russian rule, the

Mongolians had hidden religious statues, relics, and embroideries in their homes. Now independent, they were restoring the Buddhist temples and monasteries with enthusiasm. Young men and women were studying to be religious scholars. The Dalai Lama visited annually to support the revival of Buddhism.

Rather than fly back to Beijing, Gene and I took the Trans-Siberian railroad. We bought first class tickets which gave us a sleeping compartment with tiny shower-sink behind a curved door in a corner. Like older European trains, this had a corridor along one side and compartments lined up along the other side. Shortly after boarding, we were approached by two dusty young men who had been on the train for ten days, since Moscow. They asked if they could use our shower; we took sympathy on them and allowed it. The journey began in the afternoon, traversing the golden dunes of the Gobi Desert for hours. After dinner in the dining car, we crawled into our bunks, only to be awakened at midnight when the train crossed the Chinese border. The track gauge is different in China, so the wheels on each car were changed, with a great deal of noise. Some passengers went outside to observe the process, but we were too sleepy. The dining car and food service changed from Mongolian to Chinese also. At dawn, we stopped at the Great Wall for an hour so that passengers could get out and visit the wall. By noon we arrived in bustling Beijing, a day before returning to California.

The Luce Scholar wrap-up meeting in Central Asia in 1998 was an opportunity for me to observe the changes in Kazakhstan, Kyrgyzstan, and Uzbekistan since my visit in 1991. Entrepreneurship had replaced the socialist economy. Small shops appeared everywhere, even in the student cells of the ancient madrassahs (religious schools) and the open markets were bustling. People were selling everything from coca cola to antique rugs and embroideries. Enterprising blond women from Russia were plying their trade on the side streets.

Gene and I planned to trek in the Pamir mountains of Kyrgyzstan after the meeting. Four of the Scholars joined us. We hired a guide-facilitator and a small van. The convoluted borders of these countries required us to cross several international entry and exit posts. At each, our guide told us to stay in the vehicle while he took our passports in his black briefcase to the checkpoint. When border officials looked at us, we explained, "these are our children." This was hard to comprehend since our little group included one Chinese American woman, one tall black woman, one woman with curly black hair and a tall young man. Only the young man resembled Gene and me.

The ten-day trek was fun but had its challenges. The limited choices of food and utensils in the market in Tashkent forced us to innovate. There weren't many crackers or suitable bread, so we bought whole wheat flour to make chapatis. We could buy frying pans but not large pots, so had to borrow those of our donkey men. The Scholars thought we "old folks" (60 and 64 years old) would be slow hikers, but from the first day Gene and I were far ahead of them. They would arrive huffing and puffing as we relaxed by the trail. We camped in two wildflower strewn valleys and all climbed three different passes over 15,000 ft. Gene and I with one of the donkey drivers reached a summit 2,000 ft higher. The granite spires above us resembled Yosemite. The shepherds were friendly and there was only one day of rain. Two years later, in 2000, three American climbers were kidnapped in this area by rebels. To escape, they pushed one of their captors over a cliff. That saga was portrayed in a popular film.

During the five years that I managed the program most of the Scholars had rewarding experiences. Though we revised some of their assignments, I never had to move a Scholar to another country. Three times a year I had to visit multiple Asian cities. Often, I could combine this travel with my other responsibilities. For instance, while visiting Scholars in Thailand, I went to Laos to initiate re-opening an office for the Foundation. My Thai colleague and I filled our suitcases with the most attractive books from the Bangkok office and flew to Vientiane, the capital of Laos. It was a small quiet city with few paved roads. The bridge from Thailand had not yet been opened, so there was little motorized traffic. The National Librarian remembered the Asia Foundation from its previous presence in the country and welcomed us, as did the Director of the National Museum. They both spoke French. We took some books to Dong Dok teachers' college, the only post-secondary institution in the country. It has now expanded to be the National University. Programs concerned with the environment in all countries where the Foundation had a presence were also my responsibility.

In January 1999, we made our final south of the border trip, to Patagonia. Encouraged by the Chilean parents of a friend, we hiked in the Torres del Paine Park of Chile and Los Glacieres National Park of Argentina. In this, the popular summer season, all the refuges were booked. We were permitted to put our little tent near each refuge and use the indoor facilities to escape the fierce winds, buy beer, and take showers. We did not have the skills to climb the steep towers, but we enjoyed seeing them and thinking of our friends who had reached those summits.

In 2000, I was getting tired of the international travel. While most of the Luce Scholars were intelligent, hardworking young people, some were obviously privileged and self-centered. My enthusiasm for the program was waning. Gene wanted to have more time to spend at our house in the Tetons. My first grandchild was born in 1998; that was another distraction from work. I decided to retire January 2000, after more than two decades with The Asia Foundation.

Chapter 29   Consultant on Human Trafficking in South Asia

After retirement, many people become consultants, performing almost the same tasks as prior to retiring but responsible for their own health insurance, retirement savings, and other benefits. In August 2000 I was given a consultant contract to gather information on current efforts to combat trafficking in South Asia. The purpose was to develop a strategy for The Asia Foundation. The issue had been included in a new UN convention against Transnational Organized Crime and the U.S. government had announced increased concern by including anti-trafficking in its foreign policy human rights objectives. Hilary Clinton and Madeleine Albright had made trafficking a focus of their recent visits to the Indian subcontinent. My assignment would include travel to Pakistan, Nepal, Bangladesh, and India to confer with Asia Foundation staff, diplomatic and international aid personnel and meet local activists addressing the problem. My journey started in Islamabad, Pakistan, familiar territory for me due to my many years of living and working in the country. My most recent visit to Pakistan had been in 1995 when Gene was working in Lahore. In both Islamabad and Lahore, I managed to meet old friends in the evenings after my busy days of meetings and field visits with women activists and lawyers working to investigate and stop trafficking. The Foundation Country

Representative was my old friend Andy, who had been responsible for hiring me in 1979.

In Pakistan, government concern was directed towards prostitution not trafficking per se. In fact, in Pakistan there is considerable internal trafficking for forced labor (male and female), beggary and debt servitude as well as prostitution. In Lahore there is a traditional "entertainment" area in Anarkali Bazaar, where there are 1,800 registered dancer/singers, each of whom can have six students. A survey by a Canadian aid organization found that two thirds of the young women were HIV positive. The Women Lawyer's Association, War Against Rape (WAR) and a few smaller NGO's were planning methods of rescue and repatriation of trafficked young women, who were usually from India or Bangladesh. Dealing with trafficking in Pakistan is complicated by the Hadood (strict Islamic) laws which make adultery or any sex outside marriage a crime. When police raid a brothel, the women and girls working there are arrested as criminals to be punished, not victims to be assisted or repatriated. If convicted, a woman would be subject to life imprisonment, lashes or death. (If she were returned to her family, her brother or father would probably kill her to protect the family honor.) There are hundreds of women languishing in Pakistani jails after being accused of adultery or fornication (some are victims of rape.) Many of them are young women who were brought to the country and sold to brothel owners by traffickers. None of my informants in Pakistan knew of a pimp or trafficker who had been arrested. Some Pakistani activists proposed a regional film festival to raise public awareness of the issue of trafficking. The films would be translated into local languages and rebroadcast in all the South Asian countries.

Nepal was also familiar territory for me, after our many mountain adventures and my previous work with the Foundation. In Nepal the government and the nonprofit sector recognize that trafficking of Nepali woman and girls to India is a serious problem. Thousands of Nepali girls are trafficked annually. Poverty and lack of education are the underlying causes. There are few opportunities for young women to earn a decent wage in Nepal. Young men migrate or commute to India for higher pay. Traffickers tempt young women to cross the border; some poor parents are pleased to have one less person to feed at home. Once in India the promised factory or restaurant job turns into virtual slavery in a brothel. There are several active NGOs in Nepal working to reduce trafficking, by providing schools and homes for abandoned and vulnerable children. Others focus on repatriated women who need housing and vocational training as they would not be accepted by their families or their villages when they return. There is also a significant amount of domestic trafficking from poor rural areas to cities.

In India I met with representatives of the U.S. government, the Indian government, NGOs and the UN.

Many of the NGOs now involved in anti-trafficking became aware of the problem through anti-HIV/AIDs programs, which put them in contact with prostitutes. The Regional coordinator of the UNIFEM South Asia Anti-Trafficking Project and I had a very informative discussion. The UNIFEM focus was regional, introducing the topic of trafficking in regional meetings of lawyers, social welfare professionals, police, and border security staff. She told me that most countries in South Asia have adequate laws against trafficking, but enforcement is weak and tends to criminalize the trafficked person, not the trafficker.

In Mumbai and Calcutta, I was hosted by NGOs working in the brothel areas, providing safe hostels, food and clothing for the children of prostitutes, so they could go to school and would not become second generation sex workers. Without safe places for their children, some prostitutes drug them so they will sleep through the night while the mother plies her trade in the same room. While searching for children in the brothels, these NGO volunteers and members of prostitute organizations can identify young, recently trafficked girls. Rescuing trafficked girls was another task of voluntary groups. This was a hazardous and frequently unsuccessful effort. If girls were taken in police raids, the pimps or madams would often go to the police post and buy the girls back or claim to be a sister or uncle wanting to take her home. Most trafficked girls do not speak the language of the country or city in which they are captive, and they have no official documents. The Government of India gives a rescued Nepalese girl a train ticket to the border and five rupees a day for food. Unfamiliar with the country and not understanding the language, most of these girls do not arrive at their destination. If a Nepali or Bangladeshi girl who has been trafficked returns to her country, she is not welcomed back to her home village or neighborhood; she is shunned as soiled and a sinner.

Several NGOs in Nepal provide hostels and vocational training for repatriated young women. One of them, Maiti Nepal, had an affiliate in India, Maiti Mumbai. The two organizations communicate to assure the repatriation of rescued girls. Before and after repatriation there is a desperate need for safe residences for the rescued women. I identified differences in the objectives of anti-trafficking organizations: The goal of some is elimination of prostitution while for others it is prevention of forcible recruitment of young girls.

In Calcutta, I spent an informative day in the "red light" district, hosted by the prostitute's union. This group has some 62 branches in West Bengal providing clinics and marketing campaigns for use of condoms. In Calcutta itself, there were six neighborhood self-regulatory boards employing male doctors, lawyers, and accountants, as well as ex-prostitutes for clerical staff. They monitor brothels for the recruitment of girls under 18 and interview newcomers to determine if they are willingly entering the trade. These boards respond to requests from Nepal or Bangladesh to watch for specific groups of trafficking victims. However, communication across borders is often not timely or effective.

One of the goals of the prostitute's union was to have the Labor Commission recognize sex workers as service workers. Then they could advocate for fewer police raids, prevention of child prostitution, diminish the power of pimps, and have access to health care and retirement benefits. In the meantime, the organization was using the dues of its members to support clinics and other services. They had a savings plan for retirement and hoped to create a home for retired prostitutes. This group could not attract funding from donors who wanted to eliminate prostitution but had received funding for combatting AIDS. The leaders insisted that their members were the most likely people to recognize young women and girls who were being trafficked and brought to the brothels. They would be able to protect the trafficking victim and help return her to her home before she became a prostitute. Since the very young innocent trafficked girls are most desirable to customers, it would be in the prostitute's interest to reduce competition from them. However young girls are most profitable for madams and pimps.

In Bangladesh, one NGO had an interesting program: Radio announcements in train and bus stations, saying, "If you are traveling with someone you do not know or traveling against your will, go to the newspaper stand in the station and ask for the hotline of anti-trafficking." The creators of this scheme had contacted newspaper vendors to seek their cooperation. They were compensated for the cost of telephone service.

The Bangladesh Women Lawyers association was one of the first organizations to recognize trafficking and to provide hostels and training for repatriated victims, some of whom are boys who were taken to Arab countries to be camel jockeys. Throughout the region, I found officials, both national and international, focused on regulations, training of police and border personnel, raising awareness, and research. Foundations and non-governmental and voluntary groups were focused on the individual victims of trafficking and practical measures for prevention.

I submitted a report to The Asia Foundation in San Francisco and met with several staff for a debriefing. My conclusions were that trafficking was a huge and under-reported problem. The root cause is poverty and lack of employment, which is in turn related to lack of educational opportunity. More research is needed to determine patterns of trafficking within and between countries. Interventions could then be targeted effectively. Appropriate roles for the Foundation would be to support the most effective local organizations providing services to the victims of trafficking and supporting awareness campaigns. In the following years, the Foundation has supported and initiated many projects addressing the problem.

Chapter 30   Mountaineering Consultant

In the 1980's I served on the Board and as Secretary of the American Alpine Club. In 1995 I joined the committee for nominating honorary members. In the early 1900's, honorary membership was awarded to foreign mountaineers. In more recent years it had been awarded to outstanding American climbers some of whom might support the club financially. I urged my fellow committee members to renew the old tradition of international awards and recognition of contributions to mountain literature and history. I was pleased to put forward and have accepted honorary memberships for Nazir Sabir, a leading climber from Pakistan and Harish Kapadia Editor of the Himalayan Journal, an Indian. They attended our annual meeting.

In 1998 my friends in the American Alpine Club asked me to represent the club on the Expeditions Committee of the Union International des Associations Alpinists, the UIAA. This was quite an honor. I would attend biannual gatherings of delegates from mountaineering clubs around the world. We discussed issues related to expeditionary mountaineering: permits, fees, approval procedures, rescues, requirements for insurance, liaison officers, environmental protection, and safety. Because my job at the Foundation required frequent travel, I was able to attend meetings in Ireland, Nepal, and Rome without incurring travel costs. I arranged for the American Alpine Club to host a meeting in 2005 at the Climbers' Ranch in Grand Teton National Park.

Gene enjoyed coming along to the meetings in India and Rome and happy to entertain the wives of the other delegates while I was at the meetings.

In late April 2001 Gene and I went to India so I could attend the UIAA expeditions committee meeting. After the 20-hour flight we collapsed in the hostel of the Indian Mountaineering Federation (IMF) in New Delhi. During the night the electricity failed, so without air-conditioning or fans, we were at the mercy of a swarm of mosquitos. In the morning we went out for a run and bought milky tea from a tea-*wallah* squatting on the sidewalk. I felt we were home again, back in the Indian subcontinent where we had spent so many years. It was hot and dusty, there were cows wandering the streets, boys in school uniforms, rickshaws, taxis, blaring horns, Mosques and Hindu temples visible through the smog. Fuchsia bougainvillea vines contrasted sharply with whitewashed walls. We met the other delegates at the IMF headquarters and toured the facility. The library fascinated Gene because he saw books he did not have in his collection. I was amused when reading the official IMF equipment list for expeditions included "Turban cover, for those who wear a turban." You probably could not purchase that item at REI! Outside the office, there was an impressive climbing wall for rock climbers, but no one was using it; like so many things in India, it lacked maintenance and was unsafe.

Colonel Vohra, President of the IMF hosted us for dinner at the Indian International Center where the delegates to the meeting and their wives were joined by various Indian mountaineers and their wives. I was the only woman delegate. Colonel Narindar Kumar (known as "Bull" Kumar, the leader of the successful Indian Kangchenjunga expedition and Hero of Siachen Glacier battles) was hosting the meeting. Kumar presented our itinerary: Train to Mussoori (a hill station) in the morning, then on to a camp on the banks of the Ganges. There was typical chaos at the train station with turbaned luggage carriers snatching our backpacks and us ignorant of which car or seat we would be assigned. Five minutes before the scheduled train departure, Colonel Kumar, appeared with our tickets in his hand. The train was quite comfortable. Moosoori is an attractive hill station at 6,000 ft altitude, a pleasantly cool contrast to Delhi. We checked in to a good hotel. The delegates and I met all day, with me taking notes in my role as Secretary.

Meanwhile, Gene went sightseeing and shopping with the Austrian, French, Italian, Swiss, British, and Czech wives. At the festive dinner, the current Chairman from Ireland and the English delegate suggested I could be the chair of the committee except for the travel requirements. (The Chair must travel to the participating countries in between the biennial meetings.) Instead, I would continue to be Secretary. Having completed our meeting, the recreational aspect of the gathering started.

First, we visited George Everest's house. He was the Surveyor General of India who first saw and triangulated the mountain that bears his name. In retirement, he was given a modest house where he could see the snowy Indian Himalaya. Our bus continued to the banks of the Ganges River where six rafts waited to take us across the river to a luxury camp established by Colonel Kumar's trekking and travel company. There were comfortable cots in 20 double tents, toilet tents, hot showers and a large social area shaded by a parachute. We had a big dinner and a long campfire party. Bagpipers in full Scottish dress marched through camp in the morning to wake us. We drove 15 miles upriver and then rafted down the sacred Ganges, outfitted with helmets and life vests. In the calmer sections of the river, some of us jumped out of the rafts and floated along. It was a strange and wonderful experience.

Colonel Kumar asked Gene and me about our plans. We said we wanted to trek in this region, the Garwhal, and had brought our camping equipment. We planned to hire a taxi to a trailhead and hire porters in the nearest village. Sensing an opportunity, Kumar asked us how much we could spend; we were a little vague, but then he conferred with his assistant and said his company could arrange a 21-day trek for $50 a day, including road transport, porters, tents, and food. Our friend Pippa, who was working in Pakistan would join us for the first ten days and then a travel agent from England, Nancy, would join us for a week. She was evaluating the trek for clients. We would visit two of the sources of the Ganges and then hike to a point where we could see Nanda Devi, the highest peak in India. We decided it was a good offer and agreed.

Pippa met us in Rishikesh, a holy city, on the Ganges, where we visited temples and ghats. People were placing little rafts of leaves and candles in the river as offerings. I bought one to float in honor of my sister Abby who had died earlier that year. This whole region, the Garhwal, is considered sacred, so alcohol and meat are forbidden. We took a taxi five miles to the southern border of the province where butcher shops and liquor stores line the highway. We bought a bottle of whisky for our trek and beer to drink on our last evening at the hotel. Kumar's trek included tents and stoves, so the next morning, we left our backpacking tent and stove at his Mercury Travel company office and jumped into a jeep for our adventure. We camped near the Ganges River the next two nights then started trekking from Gangotri to *Gaumukh* (cow's mouth) spot where the Bhagirathi River emerges from a glacier. It is one of the main sources of the Ganges. Naked fakirs and dusty pilgrims were filling bottles with the holy water to take home as well as drinking it and splashing it over themselves. A few bedraggled western hippies were in the crowd too. Due to climate change, the glacier has retreated more than a kilometer in 50 years. The trek has become more dangerous. In 2013, the road to

Gangotri and the trail to Gaumukh were severely damaged by massive landslides.

Gene and Pippa and I were happy to proceed past the pilgrimage area to the meadows above where mountaineers were camped. The rocky spire of Shivling peak towered over our next camp, with other snow-covered peaks around. Three European expedition camps were in the meadow. The three Indian Liaison Officers in matching down jackets were "hanging out" while the climbing teams tackled Shivling and Kedar Dome. It was cool there at 15,000 ft and it snowed one night, but Kumar's large tents had foam mats on the floor. The added insulation made us very comfortable in sleeping bags. We were traveling in style. Mercury Travel provided folding chairs and a small table where we sipped whiskey while admiring the sunset. We ate our excellent vegetarian dinners in the large cook tent. Alas, somewhere between the banquets in Delhi and floating in the Ganges with my mouth open, I had picked up a nasty intestinal infection. I applied our traditional kit of remedies, beginning with Pepto Bismal, then Imodium, then fasigyn, flagyl, and the final step, Cipro, but still had several days of desperate dashes to the toilet tent which the staff put up at each camp.

We were living the "pukka sahib" life. ("pukka" means First Class). One problem with such service is the British tradition of "Bed Tea". The polite porter taps on the tent door early in the morning, saying, "Bed tea, Sahib." The problem is, Memsahib (me) desperately needs to pee. But the steaming tea is so appealing. A real dilemma, only solved by having a handy pee container inside the tent. After bed tea, the porters bring a basin of warm water for washing.

What luxury! For a few days we hiked around this gorgeous area to different climbers' basecamps. Then we headed down the valley. A reliable car (as promised by Kumar) met us to take us to the next trailhead bringing Nancy, the young woman from England. After a farewell dinner, Pippa departed in the car to return to her job in Pakistan.

We set off in the morning to trek over a high ridge to the next valley, Kedernath, where there was another tributary of the Ganges. By the time we reached that valley four days later, pilgrim season was in full swing. Rich, overweight, or ill pilgrims were being carried on palanquins by porters, others rode horses or donkeys, others were on foot. For a full day we struggled up this stone path slippery with animal dung and rain. Finally, we reached the temples and holy meadow below Kedernath peak. After a day we had enough of the pilgrim experience and walked down the trail to the paved road where another good car was waiting for us. Nancy returned to New Delhi, while Gene and I continued for the final week of our trek above one of India's few ski areas to high meadows where we had views of dramatic Nanda Devi peak, the highest point in India. Towards the end of this trip, my stomach recovered, but I had a persistent cough and runny nose. The only souvenir I bought in Delhi was a package of 20 large cotton handkerchiefs.

When I got back to Berkeley it was diagnosed as pneumonia. Antibiotics cleared it up. Gene was also ill when we returned. He had fever and dehydration, and diarrhea. The hospital isolated him in case he had brought some rare disease back from India. Three days of observation and multiple tests did not result in a specific diagnosis, but he did recover.

In 2002, my former colleagues asked me to participate in a workshop on Afghanistan. The Foundation was expecting to reestablish an office and active program in the country, after closing the Kabul office in 1980 and the Peshawar office in 1992. I was happy to join in this discussion which included several staff who had worked in Afghanistan prior to 1980, a former Ambassador to Afghanistan who was a Trustee of the Foundation, and several Afghan scholars. We shared optimism for the future of Afghanistan at that time, but all recognized the ethnic divisions and bitter conflicts of the past decades would make reconstruction of a viable political system and economy extremely difficult. As we now know, peace has yet to come to Afghanistan. A few of the institutions supported by the Foundation have endured.

Chapter 31   Grandchildren

Our first grandchild, Eric's daughter Violet, was born in 1998, in Los Angeles. She was a delightful child. Despite work and other commitments, I managed to see her every month for the first six months of her life, and several times a year after that. By the time she was eight, she could fly as an "unaccompanied minor" from Burbank to Oakland to visit us. In May 2002 we welcomed two more grandchildren. Greg and his wife had a boy, Cosmo, and Laura had a daughter, Athena. Gene and I were delighted to have them living in Berkeley so we could see them frequently. For two years, Laura and Athena lived near our house in Teton Valley, so we had a young grandchild wherever we were. In 2006 Greg and his wife had another boy, Chase. Participating in the lives of the younger generation has been delightful. I have escorted them home from preschool, elementary school, and middle school. I have met their friends and friends' families. I am pleasantly surprised when a stranger on the sidewalk gives me a look and then says, "Oh, you are Cosmo's grandmother!" Each grandchild started skiing when three years old and riding a bike at four or five. They love camping and hiking. They are all good students in school, college, and graduate school. My enjoyment of activities with grandchildren confirmed to me the wisdom of retiring at the relatively young age of 62.

In 2005, Gene and I were visiting friends in the south of France when I received a call from an official at UNIFEM (the UN agency concerned with women). She asked if I would consider a position in Kabul as advisor to the Ministry of Women's Affairs of the Government of Afghanistan for two years. I would be paid a generous salary with housing and travel allowances. I considered this offer, looking out a window at fields of lavender in Provence. I knew that the Ministry of Women's Affairs was fraught with problems. The Minister was Dr. Sima Samar whom I knew and admired. Due to her being of the Hazara minority, she was resented by other members of the government. Conservatives objected to the existence of a Ministry for Women. My salary would be sufficient to pay the annual salary of 100 teachers in girls' schools. I believe that would have done more for the status of women than my presence. Adding to that, Gene was fighting leukemia, and my mother was, at age 92, suffering congestive heart failure; plus, I had young grandchildren to enjoy. I decided that job was not for me and declined the offer. Twenty years earlier, I would have jumped at the opportunity. The Taliban have now replaced the Ministry of Women's Affairs with a Ministry for the Propagation of Virtue and the prevention of Vice.

We decided that our future travel would focus on Europe, after our 2001 experiences in India and the illnesses that followed. We had been traveling to Asia since 1962; maybe 40 years was enough. Through most of our working years, we were often apart for several weeks at a time. After I retired, we were together all the time and enjoyed every minute.

In May 2003, we joined a jolly group for a float down the Grand Canyon in three rafts and a dory. The boatmen were guides who had made many runs down the river, but on this trip, they were acting as equal participants, not guides. Gene worried that it would be "boring sitting in a raft for 18 days." It was not boring! The scenery was breathtaking, our camp sites allowed for exploration of side canyons for scenic views and petroglyphs. We stayed an extra day at three sites where the hiking opportunities were best. There were jokes and songs around the campfires, marijuana, and swimming - clothing optional- where the water was calm.

In the fall, I was expected to serve again as secretary and delegate for America at the UIAA Expeditions Commission meeting in Rome. Gene and I invited a couple from Jackson, Wyoming to join us for some hiking in the Dolomites in northern Italy before the meeting. We flew to Venice, rented a car, and drove to Cortina d'Ampezzo, where we had skied in 1961. From there we hiked to refuges where we could see iconic mountains such as the Tre Cime de Lavaredo, the snowy Marmolada, and spectacular rocky spires. We reached high points for views of the countryside and walked on rock-paved trails that had been used by opposing armies in the world wars. My father had served in North Africa and Italy in World War II. I wondered if he walked these trails.

After the hiking and two days in Venice, we bid our friends goodbye and took the train to Rome. As in India, two years before, Gene took responsibility for entertaining the wives of the other delegates while I took notes in the official meeting. The Italian Alpine club hosted dinners for us all. Gene and I then took a train to southern France to visit California friends who had a house in Provence. All this seemed more civilized, and the food and wine superior, compared with our experience at the holy sites in India.

In Provence we hiked in the Gorges du Verdun, the Grand Canyon of France. Instead of the glowing reds and yellows of the Grand Canyon, the Gorges du Verdun is limestone, white, grey, and blue. It is an impressive canyon. Many famous rock climbers have honed their skills on its near-vertical walls. While in France, I picked up a copy of the magazine "La Montagne." After skimming the articles about rock climbs and Himalayan adventures, I read an article about hiking hut to hut in one of the French National Parks, the Mercantour, at the southern end of the Alps. We vowed to return to explore the national parks of France.

Our retirement years followed a pattern: Winter months skiing in the Tetons, staying in our house in Victor, Idaho, with a week in Canada at a remote ski lodge. In spring and fall (mud seasons in the Tetons), we would be in California or traveling, and in summer, a month or two of hiking, biking, and climbing in the Tetons. Of course, we enjoyed the company of our children and grandchildren both in California and in the Tetons.

The Grand Teton Music Festival held open rehearsals at 10 a.m. on Fridays in the summer. We and a few other fanatics met at the base of the Jackson ski area around 6:30 a.m. on Fridays, ran 4,000 feet to the summit, caught the first arial tram down at 9:00, had a quick breakfast, and went to the symphony rehearsal. By 1 p.m. we had completed our athletic and cultural goals for the day and could relax. Every summer there was a running race up the same ski area. We entered it and always came away with prizes for our age categories. The race managers were old friends of ours, and we lobbied for categories such as "women over sixty" so we could compete for the prizes of clothing and shoes from sponsoring manufacturers.

Chapter 32   Illness And Death

As we enjoyed the days with friends in the beautiful country of the Dolomites and Provence, Gene complained of an irritating rash on his back. He showed it to a Pharmacist in Nice who declared it was "zona" or shingles. He was given an ointment. A few days later in Paris, Gene consulted a doctor who told him it was too late for drugs to be very effective, but he gave him a prescription anyway. Home in the USA his back continued to be inflamed. He lost weight and sleep. When we returned to our house in the Tetons for the ski season, he went to the local clinic. A blood test showed worrying results; he was advised to go to Jackson, Wyoming for a more elaborate test. On January 3, 2004, the oncologist in Jackson gave Gene the diagnosis of chronic lymphocytic leukemia.

When we returned to Berkeley in the spring, he began chemotherapy. When the treatment week of infusions was over, we asked the doctor if the disease was cured. He said "no, it is chronic, never cured." Once a month Gene would have an infusion. By August, he felt sufficiently strong to hike 12 miles into a remote area of the Wind River mountains in Wyoming (with horses carrying food and gear). With eight friends we hiked to peaks and passes for a week, including Fremont Peak, the second highest in the range. The oncologist was annoyed Gene had not followed his advice to refrain from strenuous activity and straying out of range of telephones or hospitals. Gene, however, thought it was a great trip in a beautiful area with good company.

Every six months, Gene would need more chemotherapy, each time more intense, and combining more drugs, sometimes accompanied with blood transfusions. In Berkeley, he rode his bike to the hospital for chemotherapy. I would come with the car to take him and the bike home. In the winter in the Tetons, he insisted I bring his cross-country skis so that he could ski a mile or two after chemotherapy and thereby not "miss a ski day." He skied 60 days a year until he died.

In 2005 we flew to Nice, France, met our friends from Provence and hiked from hut to hut in the Mercantour Park, crossing over to Italy for one night. On the high passes we saw fortifications from World Wars I and II. The borders in this area have been disputed for centuries between France, the Kingdom of Savoy, and Italy. The huts were large and comfortable, the food hearty, and the wine good enough for trekkers. The friendly conversations around the dinner table were carried out in French, Italian, German, and English. A special feature of the Mercantour is the Valley des Merveilles where there are 37,000 petroglyphs dating to the Bronze Age. These are very well protected; no walkers are allowed to carry trekking poles or ice axes in that area as they might damage the stone art. One evening, in a hut, we met a French foursome who spoke enthusiastically about another national park, Les Ecrins.

We hiked between two villages at the end of this trek. Just after dawn, the cafés were full of men with their dogs and guns, drinking brandy to fortify themselves for a day of hunting wild boar. As we strolled through the forests, we met three grandmothers and children carrying baskets to collect mushrooms. The combination of alcohol-fueled hunters and stooping grandmothers seemed dangerous to me. At the final village, in the setting sun, we passed a butcher shop with a table in front. On the table was a large boar half-carved, the blood dripping onto the street. I recognized some of the men from the morning café. The boar hunt had been successful, and apparently no mushroom hunters had perished.

Returning through Paris we went to the guidebook and map section of our favorite store, "Au Vieux Campeur." There we found the informative maps and a guidebook for the Ecrins park. Our ten-day hike in the Ecrins National Park in 2007 was Gene's last multiday adventure. It was a fitting conclusion to a lifetime of mountaineering and travel. We were six, Gene and I, our old friends from Chamonix, a friend from Provence, a running and hiking friend from California, a bachelor who had never been to Europe. We took the train and bus from Paris to Bourg d'Oisans to start the trek. The waiter in the hotel suggested trout, caught in the nearby river. We all ordered it. When presented with a grilled whole trout, tail curving off one side, and a shiny eye looking up, our less sophisticated friend blanched. He had no idea how to deal with it. I lifted the upper filet and grasped the tail to pull off the backbone and head. He was still too stunned to eat it, so the rest of us had added helpings.

We hiked daily enjoying the flower-strewn high altitude meadows, steep trails up and down though ski areas, charming villages in the valleys and views of the la Meige and other peaks rising to over 13,000 ft. The final few days included traversing steep shale hillsides and observing a helicopter rescue of two rock climbers, and a stay at an organic farm. At the end of the trek, Gene and I went to Nimes in southern France to see the Roman arena, city walls, and gardens. During our final days in France, the effects of leukemia became evident. Gene spent most of his time resting while I scurried around to museums and concerts with my friends. However, he managed to get to the "Au Vieux Campeur" bookstore to purchase a map and guidebook for another French national park, the Vanoise. When we returned to America, he immediately had another chemotherapy session, making him strong enough to enjoy the fall in California and some winter skiing in the Tetons. The treatments stopped being effective in the spring. On our return to California from the Tetons, we stopped to camp at our favorite desert park in Utah, Capitol Reef.

I received a call from my youngest sister telling me that our mother had died peacefully at 96. There remain many questions I never asked my mother, some more important than others: why did she and my father divorce? Someone else once told me, "Your father was not ready to settle down." That probably means he was attracted to other women. Why did she have so many children? She would have answered by asking me which of my siblings I would want to eliminate. She once referred to a woman who worked for Planned Parenthood, the mother of one of my best friends, as someone who "killed babies." That may have been her opinion, but as we children married and had fewer children, she must have realized we were using contraception. We never did have "the talk" about avoiding pregnancy. I felt it was a waste that she did not continue to practice medicine, but in her sixties, she studied special education so she could teach children with learning disabilities. She continued that work for a decade. My mother died in April 2008 when I was almost seventy years old. There were many decades when we could have learned more about each other. I moved away from home in 1956 to go to college, then returned to Colorado from 1960 to 1962, then went to Pakistan for five and a half years. In 1973, I moved to California and continued my international work.

I made a quick trip to Colorado for my mother's memorial, but Gene was too weak to come. He had no appetite and was losing weight. I knew marijuana gives users "the munchies" but Gene could not smoke. Greg made marijuana butter for him to eat. I purchased some special raviolis and served them with the butter. Gene ate only three raviolis, and I finished the rest, not wanting to waste good food. After dinner, I went to the hot tub in the back yard, but before I got to the tub, I found myself lying on the ground staring up at the stars. Realizing my position, I thought about what might be written in a police report: "Caregiver of terminally ill man found drugged, naked, wrapped in a towel, in garden."

Gene's condition rapidly declined. He died on June 17th, 2008, five days after my 70th birthday. Neither of us believed the end was so near. The death of Gene, my first love and life companion, was devastating. He had been treated for leukemia for over four years, bouncing back after each round of chemotherapy until the last. I became an orphan and a widow and a septuagenarian in two months. My life was turned upside down. However, I had my children and grandchildren and many friends and relatives for support and companionship. With their help, I organized a memorial celebration in Berkeley in July and another in Colorado in September. The statements and stories voiced at these celebrations confirmed Gene's impact on so many lives. However, I will never know how many rug dealers were missing his frequent shopping sprees or how many waiters in distant countries were relieved that he would not return with his overflowing coffee-making devices.

Gene was the love of my life and my climbing partner since I was 17. We had a warm and romantic relationship and usually slept closely together naked. When he was thin and weak with leukemia, I would hold him tight and try to transfer some of my physical strength to him. He was a firm believer in sex as an important aspect of life. More than once, I heard him say of someone who was grouchy or difficult, "He (or she) just needs to get laid." He was respectful and devoted to me, but nevertheless, several times over our forty-eight-year marriage, he had romantic encounters with other women. I also strayed a few times. Our partnership was strong enough to survive brief lapses in fidelity. He was the first man I had sex with (in the back seat of his mother's Chevrolet), but not the last. We shared high and low points—geographically, professionally, and personally—until his death in 2008. Together, we moved smoothly on rock or snow. As it is for most people who climb together, we developed a very efficient system of communication and handing over gear at belay points. He had other partners for some of his most difficult climbs, such as Shiprock, the north face of the Grand Teton, and Devils Tower, but usually we climbed together.

Gene was sincerely committed to having a family, and he was a wonderful father to our children. However, he missed the birth of Eric due to working in Pakistan and the birth of Laura, having gone to climb Mount Rainier. He was a devoted grandfather; he loved to read to his grandchildren and draw silly pictures with them. He was patient and proud to help them learn to ski. It seems unfair that he did not live to see them grow and thrive. We faced danger, challenges, and sad times together, as well as sharing the joys of children, grandchildren, adventures, and world travel. In our final eight years of retirement, we were together more than during our working years, when we were often separated. Perhaps those absences made us appreciate even more the final years together. Since his death in 2008, I have not tied onto a climbing rope. I have hiked and skied with other men, but they couldn't replace him.

The first winter after his death, his brother Jim and his wife skied with me in the Tetons. We were joined by two of his best friends as well. A year after his death, in his memory, four of us who had been on the 2007 hike made the trek Gene had hoped to do: Tour of the Vanoise National Park in France. We used the map and guidebook Gene had bought in Paris in 2007. At every turn of the path, I imagined finding him beside the trail, reading a book, waiting for me to catch up. Near one of the high passes, we came upon a flat sandy area where other trekkers had made small piles of black stones. I collected two large ones supporting three smaller stones, representing our family, a small monument for Gene.

For months, I could only feel loneliness and sorrow. Eventually, I could find joy in places we knew together and when I saw our grandchildren active in the things he loved. At his death, I did not understand the saying, "May he rest in peace." Now I have the sense that he does, though peace for him is searching for a perfect turn in the powder snow of infinity. After Gene's death and my aging, the focus of my travels evolved. I no longer seek to reach the highest point in each area, though I still admire the mountains.

In 2023, our youngest grandchild, Chase, restored Gene's 1970 all-chrome Schwinn Paramount bike for 100-mile road rides. He emulates Gene's enthusiasm for mountain biking, rock climbing, and skiing. The others continue the tradition of snow sports. Athena has added surfing to her athletic pursuits. Gene would have loved to be with them and admire their accomplishments as they became teenagers and young adults.

Gene's death was an acute loss, as was the loss of my my mother and the twins. When someone dies, they are alive one minute, and the next, they are dead. There is no in-between or going back. Other kinds of loss are chronic, like the creeping sense of loss in aging. I find my physical abilities and strength diminishing. Every year, I climb hills more slowly. What happened to the strong legs and lungs that carried me through so many marathons and to the summits of mountains?

When my son Eric, the bright, cheerful first-born, artistic, and well-educated, succumbed to drug addiction, it was a chronic loss. He had drug problems in college, but he became a competitive runner and excellent rock climber. He completed a BA degree with honors and an MBA. He held positions of responsibility in his work, married, and had a lovely child. He lost everything, his wife and child, his job, and his house with the swimming pool, to wander the streets using drugs. Lost. In 2007, Gene told him, "I never want to see you again," Eric visited me in 2021; he was helpful for a few days and then returned to using drugs and being destructive. I have lost him due to his own actions.

Chapter 33   After 70 Life Continues

"At 72, you are too old to join a dating app."

After a couple of years, I was active and busy but tired of living alone. I thought it would be good to have a partner. I looked on some dating websites and posted my photos and resume. I met several men for coffee. My brother-in-law asked me, "What if one of these guys you meet wants to have sex? I replied, "That is the point."

I discovered the first five minutes could reveal whether it was worth spending half an hour with a man. Some encounters extended to lunch if I found the man interesting. After several boring coffee dates, I saw a man on "Match.com": Travis, who said he was a linguist, a spy, and a winemaker. On my profile, I listed languages I knew, including French, Pushto, Urdu, and Indonesian. He doubted that Pushto was a real language! I corrected him, noting that it was spoken by more people than all the Scandinavian languages combined. Accepting my correction, he suggested I attend the Italian class he was teaching at the Senior Center. If I liked the class and stayed to the end, we would go out for coffee. If I did not like it, I could just depart. I observed that he was an informal teacher who was careful to include students at every level in the class. Some were clearly beginners, and others were quite advanced. He called upon everyone to participate. The students, ranging in age from 60 to 90, seemed to like him. He made it pleasant for them even if they struggled to say a few words in Italian.

I picked up the textbook and read a sentence aloud when it was my turn. I stayed through the class for the after-class coffee. I discovered through long conversations we had much in common. Our daughters had been at Berkeley High together; we might have passed each other in the hall during parent back-to-school night. He had studied at the University of Geneva two years after I. His sister used to compete in the same running races as I, and we had several mutual friends. He was not a mountaineer or a skier, but he enjoyed hiking. He played piano and guitar. I knew the words to the funny old French and American folk songs he played.

In fact, I usually knew the third and fourth verses which he did not. We began enjoying each other's company more and more. In some ways our backgrounds were very different. He had lived in Europe for several years. I had lived in Europe only one year, and in Indonesia for five years and Pakistan for nine. We had both traveled in Europe and Mexico, but I had also travelled in Africa, South America and many countries of Asia and the South Pacific. I read very fast, he read more slowly and deliberately. However, we both loved traveling in general, experiencing different cultures, and tasting different foods and wines. We seemed very compatible. A partnership after age 70 is very different from one that begins in youth. Most of life's major decisions have been made, including education, children, career, and saving for retirement.

We had both met our spouses when in our teens and married young. Gene and I right after my graduation from college; we were together 48 years until his death. Travis met his wife when they both played in the Berkeley High Marching Band. They married soon after he graduated from the University of California. She died of cancer when their daughters were five and ten years old. His experience as a parent was very different from mine.

When I met Travis, his 93-year-old mother came into my life. I appreciated knowing a lively woman of my mother's generation. Travis was committed to helping his mother and caring for his brother who was declining from dementia. Travis was different from Gene in many ways. His wardrobe was limited to blue jeans and shirts. He had a couple of suits, and a tuxedo for special events, but no special clothing for athletic activities. When I convinced him to try cross country skiing, it took strong arguing to make him put aside the cotton blue jeans for long underwear and water-resistant pants. Gene enjoyed music but had no musical skills, but Travis played piano and guitar, singing songs in several languages without the help of printed music. Gene was rather fanatic about cars. He bought a series of impractical cars over the years: a tiny Alfa Romeo convertible, a Mercedes convertible, and three BMW's. I always had one practical station wagon, however. Travis was proud of having had a motorcycle with a side car when he lived in Europe, but when I met him, he was satisfied with a used Toyota. His international experience consisted of several years in Europe plus a trip to Morocco for a family wedding. In contrast, by the end of his life, Gene had worked in twelve countries and traveled to fifty.

Travis had been a wine maker and was a respected judge of wines, invited to taste and comment on various vintages. I inherited two cases of his 1984 Fretter Wines Cabernet when he died. Some of it has aged well, but some has gone bad over the years. Travis was delighted to take charge of the garden at my house when he moved in. He established two compost systems and purchased an old lawn mower to grind the kitchen waste and garden trimmings into fine, quickly composting matter. He chose the seeds and plants and the appropriate location for each. Soon we were enjoying kale, beans, peas, tomatoes, lettuce, cabbage, chard, collards, raspberries, and many herbs throughout the year. The vegetables thrived, but the blueberry bushes and the grapefruit tree he purchased did not. This was a contrast to Gene who was not interested in gardening. When I started composting, he complained, "you are so frugal you are now saving the garbage."

The first summer we were together, Travis invited me to his family cabin at Echo Lake in the Sierra. It is a very scenic area a thousand feet above Lake Tahoe, at the edge of the Desolation Wilderness area. Around each lake are a few cabins built decades ago. His grandmother had obtained a lease for the land in 1935 and built a simple cabin on the lake shore. There is no road access, so one must hike or take a boat. I packed up my expensive mountain bike and everything I wanted to take to Idaho in my car. We planned to stop at Echo Lake for a few days. I would then drive east to Idaho while Travis returned to Berkeley on the train.

The sun was setting as we reached the lake. Travis assured me he knew the path well, so I grabbed my headlamp and followed him into the darkening forest. He strode ahead, familiar with every fallen log or rock in the trail, while I struggled along, the light from my head lamp flashing against the tree limbs. We got to the cabin, a snug little refuge, and turned on the solar powered lights. Travis immediately went out with a flashlight to the dock, put on a life vest and stepped down into the family outboard. As he roared away across the lake to get our food and luggage, I thought, "what if he sinks, drowns, or just doesn't return?" He had the key to my car packed with my bike and luggage. Of course, he returned within the hour with everything. We crawled into the cozy bedroom on the porch and were lulled to sleep by the sound of a small stream running over the rocks below us. This was the first of our annual visits to the cabin. I had been to Echo lakes three times before, in the winter, skiing from the highway and across the frozen lake to a cabin belonging to other friends. In 1983 with our children, Gene and I skied to the summit of Mount Ralston, above the lake. In the '90's I had skied with two friends across the frozen lakes, and over a pass, to pitch our tent on the ice of Lake Aloha.

Travis' daughters and granddaughters lived far away; he was happy to interact with my grandchildren. They joined us at Echo Lake more than once. He instructed them to start and steer the motorboat and paddle the canoes.

In 2011 Travis and I traveled to Europe, planning to visit places familiar to us and one place in France neither of us had visited: The Limousin region of France, where I arranged the first of many home exchanges.

In Geneva, where we stayed with Travis' friends, we strolled past the apartments where we had lived and the cafes we frequented as students, many years before. At the university campus we had coffee in the student café where the Formica tables seemed unchanged. I even remembered the location of the ladies' room in the basement.

This trip ended with a week in the Val d'Aosta, on the south side of Mont Blanc, in Italy, staying in the guest house of his Italian friends. We did some hiking on trails in the foothills, with the rock and snow of the Mont Blanc range towering over us. This was the first of several very enjoyable trips we made together. We had similar approaches to luggage and hotels. We limited ourselves to small carry-on suitcases and found modest hotels when we weren't staying with friends or exchanging homes. We rented cars, when necessary, but mostly used public transportation. Trips with

Travis included some walking on trails but no summits. I was bitterly disappointed during a 2016 trip to Italy when sleet and insufficient gas prevented our driving to the highest point in the Apennines. He wasn't disappointed at all. Gene would probably have insisted on returning the following day.

In those years, I wanted to bring my grandchildren to Europe, too. In 2013, grandchild Violet and I spent three weeks in Paris, the Loire Valley, and the Chablis region of France. I found travelling with a curious, enthusiastic teenager very pleasant.

In 2015, with Travis and my son's family of four I exchanged an apartment in Paris for my house near the Tetons. Since it was a family with four children, I figured there must be beds for six in their apartment. It was a small but efficient apartment in a great neighborhood with three metro lines, parks, and a farmers' market twice a week. I found the cheapest air fares to Paris were on July 13. (Travis flew to Germany for three days before joining us in Paris.) That meant we arrived on Bastille Day, July 14. We found the apartment, took naps, then caught the Metro across town to the Eiffel tower area. There we saw the spectacular fireworks streaming up and down the tower and arching up from nearby parks and buildings. At the conclusion of the fireworks, the crowds made it impossible to enter any nearby Metro stations, so I hailed a taxi. My son got into the seat next to the driver and I did not tell him four of us (the two boys, my daughter-in-law, and I) were crowding into the back seat. The taxi could barely move through the traffic, but we were saved from the claustrophobic crowding of thousands of people walking on streets and sidewalks.

An advantage of a home exchange with a family is that there were puzzles, games, bicycles, and skateboards at the apartment. My grandsons used them with enthusiasm. I bought museum passes for the adults and children under 18 are free, so we visited many art and science museums, an aquarium, and a museum of cartoon art. One day, with my son and grandsons I went to the Picasso Museum, the Pompidou Museum, (with its popular exterior escalators) the Arc de Triomphe and concluded at the Cluny Museum. (Boys of 9 and 13 move through museums quickly). Meanwhile Travis rented a bicycle to search for a horse meat butcher. My daughter-in-law is vegetarian, I do not eat red meat, and the grandsons are timid.

The home exchange family also had a farmhouse in Normandy, near Bayeux. They loaned us their Peugeot van to drive there. So, we had a rural French experience, including Mont St. Michel, the beaches and forests and small towns of Normandy. As often occurs in France, there was a general strike. Farmers parked tractors on the highway and piled manure on the exit ramps in protest, but we were able to wind our way through the obstacles. Due to the strike, there were not many tourists at Mont St. Michel, but we had to walk an extra mile. It was low tide, so Travis walked around the island on the sand while we explored the monastery and towers.

Travis loved travel bargains. He discovered a two-week trip to China: Beijing and Shanghai, air and hotel included, for $900 each. Except for the air pollution, it was a good trip, since I had been to Beijing several times but never to Shanghai.

Another year, he found a bargain week in Paris for less than $500, including flights. In November, out of season, of course. In 2014, he found a trip to Tuscany, air, hotel, and rental car included for less than $1,000 for two. Bargain trips are always in November when the days are short and cold. The positive side of November travel is there are very few tourists.

In 2016, a friend of mine rented a beautiful villa belonging to the actress Miriam Margolis, in Montisi, Tuscany. Travis' Italian language skill was essential for communication with the caretaker. We stayed two weeks, including an excursion to Umbria for four days. We reveled in the beauty of Tuscany. Every small town has a 400 year old church, the red poppies bloom in the green fields; the roads are lined with Cyprus trees; the vineyards create stripes on the hillsides while others are dotted with old grey-green olive trees. We enjoyed our stay so much that Travis and I rented the villa in 2018 and invited friends, family, and members of his Italian class.

In 2017, I arranged a home exchange in a suburb of Barcelona. This would be my first trip to Spain and provide a chance for my granddaughter to practice her Spanish. The Catalan family came to Berkeley and to my house in Idaho. It was a hot summer in Spain, but the beach was only 20-minute walk from the apartment. The family left a car, so we could visit the surrounding countryside and the Salvador Dali Museum. Excursions into Barcelona were best made by train. Athena and I had stopped in Paris on the way to Barcelona, so we flew nonstop home from Paris to San Francisco. A few days later, Travis and I drove to my house in Idaho to observe the solar eclipse with 14 guests. My house was in the line of totality.

After the guests departed, I found hiking familiar trails in the Tetons increasingly difficult. I could not keep up with my friends. Finally, on September 1, I drove 7 miles to the Emergency Room in Driggs, Idaho. X rays and scans indicated I had pulmonary emboli: blood clots in my lungs. I stayed overnight in the hospital and was discharged the next day with an oxygen tank. I could not believe that the lungs that had carried me above 20,000 feet would fail me on a gentle trail at 8,000 feet. We canceled our reservation for Glacier National Park and drove back to Berkeley. A week later, Travis had a stroke. 2017 was our bad luck year.

I gave up biking and downhill skiing, but continued to cross country ski and hike, using an oxygen concentrator where the altitude required it. Despite being slowed down by the effects of these health crises, we invited our Swiss friends to visit the Tetons, Yellowstone, and Glacier National Parks with us in the summer of 2019. A few weeks later, we flew to Paris. After a week with other French friends in Brittany, we took the train to Geneva then on to Chamonix. When I went in the garden of our friends' chalet in the morning and saw the sun gleaming on the snowy dome of Mont Blanc and the rocky spires of the aiguilles, I felt I had returned to my home. In Chamonix, I could identify every peak and ridge by name and point out the routes I had climbed or skied over the years. (Just as I could in the Tetons.)

Our days in Chamonix were the highlight of the trip for me, though we did continue to central France and Tours, to see the house where Travis had lived 50 years earlier with his wife. When we were not traveling, Travis and I enjoyed our local activities in Berkeley: Italian class, a French conversation group, and a hiking group. He was also very involved with his German club as I with my book club, writing group and drawing groups.

The onset of COVID-19 disrupted 2020. Among my grandchildren, one college graduation, two high school graduations, and a middle school completion went uncelebrated. The Hawaii holiday I had arranged for all had to be cancelled. There were many cancellations and postponements.

Travis and I were able to obtain vaccinations in early 2021. In March, I went to my house in the Tetons to do gentle cross-country skiing. I was elated to feel capable at a sport I had loved for decades, even though the altitude made the oxygen concentrator necessary. After this happy trip, I returned to find Travis continuing to have balance problems and general weakness.

In May, a scan of his abdomen revealed multiple metastatic lesions. His declined rapidly. Not strong enough for chemo and the cancer too scattered for radiation, there was little hope for improvement. He moved to a hospital bed in his mother's house where there were no steps. His daughters came to help with his care. During this crisis I fell at home and broke my right hip. With a quickly installed titanium hip, I regained mobility and strength, but I could not lift Travis. He decided that rather than wait for the cancer to kill him, he would order the medications for a scheduled death. Then he, my companion of a decade, died. It was a sharp, unanticipated loss from which I slowly recovered. I can concentrate on the happy memories of our time together. His death has left an empty area in my life. I am grateful that after a wonderful 48-year marriage I had the joy of another companion for 10 years. I am without a partner again but have caring family and friends near me.

My life has been full of adventure and learning, joy and sadness, summits and low points, enhanced by the love and support of my family and friends. It is not over yet. I plan to continue for as long as I can enjoy the natural world and the people I love.

Gallery

1938 New York City,
sister Josie and me.

1940 Herrick house
in Sharon, CT

With Grandmother Dr. Kenyon 1945

Mother's marriage, 1945

Clockwise from left:
Peggy, me, Josie,
Mother holding
Charles, Louise, Bill,
Jean, John, Abby 1955

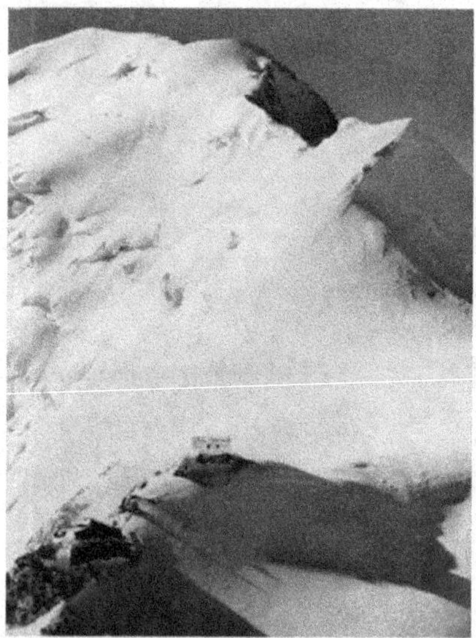

Summit ridge of Mont Blanc
with Vallot Refuge 1959

Skiing the Vallee
Blanche 1959

Mt. Kenya 1961

Peshawar roof tops 1962

On an unnamed peak
in Swat, Pakistan 1963

With Sargent Shriver,
Director of the Peace
Corps 1963

1963 in Pakistan

At Sikh temple in Amritsar
with Eric in the pack 1964

Parachinar with Babu, 1964

Grandmother with me,
Eric, sister Josie and her
daughter, Elizabeth

My father with Eric 1965

Christmas card, 1965

Climbing to a refuge
in Chamonix 1966
home leave trip

HOME LEAVE 1966: Siblings,
Mother, Stepfather, Gene,
Eric and me

Eric in the Zermatt
campground 1966

Hiking with Greg, 1968

Eric, Laura and Greg 1970

Grand Teton Climbers
Ranch 1970

Rainy season 1976
Laura and Ira

Laura in Nepal 1977

Crossing river in
Pakistan 1977

Toraja, Indonesia 1977
Burial Ceremony

1977 Nepal Annapurna
South face

Gene 1978

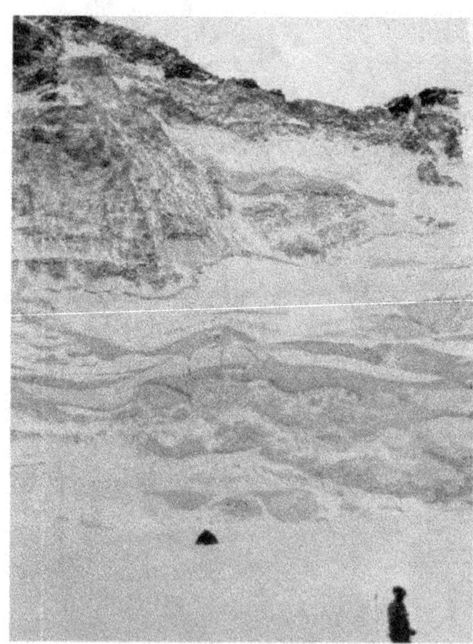

Me approaching the
tent where Mike was
unconscious, Makalu
1980. Betsy

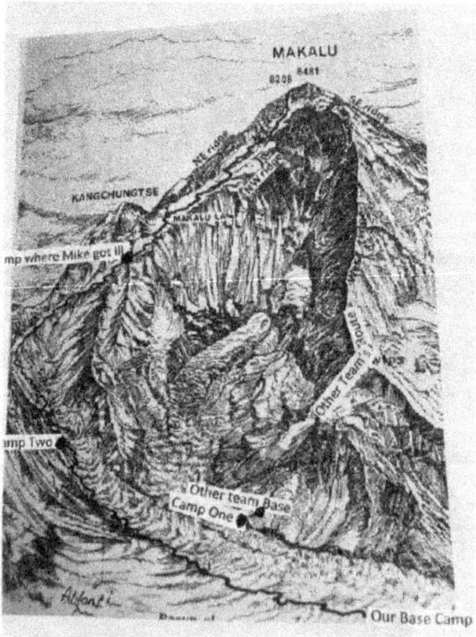

Makalu, Nepal 1980

Greg on Hispar Pass,
Pakistan 17,000 ft. 1991

Irian Jaya 1986

Alps 1987 Chamonix

1987 Irian Jaya. The older
man in traditional dress.

2006 Gene with
grandson Cosmo

Peshawar mosque

1960 to 2000

Appendix 1: Research Questionnaire

THE QUESTIONNAIRE

Number______

Married / single / other Age______ Language: Pushto Urdu Punjabi other
Economic: rural / urban
Adults in household______

shoes radio pukka house oil stove bike car
Children under 15 in household______

1. Do you keep purdah?   yes no Did mother? yes no Will daughter? yes no
2. Your age at marriage______   Mother's______   Daughter's______
3. Was your marriage arranged?   yes no Was mother's? yes no Will daughter's yes no
4. Do you approve of Talak?   yes no Did mother? yes no Will daughter? yes no
5. Do you approve of polygamy?   yes no Did mother? yes no Will daughter? yes no
6. Do you wear a burka?   yes no Did mother? yes no Will daughter? yes no
7. Do you & husband eat together? yes no Did parents? yes no Will children? yes no
8. Do you entertain mixed groups? yes no Did parents? yes no Will children? yes no

9. Do you go to the cinema?   yes no Did mother? yes no Will daughter? yes no
10. Do you go to the bazaar alone? yes no Did mother? yes no Will daughter? yes no
11. Do you work outside home?   yes no Did mother? yes no Will daughter? yes no
12. Do you ride a bike, drive car? yes no Did mother? yes no Does daughter? yes no

EDUCATION

13. Can you read?   yes no Did mother? yes no Does daughter? yes no
14. You have how many years of school?______ Mother______ Father______ Husband______
15. How many school age children in household are in school?________

383

EDUCATION (Continued):

16. Are girl children in school?   yes no

17. Should girls and boys have equal education?   yes no

18. If offered a scholarship, should a girl study at a college or university?   yes no

19. If some children are not in school, why not?   1. no school   2. too expensive
                                                              3. other reason

HEALTH

20. When ill, do you consult a hakim?   yes no

21. Do you ever go to an educated doctor?   yes no

22. Would you consult a man doctor?   yes no

23. Do you use trained Dais or a maternal health center for childbirth?   yes no

24. Do you get inoculations for yourself and children?   yes no

25. How many children do you have?______   How many died?______
      "   "   "   did parents have?______   How many died?______

26. How many children are a good number for a family?______

27. If available, would you go to a family planning clinic?   yes no

28. Have you ever been to a family planning clinic?   yes no

29. Do you approve of family planning?   yes no

30. Do you practice family planning?   yes no

Comments on any question: indicate which question is concerned.

Appendix 2: Family History

My mother and I share the middle name of Talcott. Mother was tenth generation descendent of "Worshipful" John Talcott who arrived in Massachusetts in 1632 on the ship the "Lion." He and other members of the Rev. Hooker company moved west to the Connecticut River where they established a town that became Hartford.

The family of my mother's mother, Josephine Kenyon also descended from other early settlers of America, the Shackelfords. Baron Jacques Le Fort of Normandy came to England with William the Conqueror in 1066 and was granted land. Jacques le Fort was Anglicized and became Shackelford. From 1367 to 1413, Henry de Shackleford was a gentleman in waiting to Henry IV. In 1649 John Shackelford fled to America, settling in Queens County Virginia. The land and village in England became part of the estate of the Earl of Middleton.

James Shackelford married Mary Stamps. Their son, Thomas Shackelford married Eliza Pullian; their son married Sara Eliza Harrison and moved to Missouri, their daughter Ada Eliza Shackelford married Charles C. Hemenway; their daughter Josephine Hemenway married James Henry Kenyon; their daughter Ruth Talcott Kenyon was my mother. She married William Herrick, then William F. Russell.

Appendix 3: Mountaineering Resume

Year/Area		Year/Area	
1955 Colorado	Little Matterhorn	**1960 Colorado**	Gore Range 5 pks
	Matterhorn		Belford
	Capital		Oxford
	Quandary		Vestal
	La Plata		Notchtop
	Tabeuach	**1960 Canada**	Lake O Hara
	Princeton		Wiwaxy
1955 New York	Marcy	**1961 Switzerland**	Piz Palu
1956 Colorado	Lindsey		Mt Rosa 4 summits
	Sneffels	**1961 Greece**	Mt Olympus
1957 Colorado	Sunlight	**1961 Turkey**	Taurus
	Windom	**1961 Lebanon**	Cedars summit
	Elous	**1961 E. Africa**	Kilimanjaro
	Wilson		Mt. Kenya, Lenana
	Lincoln	**1963 Pakistan**	Buni Zom
	Bross		Rosh Gol
	Democrat	**1964 Pakistan**	Barun Gol 1-3
1958 Colorado	Little Bear	**1966 France**	Aig. Argentiere
	San Luis		Triolet
	Stewart	**1966 Switzerland**	Castor
	Kit Carson		Pollux
	Crestone Peak		Breithorn
	Humboldt	**1967 Pakistan**	Tukatu
	Snowmass		Tachte-Suleiman
	Sherman	**1968 Canada**	Resplendent
	Elbert		Square Peak
1958 France	Mont Banc	**1968 Colorado**	Pikes Peak
	Aiguille du Moine		Wetterhorn
	La Nonne		Sunshine
	Gouter		Redcloud
1959 U. K.	Snowdon		Handies
	Ben Nevis		Huron
			Missouri
			Culebra
			Holy Cross
			Grizzly

Year/Area		Year/Area	
1969 Colorado	Evans	1975 Wyoming	Sawtooths
	Lincoln		Warbonnet
	Bross		Symmetry Spire
	Democrat	1976 California	Star King
	Sherman		Fairview dome
1969 Peru	Chinchey		Cathedral Spire
	Huascaran		Snake Dike, Half Dome
1970 Colorado	El Dorado Canyon		Joshua Tree
1970 Wyoming	Symmetry Spire	1976 Peru	Ranrapalca
	Teewinot	1976 Indonesia	Lombobattan
1971 Wyoming	Pingora	1977 Indonesia	Toraja
	Block Tower	1977 Nepal	Tent Peak
	Grand Teton E Ridge	1978 France	Chardonney
	South Teton		Aig. Tour
	Nez Perce		Charmoz
1971 Mexico	Ixty	1979 California	Mt Dana
	Toluca		North Palisade
1972 Ecuador	Chimborazo		Mt Sill
	Cotopaxi	1980 Nepal	Makalu II to 21,00 ft
1972 S. Wyoming	Rock climbs	1981 Alaska	McKinley to 17,500 ft
1973 Wyoming	Mt. Woolsey	1982 California	White Mountain
	Stettner		Tyndall
1974 California	Shasta		Russell
	Whitney Muir		Whitney, Muir
	Tuolumne 23 routes		Williamson
	Cathedral peak	1983 California	Langley
	Lempert Dome		Clark
	Mendlicot Dome	1983 Canada	Hawkins
	Royal Arches		Hoffman
	Lovers' Leap		Freel
	Pinnacles,3 routes		Lassen
	Yosemite Valley		Unicorn

Year/Area		Year/Area	
1984 Pakistan	Shimshall peaks	**1992 Nepal**	Gorkha-Trisuli
1984 California	Tallac	**1992 Pakistan**	Shangla pass
	Echo Lake Peak		Kalash Peaks
	Rubicon		Anniversary Peak
1985 Indonesia	Gunung Agung		Sangemarmar
	Bromo	**1992 India**	Ladakh
1987 Indonesia	Trikora	**1993 California**	Mt Lewis
	Merapi		Pinnacles routes
	Rinjani attempt	**1993 Wyoming**	Eagles' Rest
	Gunung Gede		Buck Mountain
1987 Pakistan	Hispar Peaks		Cube Point
1987 France	Brevant		Olmstead Point
	Mt. Blanc de Tacul	**1994 Wyoming**	Glory
1988 California	Thunderbolt		Buck Mountain
	Middle Palisade		Cathedral peak
	Joshua Tree		Disappointment
1989 California	Clouds Rest		Symmetry Crag
	Castle Peak		Brooks Mtn
	Round Top		Prospectors Mtn
	Split Mountan	**1995 Wyoming**	Oliver peak
	Marmot Dome		Cloud Veil Dome
1990 Pakistan	Kedam Peaks		Taylor Mtn
	Koala		Albright
	Tika Sar		Rolling Thunder
	Hushe	**1996 Canada**	Pioneer Peak
	Matitlan Pass		Mt. Sir William
1991 California	Mt. Lyell	**1996 Mongolia**	Racehorse Peak
1991 Pakistan	Kedam Valley		Thisisgun Peak
	Kachakani Pass		
	HIspar pass peak		
	Swat Peaks		

Year/Area		Year/Area	
1997 California	Rock Creek climbs	2002 Wyoming	Cody
	Lovers' Leap		Beard
1997 Wyoming	South Teton		Spearhead
	Housetop		Fred's Mtn
	Fossil Mtn		Pinnacle
	Woodring		The Wall
	The Wedge	2002 Arizona	15 Grand Cny hikes
	Jedediah Smith		Humphries Peak
1998 Canada	10 ski ascents	2003 Italy	Dolomites hiking
1998 California	Black Kawiah		Piz Boe
1998 Kyrghystan	Aktu Bek	2003 Colorado	2nd Flatiron
	Karasu	2004 Wyoming	Taylor
1999 Chile	Paine Tower hike		Blacktail Butte
1999 Argentina	Fitzroy Hike		Mt. Moran
1999 Wyoming	Shadow Mt.		Fossil
	Alice		Elephant Head
	Fox Creek		Fremont Peak
	Garns		Jefferson Peak
	Breccia Peak	2005 Canada	Amiskwi ski climbs
	St. John	2005 Wyoming	Peaked mtn
1999 India	Gocha Ła		Rammel
2000 Wyoming	Mt. Hunt		Jackson Peak
	Sheep Mtn		Table Mtn
	the Jaw	2005 France	Mercantour point
	Two Elk		Col Guillet
2000 Colorado	Long's peak		Col Sublime
	Pike's peak	2006 Canada	Campbell Icefield
2001 Canada	6 ski ascents	2006 Montana	Lions Head
2001 India	Sir Everest peak	2006 Wyoming	Various
	Kedar Dome base	2007 France	Les Ecrins Traverse
	Shivling meadow	2007 California	Bay Area Ridges
2001 California	Trans Sierra ski tour	2007 Yosemite	Tuolumne rock climbs
		2009 France	Vanoise Park